WHAT PEOPLE A[RE SAYING ABOUT]
Search N[ever Sleeps]
By Jon[athan Guy]

"**Search Never Sleeps** is a must-read [for anyone interested in SEO]. [It is] a well-written, unique perspective of SEO in plain English, by a leading expert in the field. Jonathan's encyclopedic knowledge and experience of SEO shines through the chapters.

The simple way in which SEO concepts are explained has greatly improved my understanding of this formerly mysterious subject. It will undoubtedly be of value to any small business owner commissioning future SEO projects. Jonathan refers to the importance of understanding the concept that 'people buy benefits not products', and cites examples to increase the reader's knowledge of how this applies to SEO.

I also particularly enjoyed learning the background of how SEO has evolved over the years and how data can eventually become 'meaningful intelligence.' A thoroughly recommended read, very useful to me and my franchisees."

Mike Hanrahan, Franchisor, Maid2Clean Franchise Limited

"Being the owner of an IT business, I always sort of knew I should be doing something about SEO on my website. However, I was completely put off by the apparent technicalities of applying this from the books I had read and even more so by the constant barrage from charlatans claiming they could get my company to #1 on the search list (How could they get everyone to the top and keep them there?). **Search Never Sleeps** is a refreshing change from anything I have seen previously. It is written in layman's terms and explains clearly and succinctly not only what it is but why I need it and, if I was so inclined, how I could implement it myself. Time to finally do something about this SEO wizardry, I think!"

Paul Brooks, Managing Director, Antar Information Technology Ltd

---

"One of the great things about **Search Never Sleeps** is it's easy to follow and understand as opposed to being overly technical. It also gives very useful information relating to common myths of SEO, which I found particularly interesting!"

Gary McDermott, Managing Director, SSO International Freight

"Having spent years trying to understand SEO by reading whatever the "big guns" put out, only left me further confused and then hesitant to try anything.

This refreshing approach, in simple terms, gives you the knowledge to understand what is really needed and how to implement the strategy across your website to improve."

Beverley Flynn BA (Hons), Director, Insight Investigations

"Having a cursory knowledge of SEO, I found that **Search Never Sleeps** dealt with the potentially complicated aspects for me, in a way that I could totally understand. The 3 Rules of Google made total sense."

Ian Gregory, Business Coach, Cheshire Business Forum

"**Search Never Sleeps** is a great read that will change your online business trajectory. There are excellent tips that are simple to follow and simple to implement. Highly recommended."

Benet Slay, Angel investor and drinks entrepreneur

"I found your premise of SEO and your 3 rules quite interesting. I have been involved with computers since the late 1970s and built my own small business online web presence in the early 1990s. Gaining exposure in any search engine has been the priority for decades and you have a very readable way of explaining what the parameters are and how to maximize SEO results. Your style is easy to follow and your everyday language will help take the mystery out of this for many who attempt to create their own identity online."

John Armstrong, Armstrong's Stamps, Ontario, Canada

"A refreshing, no-nonsense, common sense look at SEO that cuts through the usual smoke and mirrors. What you do get is solid, down to earth advice on what you really need to know about SEO and how it can work for your business."

Phil Lund (MCIM), Marketing Manager, Timberwise (UK) Ltd

"A great read for non-techy entrepreneurs, it demystifies the world of SEO. I particularly enjoyed The 3 Rules of Google."

Steven Ward, Managing Director, Award Signs & Business Gifts

"An insightful and refreshingly different view on SEO, from an experienced marketer, rather than a digital guru. This book a grounded in solid marketing practices, a focus on the customer rather than the algorithm, and written in a style that makes it an easy, informative, and compelling read. **Search Never Sleeps** gives you the how, but more importantly, the customer-driven value and why of SEO."

Frank Reynolds, B2B Software Marketer, Corporate, SME and Start-Up

---

"I often look for 'go-to' reference books for digital marketing topics, and I've found a new best one! **Search Never Sleeps** explains SEO really well. There are many good books on this topic, but they tend to deal with just the what and how. This book is the first one that I have read that also deals with the why.

Too often, business owners focus on getting to number one on Google but rarely focus on why or search for the right keywords or phrases for their business.

It also throws in some interesting background and history to contextualise everything. Many misconceptions are also unraveled, and 'The 3 Rules of Google' give you a simple framework for your SEO strategy."

Richard Dawson, Digital Marketing Coach

"**Search Never Sleeps** is a must-read guide for anyone looking to boost their online presence. The book takes a conversational and approachable tone, making it perfect for beginners in the world of search engine optimisation (SEO).

It is particularly suitable for small and medium-sized enterprises (SMEs) and business owners who are new to SEO. The book assumes little to no prior knowledge and guides readers through the intricacies of search engines in a clear and concise manner.

The author's clear explanations and actionable insights will undoubtedly help SMEs navigate the ever-evolving world of SEO, driving organic traffic to their business and boosting their online presence.

Search Never Sleeps is a must-read for anyone seeking to unlock the potential of search engines and harness their power in the digital realm."

Stuart Waddington, MD & Founder, TDL

"Jonathan Guy has written a book that packs a lot of punch on a topic close to his heart. His SEO knowledge and experience is reassuring and his passion is compelling. As a business owner who deploys SEO, it's a fascinating read on its history and how we should be thinking about it and using it now.

It provides invaluable insights and ideas on how to develop successful SEO strategies with greater confidence. If you are interested in furthering your use of SEO for your business but are confused as to what to think about it, or where to start, **Search Never Sleeps** is for you."

Penny Haslam, MD, Bit Famous - Executive Coaching and Training

---

"A refreshingly easy-to-understand insight into the complex world of SEO, taking the reader through a step-by-step history of their origins and myths. Drawing on the author's considerable sector knowledge and experience, the use of case studies brings the narrative to life. The examples and tips for growing sales by maximising e-commerce effectiveness is a must-have for anyone who wants to grow their business."

Gary Dixon, Independent Consultant

"Have you ever felt bamboozled by the world of e-commerce? Do you want your website or product to be at the top of search rankings? What is e-commerce anyway?

There are many self-help books out there about SEO and what needs to be done. Many are jargon rich (like.... SEO...) and don't feel like they wait for the reader to come on board for the ride.

What Jonathan has written is a guide that brings you into the mystical world of computer marketing. Jonathan has decades of experience in marketing and SEO. He has built up a successful company that takes company sites and gets them high up the search engine ratings. Who doesn't want to be top of the search list? Let's face it, when we do a search, how many of us scan far down the results page for what we need?

Jonathan's style is very engaging. He breaks down the concept and the jargon without patronising the audience. He explains what is going on, how and why, and what you can do to make your product shine that bit brighter out there.

It's not a quick fix, it takes work. It's not even a dark art – even though for most of us, it feels that way...

With a structured approach using simple but effective illustrations, Jonathan engages his audience and provides the answers. Inform, educate, entertain... can't get better than that!"

Geraint Roberts, Author

"*Search Never Sleeps* presents a clear articulation of the practice of SEO, written in an easy-to-follow style which I found both informative and engaging.

I loved the Takeaways, and the reminders that you should always approach each solution with your consumer top of mind.

An enjoyable read, and clear signposts of what 'good' looks like."

Marcus Hall, Managing Partner, Essence/Mediacom North

"A refreshing, new perspective on digital marketing and SEO in particular. Unlike the vast majority of other SEO resources, **Search Never Sleeps** focuses on the marketing rather than the digital aspects of digital marketing. This book goes back to basics, explaining why website owners should build a well-structured, customer-friendly website and how this approach should ensure that their website is ranked well by the search engine algorithms. It covers everything from how search engines work, and how to use this knowledge to better structure your website, to key things to consider when building product pages to both appeal to customers and rank well in search results. This accessible book talks to website owners in plain English, avoiding technical jargon wherever possible and explaining terms where necessary. It will be an invaluable tool for all website owners, from microbusiness owners building their first website to sales directors responsible for corporate websites. I defy any reader not to come away with a list of action points for their website."

Jae Rance, Managing Director, ScratchSleeves

"**Search Never Sleeps** is a comprehensive and user-friendly guide that demystifies the complex world of SEO. Written with a broad audience in mind, this book offers a practical and step-by-step approach to understanding and implementing effective SEO strategies.

Authored by Jonathan Guy, a recognised expert in the field, **Search Never Sleeps** covers all the fundamental aspects in a concise and easily digestible manner. The book starts by explaining the basics, such as what SEO is, how search engines work, and why SEO is essential for online success. From there, it gradually progresses to more advanced topics, providing readers with a solid foundation to build upon.

One of the key strengths of this book is its ability to break down complex SEO concepts into simple terms. It uses plain language and avoids excessive technical jargon, ensuring that even readers with no prior knowledge of SEO can follow along. The author provides real-world examples, case studies, and practical tips throughout the book, making it easy for readers to apply the strategies and techniques discussed.

A standout features of **Search Never Sleeps** is its emphasis on ethical and sustainable SEO practices. The author frequently stresses the importance of using 'white hat' techniques that comply with search engine guidelines and prioritise user experience. This approach ensures long-term success, and minimises the risk of penalties or negative impacts on website rankings.

Overall, **Search Never Sleeps** is an invaluable resource for beginners who want to navigate the intricacies of SEO effectively. Its clear explanations, practical examples, and ethical approach make it a must-read for anyone seeking to improve their website's visibility and drive targeted traffic. Whether you are a small business owner, a marketing professional, or a website owner looking to enhance your online presence, this book will serve as your ultimate guide to SEO success."

Andy White, MD, Jawline Ltd

"If you're in business, understanding the language of digital marketing and its holy grail of search engine optimisation is not optional. Today, five million of the UK's six million businesses have a website. Nine out of every ten households shop online, more so since lockdown. And it's not going away.

Fortunately for UK plc, Jonathan Guy knows his subject. The founder of an award-winning digital agency, he's spent half a lifetime creating marketing solutions to help businesses grow. His new book, **Search Never Sleeps**, offers unique insight to beginners and experts alike in their quest to crack the code of digital marketing.

Search Never Sleeps acknowledges the role played by Google in SEO but offers a warning to those who believe sleight of hand will bring rewards: Don't try and beat Google or cheat Google, the book argues, because Google always wins. Work with it and you can achieve the right outcomes for your business.

Ultimately though, what separates **Search Never Sleeps** from the rest of this crowded field is the recognition that Google – for all its ubiquity – has limitations. Search is nothing without Google but – because it's just a machine – Google is nothing if it can't understand what people want. Effective SEO, like all forms of marketing, depends on how well businesses know their customers.

Knowing your customer...now there's a thought!"

Steve Chambers, Lecturer in Strategy, Manchester Metropolitan University

To Ian,
Here's your first edition —
Signed! Jonathan

If your business depends on being found online,
this is the book for you

Search Never Sleeps

Learn how **three simple rules** can change
the way your website is found

Jonathan Guy

Search Never Sleeps
By Jonathan Guy
ISBN: 978-1-8384258-9-0

Copyright © 2023 Jonathan Guy

Jonathan Guy asserts the moral right to be identified as the author of this book, in accordance with the Copyright, Designs and Patents Act 1988.

All rights reserved. No part of this publication may be reproduced, stored in a retrieval system, or transmitted in any form, or by any means, electronic, mechanical, photocopying, recording or otherwise, without the prior written permission of the publisher.

Copyeditor and proofreader: Siân-Elin Flint-Freel
Book design by Tanya Back, www.tanyabackdesigns.com
Cover design by Gabriella Guy: Millennial Burnout
Back cover photograph by Andrew Collier: Just Headshots

Printed by Lagan Valley Publishing

All information, methods, techniques and advice contained within this publication reflect the views and experiences of the author, whose intent is to provide readers with various choices and options. We are all individuals with different beliefs and viewpoints, therefore it is recommended that readers carry out their own research prior to making any such choices. While all attempts have been made to verify the information contained within this book, neither the author nor the publisher assume responsibility for any errors or omissions, or for any actions taken or results experienced by any reader.

Google and the Google logo are trademarks of Google LLC.

To Emma, for always having my six.

Table of Contents

Author's Note 15
Preface 17
    The myths of SEO 20

Chapter 1 - Introduction and History 23
    The definition of SEO 26
    Why should SEO be important to you? 29

Chapter 2 - The 3 Rules of Google 33

Chapter 3 - The three key areas of SEO 43

    On-Site 44
    How should I organise my website so Google can rank me well? 54
    Meta data - what it is and why is it important? 55
    Page Titles 58
    Header Tags 61
    Meta Descriptions 66
    Image Alt Tags (or Alternative Text) 70

    On-Page 75
    It's all about Rule 3 78
    How do I create a great website page? 86
    What makes great content? 96
    Keywords and phrases 99
    Images 104
    Internal and External links 105
    E.A.T. 108
    Bounce Rate 113
    UI/UX - you what? 116

    Off-Site 120
    Link building and the voice of the crowd 120
    What exactly is a 'backlink'? 123
    How do I get people to link to my website? 129
    The value of backlinks 131
    What does a natural link profile look like? 138
    A quick guide to Link building strategies 141
    Press and PR Activity 151
    How to create links from your website 153
    How to create internal links within your website 157

Should you buy links? 171
Google penalties – what is a manual action
and what can I do about it? 172

Other SEO Fundamentals **176**
Which website platform is best for ranking? 177
Sitemaps 179
Schema Markup 182
Website Security 189

Chapter 4 - Local SEO **199**
What is local search and why is it important? 199
Google My Business 203
Google Reviews - how to get them and how to manage them 212
Managing Google (and other) reviews 215
Other local signals to help customers find you 225

Chapter 5 - E-Commerce **227**
Should I have an e-commerce website? 229
What is the best e-commerce platform? 230
How do I optimise my e-commerce website? 235
Should I use Google Shopping? 242

Chapter 6 - How to build a better website **247**
Things to consider before you create your own website 248
How to work closely with your developer 250
Fifteen things people get wrong on new websites 256
What is your website worth? 260

Chapter 7 - Google and The Future of Search **265**
Why do we need search engines? 268
Why do we need websites? 273
The rise of machine learning 276
The importance of privacy 280
Will there be a need for search engine
optimisation in the future? 284
Should you use an SEO company? 292

Chapter 8 – Resources and Tools **297**

Appendix - Checklist for website development **303**

Glossary of Terms **307**

About the author **316**

Acknowledgements **317**

Table of Figures

Figure 1 – The relationship between data, information, and intelligence 25
Figure 2 – Do you know what this symbol means? 26
Figure 3 – Percentage of users who click on each position of the search results 30
Figure 4 – Google crawl of a website. Note the spike in early 2021 46
Figure 5 – Google search results showing just two of the websites listed have the correct answer 47
Figure 6 – Google results in June 22 after the price rise in the cost of stamps to 68p 48
Figure 7 – Google's answer to 'What's the most valuable stamp in the world?' 51
Figure 8 – The same search query three days later – notice the difference? 53
Figure 9 – How to examine the source code of any webpage 56
Figure 10 – Meta data on a webpage 57
Figure 11 – An example of a Title Tag 58
Figure 12 – Descriptive title tags help Google and users understand what the page is about 59
Figure 13 – The Dash and Pipe symbols on a keyboard 60
Figure 14 – Meta Descriptions are an essential part of SEO 67
Figure 15 – Google may pick something different to show as your meta description 67
Figure 16 – Revising a meta description 68
Figure 17 – Proof that Google decides what to show in your meta description 68
Figure 18 – Testing a url has been indexed 69
Figure 19 – Bing's Meta Description 69
Figure 20 – How would you describe what's in this picture? 70
Figure 21 – Google Image Search 71
Figure 22 – This is what Google thinks my picture shows 72
Figure 23 – Adding image alt text 74
Figure 24 – Google relies on you to tell it what each picture shows 75
Figure 25 – What does this number plate say? 79
Figure 26 – Keyword Density 80
Figure 27 – Things Google says you should NOT do 85
Figure 28 – Does your website include this well-used phrase? 87
Figure 29 – Phrases such as this are not unique or helpful to users 88
Figure 30 – Example website hierarchy 89
Figure 31 – Search phrases, not keywords, in Google Search Console 100
Figure 32 – (not provided) and (not set) in Google Analytics 101
Figure 33 – Change, Measure, Analyse recurring loop 111
Figure 34 – High bounce rate does not automatically mean user dissatisfaction 115
Figure 35 – What is UI/UX? 117
Figure 36 – How Yahoo's home page looked in 1999 121
Figure 37 – Google's home page in 1999 122
Figure 38 – A snapshot of the Resources page on my website 124
Figure 39 – The link on that page, highlighted in blue 125
Figure 40 – Moz Beginners Guide to SEO 125
Figure 41 – Where to find 'Links' in Google Search Console 126
Figure 42 – Google Search Console showing which websites link to your website 126
Figure 43 – Full list of websites linking to me, taken from Google's Search Console 127
Figure 44 – Full list of websites linking to me, taken from Ahrefs 128
Figure 45 – Mathematical relationship between websites (Image courtesy of Wikipedia) ... 130
Figure 46 – A Google search for 'the importance of anchor text' 136
Figure 47 – 10 different types of anchor text 137
Figure 48 – bbc.co.uk 139
Figure 49 – eBay.co.uk 139

Figure 50 – telegraph.co.uk 139
Figure 51 – next.co.uk 139
Figure 52 – BBC anchor text 140
Figure 53 – Next anchor text 140
Figure 54 – The options to create different types of links in WordPress 154
Figure 55 – The 'home' button is an internal link 157
Figure 56 – Structural and Contextual internal links 158
Figure 57 – Spammy forum comments 161
Figure 58 – More spammy forum comments – these are clearly automated 161
Figure 59 – Spam forum comments with the link in the username 162
Figure 60 – Example of a low-quality Guest Post 162
Figure 61 – An example of a link directory 163
Figure 62 – Another cheap link directory 163
Figure 63 – Disavow Links in Google Search Console 166
Figure 64 – The correct way to disavow a domain 167
Figure 65 – Security & Manual Actions in Google Search Console 173
Figure 66 – Google Manual Actions 173
Figure 67 – A typical website sitemap 180
Figure 68 – A badly configured sitemap 181
Figure 69 – A typical schema hierarchy 183
Figure 70 – Example of schema 184
Figure 71 – Google's Structured Data Markup Helper 185
Figure 72 – Schema tagging of a page 185
Figure 73 – Search share by desktop v mobile over time – Copyright Statcounter 187
Figure 74 – Google Safe Browser warnings – 1998-2022 190
Figure 75 – WordPress Plugin Directory 195
Figure 76 – An example traffic light system from an SEO plug-in 196
Figure 77 – The history of 'near me' searches on Google 201
Figure 78 – Search for 'Plumber near me' 206
Figure 79 – The wider map for 'Plumber near me' 207
Figure 80 – The same search for 'Plumber near me' when I tell Google where I am 208
Figure 81 – The review that appears on their profile is two years old 208
Figure 82 – A refined search for 'Commercial Plumber Boiler Servicing' 209
Figure 83 – Options in the Google My Business dashboard 210
Figure 84 – How to ask people for reviews 214
Figure 85 – Serenata Flowers Northwich landing page 220
Figure 86 – Serenata Flowers Runcorn landing page 220
Figure 87 – Northwich data on the Northwich page 221
Figure 88 – Runcorn data on the Runcorn page 221
Figure 89 – Local testimonials on the Runcorn page 222
Figure 90 – E-commerce platforms used for the top one million websites, courtesy of BuiltWith 230
Figure 91 – Pros and cons of hosted versus independent e-commerce solutions 233
Figure 92 – Breakdown of the platform types of the top one million websites 234
Figure 93 – Google Shopping result for "ladies red stiletto shoes" 243
Figure 94 – Google search results for 'lorem ipsum' 253
Figure 95 – Google search result for 'how to improve gut health' 270
Figure 96 – TikTok search result for 'how to improve gut health' 270
Figure 97 – Google search for 'Blue Air flights' 274
Figure 98 – The expanded search box for 'Blue Air flights' on Google 274
Figure 99 – Blue Air's home page offering a range of services, not just flight bookings 275
Figure 1 – The relationship between data, information, and intelligence (from page 21) 278
Figure 100 – Google trend of searches for 'privacy' 283
Figure 101 – Google search trends for 'Covid-19' 287

Author's Note

"Why is it called 'Search Never Sleeps'?" asked one of my reviewers. I must confess, the question left me stumped for a moment; after all, it was obvious, wasn't it? Apparently not, according to my friend. It's probably right, therefore, to explain where the phrase came from.

Several years ago, when I was delivering a talk on search engine optimisation to a room full of business owners, someone asked me why the Google search results seemed to change all the time. My answer was simple, it was because search never sleeps. From there, the phrase stuck and from that point on we started to use it within our business. The reason for recalling this now is to explain to you the significance of the title.

I found that search never sleeps was a useful way of describing both the behaviour of the search engines and the actions of those website owners determined to rank well on Google. Every day, Google is asked billions of questions globally and its never-ending quest is to deliver the correct answer to every question, all the time, in under one second. To do that – as you will discover in this book – it deploys an army of bots to search the internet to help it understand and put into order the information that is available. This 'crawl' process, much like our constant questions, never ends. On that basis, search never sleeps.

Similarly, of those who set out to ensure their websites rank well on Google, there is a subset who allow themselves to be completely immersed in search engine optimisation. They study every nuance of the Google search results, track and measure every change that occurs and fixate on minutiae in the search algorithm changes in the hope that it will lead to a competitive advantage. There is an entire industry that has built up around this and several well-respected websites who track all the daily comings and goings in the world of search. The work they do is invaluable and often leads to breakthroughs in understanding, allowing business owners to adjust their websites to appear more frequently in search results. For these people too, search never sleeps.

For the vast majority of us though, there simply aren't enough hours in the day to get that involved. Business owners in particular have a hard enough time running a business and making a profit without worrying about how Google is changing its algorithms (which it does approximately four times a day). It's about finding a system that doesn't take too much time, is easy to understand and that gets the best results for the least amount of effort. Hence my **3 Rules of Google** in Chapter 2. These three rules are designed to help you make sense of the never ending and ever-changing world of search and to give you a solid platform to ensure your business thrives, despite the fact that search never sleeps.

The other obvious manifestation of search never sleeping is that since I wrote this book in 2021 and 2022, despite rewriting several parts as I went along, changes have happened as we go to press in 2023. The first of these changes is that Google have changed EAT (see Chapter 3 for the details on this) to become EEAT.* A small but subtle change that doesn't materially affect what I have written but does render it out of date.

The second glaring change is that a company called Open AI released an Artificial Intelligence programme called ChatGPT which has made headlines around the world. In the search engine optimisation world, it led to a flurry of speculation and wildly differing opinions as to what this means for our industry. I may be completely wrong, but right now I see nothing changing, certainly in the immediate future. Over time, I am sure there will be some kind of impact but everything I have written in this book still stands, irrespective of this development.

There are, of course, more examples where things have changed, but these two alone should be enough to demonstrate that for anyone who owns a website, search never sleeps.

---

* In December 2022, about a week before Christmas, Google announced on its blog that their acronym EAT (expertise, authoritativeness, and trustworthiness) was changing to become EEAT by including the word 'experience'.

Preface

You might think that by now, everything useful that could be written about the basics of Search Engine Optimisation (SEO) would already have been written. But you'd be wrong.

Sure, there are some useful resources out there, including one from Google which explains how to play nicely with their search engine,[1] and the wonderful *Beginner's Guide to SEO*[2] from the people at Moz.com, who are specialists on the subject. The Moz guide is so handy we even use it as a starting point when anyone asks us what they should do to understand SEO. The industry has developed a pretty poor reputation as being something of a Dark Art or a practice shrouded in smoke and mirrors.

As Moz say at the start of their guide:

> **"The world of search engine optimization is complex and ever-changing, but you can easily understand the basics, and even a small amount of SEO knowledge can make a big difference."**

---
1 https://developers.google.com/search/docs/beginner/seo-starter-guide
2 https://moz.com/beginners-guide-to-seo

I totally agree with this sentiment, and from my point of view, helping people understand what SEO is all about is fundamental to the work I do. After all, if a customer doesn't know what I am doing for them, then how can they know if I'm adding value?

At this point, I suppose it might be useful for me to say a bit about what it is I do and why I have an opinion on this. As you will no doubt have seen from the cover, my name is Jonathan Guy and for the past twelve years I have run my own SEO company in the UK. Prior to that, I worked in advertising and marketing for a quarter of a century and now, with coming up to forty years' experience in this field (having been a chartered marketer for over half of that time), I find that I fundamentally disagree with some of what is considered to be 'common knowledge' in digital marketing.

The main issue I have with many of the available guides, books and checklists is that they all start with some basic assumptions. Assumptions I believe to be flawed. Not least amongst these is the assumption that you, as a business owner, should be doing any or all of this. Of course, it needs doing, but by whom is the question? I'll cover this in more detail later in the book. What I want to do is to give you a slightly different view of search engine optimisation, one I've not seen in any of the literature I've read to date.

To explain what I mean, take the simple task of searching on Google for how to do search engine optimisation.

When I searched in 2021 on Google for 'SEO Guide' I got the following results. (Let's ignore the advertisements for now; after all, this is about SEO.)

- SEO Basics: Beginner's Guide
- SEO Starter Guide: The basics
- Beginner's Guide to SEO
- A Complete Guide to SEO
- SEO Basics: A Beginner's Guide
- Essential Guide to SEO
- SEO in 2021
- SEO Guide: Everything a beginner needs

and so on...

You can see a picture emerging here. I found over 20 of these guides, all pretty much saying the same thing. Whilst each of these guides has its merits, if you read them, you will see that they all repeat the same material. They explain what everything is and what you need to do, but more often than not, they don't explain *why*. They fail to give you any context and no real sense of what making these changes will do for you. That's a real issue for me, as it is only by understanding *why* you are doing it that you will be able to understand *how* it will benefit your website or your business.

So, I decided to produce this book. It started life as 'an alternative guide', but over time morphed into something quite different, something that goes beyond the 'what' and firmly into the 'why'. It asks some difficult questions about why we are doing this. I will cover the basics of SEO. Yes, I feel it's important to cover the basics, but not in the same way everyone else does. In this book, I will show you what needs doing, why it needs doing, and most importantly, what people *don't* tell you. And I will do so in plain English. So much of what has been written previously is full of jargon with, in some cases, no explanation of what it means. Jargon created by people who understand this kind of stuff, not people like you and me who prefer things to be in plain English. This guide has been designed to be easy to read and to understand. Where I do use jargon – and in places I am going to have to do so – I'll translate it into something everyone can understand. At the back of the book, I've even included a chapter of resources and a glossary of terms that will help you, should you be inclined, to give some of this a go yourself.

The pages in this book will give you everything you need to know to make an instant difference to your website, and hopefully the encouragement to give it a go and transform the way your website appears in search. Along the way, I will show you the impact these actions have in the real world. Whilst I can't name all the companies involved, I can tell you that the examples in this book are all real-life examples.

This 'alternative' guide is built on the premise that pretty much each one of us uses Google on a daily basis. Every day we ask it millions of questions and every day it returns the results we are looking for – and those results are pretty much spot on. But when was the last time you questioned why it happens that way? What is it that makes Google such an effective search tool and why does it seem to know the right answers to your questions? And how does it know, before you do, what you are looking for?

I'll answer these, and more questions like it, in *Search Never Sleeps*.

The myths of SEO

There are so many myths surrounding SEO that it makes sense to cover some of these early on in proceedings, just in case you are labouring under any misconceptions. Time and again I am approached by firms who aspire for their business and website to 'be number one', 'beat my competitors' and 'make my website appear whenever people are looking for what we do'. Overriding all of this is the urgent demand that all of this needs to happen within a few weeks. Whilst these are common goals across many businesses, they are not specific or measurable and the timescales here are definitely unrealistic!

Getting to number one is a great aspiration for any website, but for which keywords or phrases? What is important for your website, and more importantly, what are your customers typing into Google? It might not be what you are thinking.

Previously, it was possible to get to 'number one' for a keyword within a few weeks, but if it was for a particularly competitive keyword then the only way to do this was to cheat the search engines. Some firms found this an acceptable solution, but as the search engines always catch up with this and penalise the site, it is a short-sighted and ineffective strategy and not one I recommend you pursue. Google has, and continues to change the way in which searches are presented, which means that SEO is not a 'tick box' exercise; it is a moveable feast and aspirations to be on 'page one' for an undefined and unquantified number of keywords or phrases in a very short timescale is unrealistic and generally leads to disappointment. Furthermore, as every keyword has different competitors, then it is perfectly possible to be successful with some and not others. The exception does not prove the rule; the lack of top search results on certain terms does not prove 'it isn't working', merely that it requires either a different, longer term or more innovative approach.

Finally, organic search positions are important but are not the only measure of success. They should be considered as part of a holistic approach and one of a number of metrics by which a business can measure success.

After all, wouldn't customers converted be a better yardstick?

The following is a representative sample of some of the myths that you can and will hear being repeated about search engine optimisation. Some of them might make you stop and think – and if so, good. Throughout this book, each of these will be dealt with, so when you get to the end you will understand not only why SEO is important, but what you need to do to make it work for you and your website.

> **Some of the most common myths of SEO**
>
> The more keywords you have on the page, the better
>
> Being active on social media helps SEO
>
> Spending money on Google Ads will improve your rankings
>
> Backlinks are unimportant
>
> Content is unimportant
>
> Google will penalise you for duplicate content
>
> SEO is the only thing you need to do to get your website to make money
>
> SEO is a replacement for good solid professional marketing
>
> It's a tick box exercise
>
> It's a 'quick' process to get your website on the 'front page' for an indeterminate number of phrases or keywords
>
> You have to be number one to get customers
>
> SEO doesn't work (or SEO is dead)
>
> SEO is a dark art with smoke and mirrors

This is not a definitive list. Every week I hear something new, usually in an email from someone trying to sell me something, and in pretty much every case, it's nothing more than their opinion. Sadly, this type of information is rarely checked, and as you will see later in this book, some of it comes to pervade the literature without anyone questioning where this idea came from in the first place. If it sounds plausible, too many people are willing to believe it without checking, but experience tells me that most of what SEO's do for a living hasn't changed that much in twenty years. The important things then are the important things now, and whilst Google may have changed how it ranks websites, it's always held true to the same principles. I'll cover those principles later in this book, but for now I simply urge you not to take everything you already know at face value. Read on and you might just be surprised.

CHAPTER 1

Introduction and History

When did SEO start?

SEO is generally considered to have started in the mid 1990s. In fact, dates seem to range from 1990 to 1997, and no one seems to be able to agree on a fixed point in time. The bottom line is that it can only have started once there were websites and search engines, and as the first search engine was Archie in 1990,[1] it can't possibly be any earlier than that.

That's not the only thing there is some disagreement about. Even the definition for SEO is the subject of much debate. I will return to that later, but for now, let's just say that SEO is about helping your website rank higher in the search results of a list of websites.

The first publicly available search engines were WebCrawler and Lycos in 1994, so logically, this is probably the likely earliest date. Knowing the type of people who were interested in websites back then, they would definitely have been interested in seeing how they could change the position of their website on any list.

---

1   https://en.wikipedia.org/wiki/Search_engine

But in January 1995, everything changed when Yahoo introduced a search function to their Yahoo Directory. For those of you old enough to remember dial up Internet, you'll remember that Yahoo was the start page for many people. The page used to build very slowly, line by line. Halfway down the page, along with the news headlines, weather and stock prices, there was a little 'search' box which you could use to find stuff online.

As more and more websites started appearing, people found they could search for and find what they wanted. Thus, there was more interest in the order in which websites were listed as a result of the search. And SEO was born.

Who needs SEO anyway?

The simple answer to this question is anyone with a website, but the more detailed answer is anyone with a need to communicate electronically with anyone else.

Back in 1999, Tim Berners-Lee, the man who is credited with inventing the World Wide Web, wrote a fascinating book entitled *Weaving the Web*, in which he described how he envisaged linking computers together into a network, which would encourage and enable data and ideas to be shared. In short, the principle he championed was that if we could link all the computers in the world together and share what we knew, then in theory it would be possible to solve almost any problem facing humanity. What he didn't envisage was quite so much data being available in such a short space of time. So much, that without some kind of organisation, it would be impossible to find what you needed.

Enter Google, with its mission statement to "organize the world's information and make it universally accessible and useful", and you have the elements needed to enable the global sharing of information. Except we haven't really seen that happen yet. Part of the problem is that much of the information that might be useful in problem solving is either hidden (meaning Google cannot access it), or if Google can access it, it can't make sense of it. And if they can't make sense of it, then it can't be organised into something easily accessible by others.

The problem isn't going away either. With more and more data becoming available every day, the issue isn't about what we know, it's about how we access, store and share what we know. This is precisely the problem that SEO is set up to help solve. By organising data in a more efficient manner, making it accessible and searchable, the goal of global knowledge sharing is a step closer.

It doesn't matter if you run a business and your website is essential for driving trade, or a charity where you communicate with your supporters and get your message out, or even a hobby site where you like to share what you know with others, without the data you produce being optimised in some way, it will be hard for both search engines and people to make sense of what you are saying. But with a little bit of effort and a clear understanding of what you are doing – and why – then you can help your website rank better in more searches and provide more helpful information to more people.

Early on in my career, I developed a simple model which illustrates that we have too much of what we need the least and not enough of what we need the most (Figure 1) .

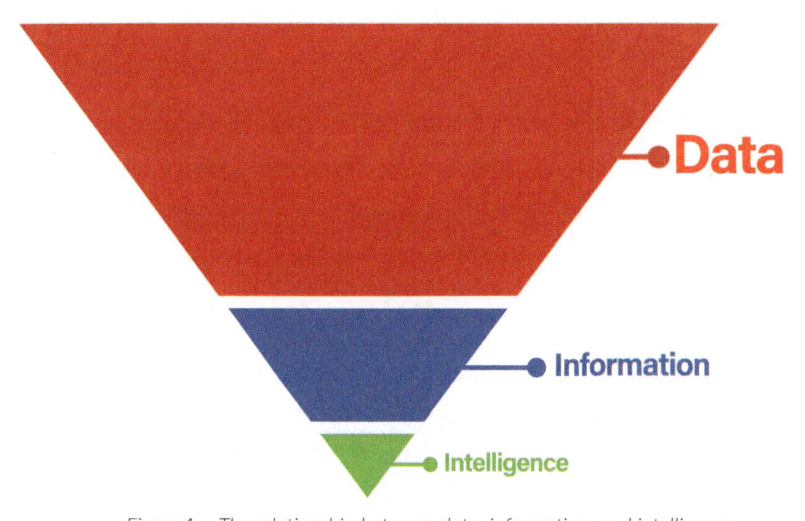

Figure 1 – The relationship between data, information, and intelligence.

The world is awash with data. We have data coming out of our ears as everything electronic these days creates more and more data. There are some tools out there which take that data and present it in a more manageable format, such as Google Analytics[2] (a free programme from Google that allows you to see how many people visit your website), but there are precious few programmes out there that take us to the final step, providing some intelligence.

---

2   https://analytics.google.com/analytics/web/

As an example, imagine the dashboard of your car. Countless hours have gone into its design to make sure that as a driver, you have all the information you need in front of you. Your car engine management system constantly monitors dozens of different sensors, all of which produce data. That data is only shown to you as information if you need it to drive the car safely, such as your speed. If something goes wrong, however, your dashboard will flash up a warning light, like the one shown in Figure 2. But here's the problem: It's giving you information, but do you have any idea what it means?[3]

Intelligence, particularly actionable intelligence, is still the rarest of commodities in this world, and this is where SEO comes in; because optimising data means it can become information, and from information, we can start to derive some real intelligence.

Figure 2 – Do you know what this symbol means?

The definition of SEO

If we accept that SEO has been around for at least 25 years, you'd think that by now there would be a single definition on which everyone agreed? After all, it can't be that difficult, can it?

Once again, it seems people can't agree.

Top of Google's search results is this one from Oxford Languages:
"the process of maximizing the number of visitors to a particular website by ensuring that the site appears high on the list of results returned by a search engine."

Moz says:
"SEO stands for Search Engine Optimization, which is the practice of increasing the quantity and quality of traffic to your website through organic search engine results."

There are dozens more definitions like this, and whilst they are similar, they have subtle differences. Which is fine, but they miss the basic point. They miss the

---

[3] When it was first introduced, it was to indicate that the alternator was malfunctioning and therefore, the battery was not charging. In practice, it usually meant that the fan belt had snapped, for which the roadside fix was to fashion a new one from a spare pair of ladies' tights (I kid you not). Today, this symbol means a huge range of things, depending on what type of vehicle you drive. From a misfiring spark plug to a blocked diesel particulate filter, and over twenty other different faults are all reported by this one symbol. No wonder motorists are confused.

fact that it's not about *quantity* and *quality* of traffic – those are a by-product of the work that is done.

It's all about the search engine.

> My definition for SEO, which I have used for many years, is:
> **The process of structuring data on your website so search engines and humans can read and understand it.**

This is important.

The clue is there in the name — search engine optimisation. It's about optimising for search engines. Full stop.

If it's done properly, what happens after you have optimised your website is you get more visitors to your website and more people who want what you are selling, but to do that you need to have understood in the first place what both the search engines and real people are looking for.

Because, despite the focus on search engines, they never buy what you are selling.

People do.

Think back to the days before the internet, when we all relied on printed advertisements to promote a business. Back then, would you have created an advertisement based on the technical specifications of the publisher, or would you have created an advertisement with the message you wanted your customers to read?

Sure, you needed to make sure you *met* the technical specifications of the paper, but that was after you'd decided on the message and design. Because back then we accepted that the paper was just the vehicle for delivering your message, not the most important thing. Strangely, however, people seem to think that it's all about Google these days and they forget about the real reason for doing this – customers.

So, whilst search engine optimisation is focused on optimising your website for search engines, underpinning that work is *optimising for people*, and in doing so, making sure you meet the technical specifications of the vehicle people are using to find you. When it was decided that the vehicle was more important than the message, I don't know, but I do know that it has dominated thinking for far too long and we need to break free of this constraint to propel businesses forward.

Why SEO became a byword for cheating

When I first set up a digital agency back in 2011, I was fascinated by the way websites appeared at the top of Google. I worked alongside someone who had grown up with SEO and knew pretty much every trick in the book. Knowing him as I do, I'm convinced he may have invented some of them himself! Together, we started the agency from scratch and in a very short space of time, were able to get websites ranking well on Google.

But whilst doing this and researching not just what to do, but how to do it, I was struck by one compelling thought: time after time, most websites at the top of the search results were cheating. Being able to understand the technicalities of SEO, I could see the tricks others were using to get sites above those of our customers. I quickly realised that it was nothing to do with the quality of the website, nor its attractiveness to end users, but simply a function of money and understanding. And in many cases, it was about how many cheap links one could purchase from somewhere in the Far East.

Given that at that point I had spent 25 years in sales and marketing, it seemed strange that we had abandoned pretty much everything we knew about sales psychology and marketing principles in favour of hammering a single page with multiple mentions of the keyword you wanted to rank for, and then paying for a load of links. Not only was this anathema to me, but it also went against Google's Webmaster Guidelines,[4] which specially prohibited many of the practices other firms were using. You see, it wasn't about playing fair, it was about winning. The more customers you got to number one, the more customers wanted you to do the same for them. It grew so large that some firms had their own offshore link farms, run by expats, responsible for creating millions of links to customer websites to boost their rankings.

It was madness.

Google knew this, and within a couple of months of me starting the firm, they tried their best to put the lid back on Pandora's box with the introduction of

---

[4] https://developers.google.com/search/docs/advanced/guidelines/webmaster-guidelines

the Panda and Penguin[5] updates. When this happened, there was a seismic shift in the SEO landscape. Websites with millions of links were penalised and disappeared overnight from the search engine results pages (SERPS). Firms who had been using these tactics found themselves in dire straits and were besieged with angry customers whose livelihoods had just been wiped out.

Fortunately, as we'd never engaged in any of these practices, we were spared this and indeed, our customers' websites started to thrive. In part, this was because of the framework on which we had operated since the start. I refined these into three simple rules which, even today, are the foundations of what we do in the business – **The 3 Rules of Google**. I'll talk more about them in Chapter 2.

Why should SEO be important to you?

It's an interesting question. Why should anyone worry about search engine optimisation? Well, if you own a website of any size, the chances are you will want it to appear when people look for you. If you do, then you need to worry about SEO. But there's a pretty good chance that you've never worried about SEO before. Most people don't give it a second thought and, in truth, many website owners (even if they know of it) tend to dismiss it as something that needs doing later – if at all.

As a website owner, the uncomfortable truth is that you can't afford to ignore it. As my mother used to tell me, ignoring it won't make it go away. Like homework that needs doing, tax returns that need filing and meter readings that need logging, a lack of enthusiasm or urgency on your part doesn't diminish the requirement for the job to be done. But why should you bother? Why take time to optimise your website and why spend any money on something as intangible as this?

To answer these questions, let's take a look at the logic of optimising your website, starting with scale. According to Government statistics,[6] the number of private sector businesses in the UK at the start of 2019 was 5.9 million, an

---

5   Panda was the name given to a Google algorithm update that was specifically developed to reduce the appearance of low-quality, thin content in the search results. Penguin was the name given to a similar algorithm, specifically aimed at penalising websites with unnatural backlinks pointing to them.
6   https://www.gov.uk/government/statistics/business-population-estimates-2019/business-population-estimates-for-the-uk-and-regions-2019-statistical-release-html

increase of 3.5% on 2018; more than 200,000 additional businesses in a single year. The number of businesses in the UK with a website runs at just under 85%,[7] but as this figure is from 2019, it won't take into account the impact of the 2020 and 2021 lockdowns and the drive to appear online.

So, just under six million businesses in the UK and over five million of them with websites. Marry that with 96% of all households in the UK having Internet access and 87% of all adults having shopped online in the past twelve months[8] and you can see that if you are in business, having a website is critical. But here's the problem: there's only one top spot on Google. There may be a dozen solicitors in your local town, but only one of them can appear at the top of Google. And if you've ever wondered how they do it, I can tell you – it's SEO.

The prime reason for doing any work on optimising your website is that it gets you in the game.

But let's look at what happens when people arrive on Google. What then? It's all about Click Through Rate (CTR). CTR is described as the ratio of users who click on a specific link, compared to the number of total users who view the page as a whole. In other words, if 100 people looked at a page and 40 clicked on one link, that link would have a 40% CTR.

A 2020 study by Ignite Visibility,[9] found that for non-branded clicks (i.e. searchers are looking for what you do, not who you are), over 40% of people clicked through to the website in first position. What's more, positions two and three were also impressive, with

Position	% of Clicks
1	43.43%
2	37.36%
3	29.90%
4	19.38%
5	10.95%
6	10.00%
7	5.28%
8	4.13%
9	4.13%
10	3.11%

Figure 3 – Percentage of users who click on each position of the search results.

---

7   https://www.statista.com/statistics/282241/proportion-of-businesses-with-a-website-in-the-uk/
8   https://www.ons.gov.uk/peoplepopulationandcommunity/householdcharacteristics/homeinternetandsocialmediausage/bulletins/internetaccesshouseholdsandindividuals/2020
9   https://ignitevisibility.com/google-ctr-by-ranking-position/

37% and 30% click through rates respectively. These rates slowly decrease until you reach the tenth position, by which time just 3% of the people who see that page will click on the link (Figure 3).

It's simple. The higher you are on Google for a search query, the more clicks you will get to your website. There's nothing new in this statement, but what is worth noting is that every study I have read in the past twenty years has concluded the same thing. Where you are in Google's search results matters, and search engine optimisation can help you influence that.

There are, of course, other compelling reasons why you should be interested in SEO. For a start, it helps with branding. The more people see your company name in their search results, the more likely they are to remember you when they need the product or service you sell. It also helps you stand out against your competition, which reinforces the chances of customers coming to you, not them.

I tested this a few years back with one of our customers who was running paid (PPC) advertising on Google at the same time as regularly appearing in the top three for most of the search queries they wanted. In Google's PPC advertising reporting there is a clever report called the 'Paid and Organic report', which I used to see if their advertisement and their organic listing were shown at the same time to someone searching on Google.

> **PPC Advertising**
> Pay Per Click (PPC) advertising is an online advertising model, where advertisements are served to potential customers and the advertiser is only charged when someone clicks on the advertisement.

What I discovered was that if their organic listing appeared somewhere on the page where the paid advertisement was at the top, the click through rate was 3% higher. Three percent might not sound like a lot, but to them it was worth thousands of pounds every time, so every percentage point counted. If your name appears repeatedly in the search results, people will take note of your brand. It's the old saying that 'nothing works quite like repetition; I said nothing works quite like repetition.'

And finally, if you aren't already convinced that SEO is of value to your business, consider the valuation of your business when you come to sell. I'll cover this in more detail later in this book, but for now, let's just explore the headline idea that your website might be valuable.

Many business owners dream of an exit where they get to sell their business and leave with a large sum of money in their bank accounts, but few actually have a concrete plan of how to do this. Even more astonishing is that even fewer of these owners seem to have any concept of what a buyer would find valuable and only a tiny subset of the first group considers their website to be a business asset. In a great many sales, the website has no separate valuation and does nothing to add to the final exit multiple, but occasionally, there are businesses who get more when selling their business precisely because the website has value. And it can mean thousands more on the selling price, just by spending a little time and attention on something as basic as SEO.

Takeaways:

The higher you appear on Google, the more people will visit your website.

The world is awash with data, but short on intelligence.

SEO will help you rank higher on Google and other search engines.

CHAPTER 2

The 3 Rules of Google

I t's probably a bit too easy to list the three rules without giving you any background. In fact, if I did that then you'd probably say 'well, that's just obvious'. Trust me, back in 2011, it was anything other than obvious. Most customers I spoke to were desperately confused as to what SEO was and how you did it. Many had tried to understand it, and some had even read Google's guidelines, but were flummoxed when it was clear that following them wouldn't get the job done. It was time to simplify the landscape, so I created **The 3 Rules of Google.**

Before we go into them, it's worth stating the obvious. These 3 Rules aren't a magic bullet. They don't cover everything you need to know about SEO, and they won't, on their own, get your website to number one. However, the rules give you a framework around which you can hang everything else.

So, without further ado, here they are:

➡ **Rule 1** - **Google is just a machine**
➡ **Rule 2** - **Nothing, but nothing, beats great content**
➡ **Rule 3** - **One page, one keyword or phrase**

Simple, eh? Let's dive into these and understand more about where they came from and why they are important.

Rule 1: Google is just a machine

Have you ever tried searching 'What is Google?' on Google?

I didn't think so.

Everyone knows what Google is, right? Or do they?

The top result on Google currently says: "Google is an American company that is most commonly known as a search engine."

Well, that's two things already: a company and a search engine.

Further down the results it is also described as:

"Google is a multinational, publicly-traded organization."

"Google definition: the proprietary name of a leading Internet search engine, founded in 1998."

It's also a verb – "I googled your company...",

an adjective – "Let's make the entire database googleable...",

and a noun – "Let's try and improve our website's googleability..."

It can be used in past, present and future tenses, and it is one of the world's best-known brands. On top of all that, it's developed a persona, which means that people will sometimes tell you that they can't do something because 'Google won't like it' or 'Google doesn't allow it'. Much like being in a large organisation when you are told that 'senior management would say no' before anyone has even asked senior management what they think, Google is perceived as being a kind of authority figure.

On the darker side, Google can be perceived as an out-of-control corporation, a monopoly, or the thing that killed printed newspapers. That it gathers and controls your personal data and is akin to Big Brother.

On the flip side, it can be seen as a tool which empowers the world, a force for good, and with a motto of 'don't be evil' at its core, a champion for the little guy.

And the crazy thing is, all of these could be correct.

Little wonder therefore, that when people try to optimise their own websites, they are faced with a morass of conflicting ideas, emotions and sentiments which can colour their judgement and actions.

Which is why Rule 1 is so important.

In the context of SEO, Google is just a machine.

True, it's a very clever machine, and as I write this in 2022, best guesses suggest that around 60% of the current algorithm is now artificial intelligence, driven by Google's machine learning programme known as Rank Brain. On top of that, there's no one individual who is the keeper of the 'secret recipe', who knows and understands how the 'magic' algorithm works – or to be more accurate, algorithms, plural.

If you stop thinking of Google as having a personality, or being magic, and start to think of it like the engine of a car, it becomes easier to understand.

Car engines these days are 'magic'. If, like me, you've lifted the bonnet recently, you'll see that gone are the days when you could spend a Sunday afternoon tinkering to improve performance. Most modern engines now require a laptop to be plugged in to perform diagnostic tasks, and replacing or tweaking anything is far from easy. But at its heart, it's still an engine, and performs exactly the same job as engines did thirty years ago. You add petrol, water, oil, and a spark and off they go, powering you to your destination.

Google is very much like that engine. It's ready for you any time you want it to go and will help you arrive at your destination (the correct answer to your query) whenever you like. All it needs is your spark of imagination to ask it the question and it powers you to your answer.

And much like car engines, you don't need to know how it works for it to get you to where you want to be. But when you stop thinking of it as an engine and start to imbue it with personality and powers, then it stops being something you can optimise and becomes something else.

So, for the purposes of SEO, my advice to customers is to always treat Google as a machine.

And if you ever get confused by SEO at any point, refer to Rule 1.

Rule 2: Nothing, but nothing, beats great content.

Back in 1996, a much younger Bill Gates, still driving Microsoft forwards at that time, wrote on their website: "Content is where I expect much of the real money will be made on the Internet, just as it was in broadcasting."

Taken today as almost a given, everyone has an opinion about content in the context of websites. But my interest came from much further back than that, from pre-Internet days. I grew up with print advertising and my 'bible' was David Ogilvie's *Ogilvie on Advertising* which, if you've never read it, is a highly recommended read. Wikipedia today says he is known as the "Father of Advertising", and whilst it's a nice label, it might be more accurate to say he is the "Father of *Modern* Advertising".

He took the advertising industry and not only changed the way advertising was created, but more importantly, how it was measured. He was one of the first people in the business to ever talk about data and research with as much fervour as the creative design. His methods and principles inspired generations of adverting executives, and no doubt, influenced what was later to come with the Internet.

He was perfectly at ease writing at length about the benefits of a product if he felt the advertisement needed it, and he was meticulous in his headline creation. He realised, from his background as a researcher, that different people were looking for different things (even in the same product), and his job was to create a compelling narrative that would persuade them to buy. Essentially, it wasn't about glossy pictures of the product (though they often helped), it was about the content.

Fast forward from the 1960s and 70s (when he bestrode the advertising world as a colossus) to today and I'm sure there are elements of the online advertising space that would have appalled him. From tawdry click bait display advertisements, such as those seen on your local newspaper website, to restrictive headlines defined not by creativity, but by character length, there's lots wrong with what happens online today. But within that are signs of the advertising world he helped create.

Given a website as a canvas, some people have embraced the opportunity that extra space provides and have been able to create content that speaks to their customers in new and compelling ways.

And this content sells.

Bill Gates may have envisaged something slightly different back in 1996, but today, search is predominantly about content. Even if you have technically the worst website in the world, if you have the right answer to the question being asked, you can still rank well in search.

To better understand how important content is in search, you need to consider what Google is trying to do. If we go back to Rule 1, we know that Google is just a machine. It's designed to do one thing and that is to find the right answers to whatever queries you ask of it. How it does that is to gather an understanding of everything it can find on the Internet and store that information somewhere easily accessible. In simple terms, when you ask it something, it looks in its index to see if it can find the right answer.

But what if there is more than one 'right' answer? How should it prioritise them?

Well, currently it uses a range of factors to determine which page ranks where, but for simplicity, let's assume that the two main ones are backlinks and content.

> **Backlinks (links)**
> Any electronic link from one place on the Internet to another.

Links are important as this is the foundation on which Google built its empire. The genius of the idea that sparked Google's success was that instead of just taking all the content that was on the Internet and returning it in an order based on how many times a word or phrase appears on a page, they looked at how many people found the page useful. But how do you judge what people find useful?

Larry Page and Sergei Brin, prior to founding Google in 1998, researched this as a project at Stamford University and tested this idea by analysing the number and relevance of pages that linked to each other across the Internet. What they found was that most people who linked to a page did so because they thought it would help their readers. If they were writing about a great restaurant, they would include a link to the restaurant website so anyone wanting to get the same experience could just follow the link. As part of their research, they also established that not all links were created equal. As an example, a link from the *Wall Street Journal* would generally be regarded as more valuable than a link from a local greengrocer, and so the concept of link equity was created. These ideas were critical to the development of Google as a search engine. Given that their search engine produced much better, more relevant results than other search engines, it became clear that more links, from better websites, meant websites or webpages would rank higher. And with that knowledge began the industry of buying backlinks to manipulate Google's search results.

> **Buying Backlinks**
> Purchasing a link from another website with the intention of inflating the importance of your website or page.
> This is strictly forbidden by Google.

This worked to a greater or lesser extent, right up until the Penguin update of 2012, when this type of link manipulation was called to a halt. And whilst links are still important, these days you can rank top for a query without links if you have the right answer to the question being asked.

> **Penguin**
> Penguin was the name given to a series of ten algorithm changes made by Google between 2012-2016, that sought to reduce the amount of manipulative link schemes. These schemes were founded on creating large volumes of links that could be directed to any website with the intention of helping it rank better in the search results.

Which brings us back to content.

Love it or hate it, content is King. In the case of getting your website to rank, you won't do it without the right content. There's a really good book on how to do this called *They Ask, You Answer* by Marcus Sheridan. If you want to understand just how important content is, immerse yourself in this book or just carry on reading and I'll talk in more detail about what makes great content in Chapter 3.

Rule 3: One page, one keyword or phrase

Actually, I have tweaked this rule since it was first published.

When I first went to print with this in 2012, it was 'One page, one keyword', but since then, Google changed the way it ranks websites by dropping the focus on individual keywords and focusing more on 'search phrases', so a small adjustment was needed.

But what does this *actually* mean? Why is it important to just have one word or phrase on a page and how does that work in practice?

Well, you will come across this in other walks of life, as the principle has lots of different guises. Sometimes you'll hear people say, 'Stick to the knitting' or 'Make the main thing the main thing' or 'Do one thing at a time'. All these sayings are based around the same, simple principle, which is that to do something really well you need to focus on it.

And in SEO it's no different.

Part of the problem stems from the way people were sold websites in the early days. I recall developers offering to build people a basic six-page website and then charging extra for every additional page you added on. Of course, this was in the days before the advent of WordPress and other self-publishing frameworks. Customers did what they had done for years before; they stuffed as much as they could into as small a space as possible. Partly, this has its roots in the days of print advertising. As someone who sold advertising space, I have seen, time and time again, customers trying to squeeze a quart into a pint pot and being told, 'Yes, I like the design, but can we make it half the size?'

Print advertising was always based on the space it took and so people became accustomed to trying to get as much as they could into a small space. Some buyers took immense pride in driving down the cost of their advertising by achieving the impossible in space terms. Nowhere was this more evident than small businesses and traders, who would regularly be faced with the issue of limited budget but unlimited ambition.

Take, for example, the local builder. Often, he would not just be a builder, but also specialise in one or more other trades. Sometimes it was roofing, sometimes it was plastering, but whatever else they were good at, it wasn't just straightforward building work. When they advertised in the newspaper, they would simply put in one advert containing all the trades they could provide, on the basis that if they were in the classified section, anyone looking for a tradesman could see what they did. When it came to directories, however, they had a problem. Directories were classified and they separated trades into different areas. Users were expected to look under 'B' for Builders and 'R' for Roofers. And they did. So, what of the builder who was also a roofer? Typically, the sales representative would suggest to them that they needed two advertisements: one for building and one for roofing. Equally typical was the builder who would see this as them being gouged for extra money and simply do what they did in the newspaper – put everything into the one advert. The end result? They got the type of work dictated by the classification in which they advertised, and no one called them for their other sides of the business. This was an annual cat and mouse game and businesses up and down the country played it daily with sales reps.

Enter the Internet, followed by websites, and suddenly the game changed. Except that it didn't for these local tradespeople. They still did what they had always done. Faced with a developer who wanted extra money for more pages, they simply crammed everything into the smallest possible space. In short, they took their classified advertising online in the form of a website and crammed everything they did into as few pages as possible. And in most cases, the website tanked.

What they had missed (and what most people missed) was that even though it didn't have headings, Google was a classified directory. If you wanted a builder, it would show you builders. If you wanted a roofer, it would show you roofers. And whilst it would show firms that did both trades, as a preference it showed you pages on websites that best met what you were looking for, as that page focused exclusively on that topic. And as more people became familiar with the way Google worked, they started to be more specific with their searches. Instead of looking for a roofer, they looked for a flat roofer or a slate tile roofer or someone who repaired chimney stacks. Search fragmented and the tradespeople's crammed websites became less and less relevant.

Hence Rule 3: one page, one keyword or phrase.

These days, when I talk to customers about website creation and optimisation, I talk about tailoring the user experience so that people who search for what a business does can find that page. And on that page, the business can talk about not just what they do, but how and why they do it, as well as lots of other things – as long as those things are all about the same topic. And of course, we need to explain to the person searching why they should choose the company they are reading about on the website. In short, you need to sell them the benefits not just the product.

And these are my 3 Rules of Google.

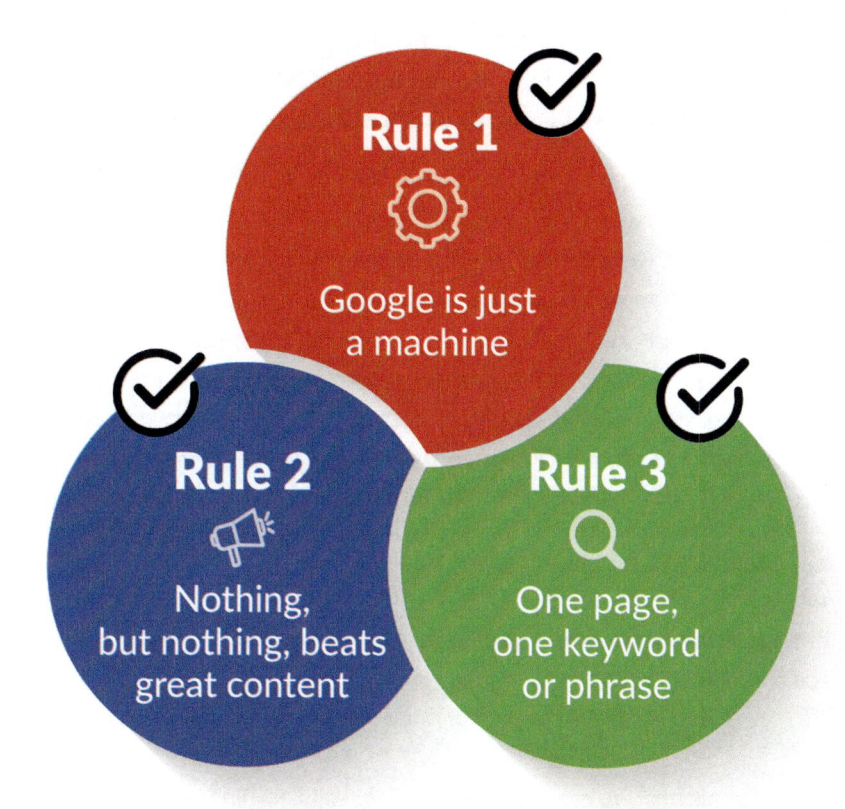

Rule 1: Google is just a machine

Rule 2: Nothing, but nothing, beats great content

Rule 3: One page, one keyword or phrase

When put in those terms it's quite straightforward. Create a website, give each product or service its own page and make sure you write good content that people will want to read.

Sure, there are the small matters of backlinks, internal interlinking, and technical SEO, but these come very much on the back of the 3 Rules.

As I said earlier, in the days before Google, people naturally linked to other websites and webpages *because they were useful*. It was like giving someone a personal recommendation. You'd only put your name to a recommendation if you knew (or at least thought) that your friends would benefit from that recommendation. And those links are what helped Larry Page and Sergei Brin create Google; by understanding that it wasn't just about how many times you could count the word you were searching for on a page, it was about usefulness and utility.

Search Never Sleeps

And the technical side of SEO? Ironically, this also comes from the 3 Rules. Even the worst optimised websites will still get crawled by Google and therefore they will be ranked. Somewhere. For something. Generally, not very highly or well, but they will get ranked. But if you have implemented the 3 Rules first, then your chances of appearing in the search results is greatly increased.

In the next chapter, I'll cover some of the technical elements of SEO and demonstrate that it's much easier to write a title tag if the page is only about one thing. Likewise with images on your website that show a single thing which is clear to see and understand. Even schema markup (more on this exotic sounding task later) requires that each page is clearly identifiable as being about one thing. Google relies on this, and it relies on us – you and me – to ensure that what it is being presented with on a website is easy to crawl, read and understand. If you ever have to sit one of Google's exams for its pay per click advertising, you can see how important this is to the company. These are the sort of questions asked:

If Mary is looking for a pair of red stilettos shoes, is it better to show her a page:
- of men's and women's shoes
- of a range of women's shoes, all of different styles
- of red stilettos shoes

I think you can guess the answer.

And at the end of this, you can now see that it's really nothing to do with Google, it's about people. It's about how people behave and how they react. In truth, they only use Google because it's useful. Because when all is said and done, Google is a vehicle for them. A bridge between buyers and sellers. In fact, Google is just a machine.

Takeaways:

Remember, Google is just a machine.

People, not machines, buy what you are selling.

A small amount of time spent optimising your website will pay huge dividends in the long run.

CHAPTER 3

The Three Key Areas of SEO

You might recall that in Chapter 2, I talked about Google being like a car engine and if you have looked under the bonnet of your car recently, perhaps to top up the windscreen washer bottle, you might have been silently grateful that you don't have to service it. Like Google, modern engine compartments look far too complicated to me.

When I got my first car back in the 1970s, things were a lot simpler. I could open the bonnet, name many of the components I was looking at, and if the car was struggling, possibly fix it myself at the roadside. There were a handful of moving parts I could affect and a short list of suspects if anything went wrong with the car. And when you got a new fault, one that required a garage, you learned from them not only what the problem was, but how to fix it at the roadside in case it happened again. These days, I can't even see the engine. When I open the bonnet, I'm faced with a big plastic panel that covers the entire engine compartment which, I have to say, makes it look aesthetically pleasing, but frankly, I wouldn't know where to start if anything went wrong.

The good news, however, is that I know some great mechanics. People who do this for a living and know not only where to start, but what to do and in which order. So, once a year, I hand them the keys to my car and it gets serviced and returned to me in tip-top condition.

Now, I say this because when you first lift the bonnet on your own website, you may well be tempted to dive in and try to fix things. And if your website is brand new, you have no traffic and there's nothing to lose, then why not go for it? Read the guides, understand the basics, and give it a good go yourself. If you break it, you've lost nothing but have probably gained some useful experience.

But, if you have an established website that delivers regular traffic and that ranks well on Google, even if it's just for your company name, then how do you know that any changes you make won't have an adverse effect? This is where a little knowledge can be a dangerous thing. So, before you dive on in, you probably need to understand what the consequences of changing things might be. And to do that you should be aware of the three areas of SEO and how they link together. They are quite easy to remember, and they are:

On-site
On-page
Off-site

On-site is all about the technical bits you find on your website, On-page is all about the content and how users see your website, and finally Off-site is all about the things that happen away from your website that influence how people see it and find it.

These next sections will deal with each of them in turn and blow apart some of the myths and misunderstandings that you'll find in existing SEO literature.

On-site

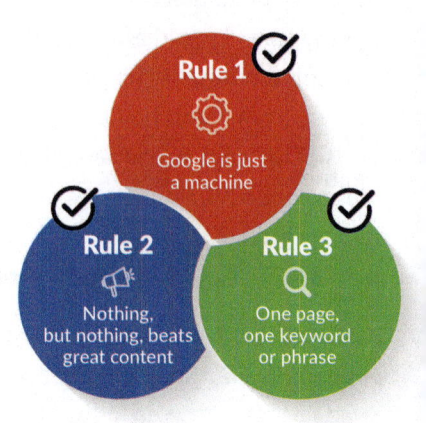

When I talk about how to understand SEO, I generally tend to start with On-site SEO first, often referred to as technical SEO. This is not because it's any more important than the other two areas, but because it links neatly with Rule 1, and if nothing else, I like the symmetry. Remember, Rule 1 is 'Google is just a machine', so what we are looking at here is how the 'machine' will see your website.

The easiest way to visualise On-site or technical SEO is as all the bits of your website that the machine will see, read, and understand. Of course, when I use the word 'see', it's a bit of a misnomer as we have to remember Rule 1 again, which of course means that Google and its crawlers have no senses. Google can't actually 'see' anything in the way humans see things and it can't smell, hear, taste, or touch them either. It's important to remember that whatever you do, this bit is all about the 'machine'.

What it can do very well is read. Google crawls and reads your website on pretty much a daily basis as it wants to know not only if you've added anything to your website but also if you've changed anything. It's a hungry beast and it feeds on fresh information.

Google Crawl, Index and Ranking

I suppose I had better start by explaining what a 'Google crawl' is, and more importantly, why it is important. Google describes its crawl like this: [1]

"The first step is finding out what pages exist on the web. There isn't a central registry of all webpages, so Google must constantly search for new pages and add them to its list of known pages."

So, it's a process of finding out what pages exist on the web. And they do that by using bots. I always find it helpful to imagine them like the Sentinels (or Squiddies) from the Matrix film franchise. They go out into the environment (in this case, the web) and examine everything they encounter, probing and interrogating to establish whether there is anything of value hiding in the websites they find. I know this makes them sound quite sinister, however in reality, these bots from Google are anything but.

Once the bots find a url they can latch onto, they crawl the website and try to gather information on what they find to 'report back to base'.

URL
A url is a Uniform Resource Locator, otherwise known as a website address.

[1] https://developers.google.com/search/docs/beginner/how-search-works

The following graph (Figure 4) shows a snapshot of Google's crawl of one of my websites. As you can see, there is a pretty much constant background crawling of this website (the line rarely goes to zero), and at certain times, such as the turn of the year, the bots crawled my website more frequently. Why? Well, because that was when I added a single new piece of content that was not only accurate and relevant, but timely as well. It was something people were looking for in the first two weeks of 2021 and I had the correct answer. Google found the new

Figure 4 – Google crawl of a website. Note the spike in early 2021.

information as part of its regular crawl, it recognised that this was the answer to a search query that it had started to see a lot more, and it came back to see if I'd written anything else on this subject or added to my original answer. As you can see, after a few days, it realised that I had nothing more for it, so it reduced the crawl frequency.

But what does Google do with the information it has found?

In this case, it found that I had written something that appeared to be (and was) the correct answer to a search query it was seeing a lot more at that time. So, what it did was index my content, knowing that when the time came that someone was asking that very specific question, it should show them my website as a precise answer to that question.

For those of you wondering what the 'correct answer' was, on 1 January 2021,

Royal Mail raised their prices for first and second class postage stamps. Normally they do this in March, so it was a bit of a departure from the norm. On my website, which is all about postage stamps, I wrote the answer to a question lots of people were asking, which was, 'What is the price of a second class stamp?' and unsurprisingly, it ranked immediately.

To illustrate the point, here's a snapshot of the Google search result from June 2021 (Figure 5), six months after I made the change. It shows quite clearly that even though my website is tiny and has no authority, it is being shown at position seven in the search results and is one of only two websites that are showing the correct answer. Ironically, the top two search results don't answer the query but

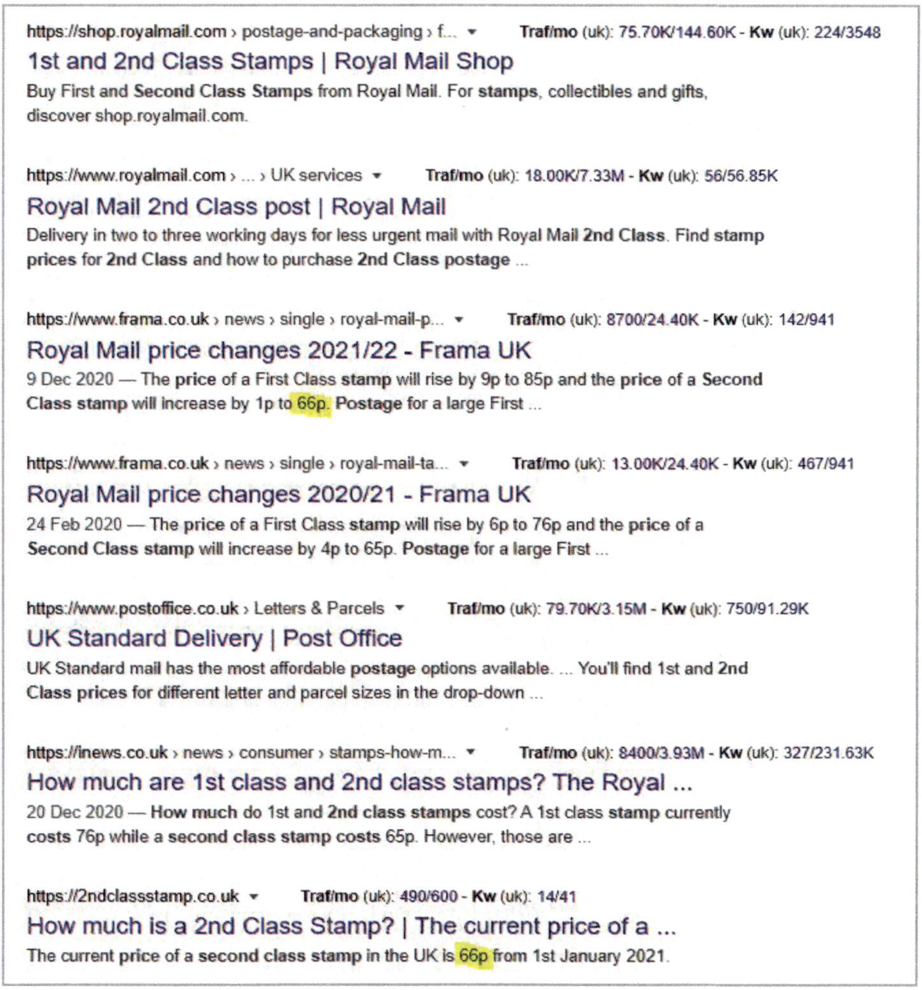

https://shop.royalmail.com › postage-and-packaging › f... ▾ **Traf/mo** (uk): 75.70K/144.60K - **Kw** (uk): 224/3548
1st and 2nd Class Stamps | Royal Mail Shop
Buy First and **Second Class Stamps** from Royal Mail. For **stamps**, collectibles and gifts, discover shop.royalmail.com.

https://www.royalmail.com › ... › UK services ▾ **Traf/mo** (uk): 18.00K/7.33M - **Kw** (uk): 56/56.85K
Royal Mail 2nd Class post | Royal Mail
Delivery in two to three working days for less urgent mail with Royal Mail **2nd Class**. Find **stamp prices** for **2nd Class** and how to purchase **2nd Class postage** ...

https://www.frama.co.uk › news › single › royal-mail-p... ▾ **Traf/mo** (uk): 8700/24.40K - **Kw** (uk): 142/941
Royal Mail price changes 2021/22 - Frama UK
9 Dec 2020 — The **price** of a First Class **stamp** will rise by 9p to 85p and the **price** of a **Second Class stamp** will increase by 1p to 66p. **Postage** for a large First ...

https://www.frama.co.uk › news › single › royal-mail-ta... ▾ **Traf/mo** (uk): 13.00K/24.40K - **Kw** (uk): 467/941
Royal Mail price changes 2020/21 - Frama UK
24 Feb 2020 — The **price** of a First Class **stamp** will rise by 6p to 76p and the **price** of a **Second Class stamp** will increase by 4p to 65p. **Postage** for a large First ...

https://www.postoffice.co.uk › Letters & Parcels ▾ **Traf/mo** (uk): 79.70K/3.15M - **Kw** (uk): 750/91.29K
UK Standard Delivery | Post Office
UK Standard mail has the most affordable **postage** options available. ... You'll find 1st and **2nd Class prices** for different letter and parcel sizes in the drop-down ...

https://inews.co.uk › news › consumer › stamps-how-m... ▾ **Traf/mo** (uk): 8400/3.93M - **Kw** (uk): 327/231.63K
How much are 1st class and 2nd class stamps? The Royal ...
20 Dec 2020 — **How much** do 1st and **2nd class stamps** cost? A 1st class **stamp** currently costs 76p while a **second class stamp** costs 65p. However, those are ...

https://2ndclassstamp.co.uk ▾ **Traf/mo** (uk): 490/600 - **Kw** (uk): 14/41
How much is a 2nd Class Stamp? | The current price of a ...
The current **price** of a **second class stamp** in the UK is 66p from 1st January 2021.

Figure 5 – Google search results showing just two of the websites listed have the correct answer.

are there by virtue of the fact that they are Royal Mail, who you might reasonably expect to have the correct answer to this question. This illustrates Rule 2, which shows that nothing, but nothing, beats great content. In this case, it's having the right answer to the question and as such, my tiny website is only beaten by Royal Mail, Frama, The Post Office and *The Independent*. Incidentally, two of the answers shown in the websites above me are incorrect. The only reason they appear higher is that the websites have 'authority' (more on that later) and had previously, at one time, been correct.

Fast forward to June 2022 and the price had gone up (again) so I updated my website accordingly. This time I'd made it to position 4 (Figure 6), surrounded by far more authoritative websites than mine.

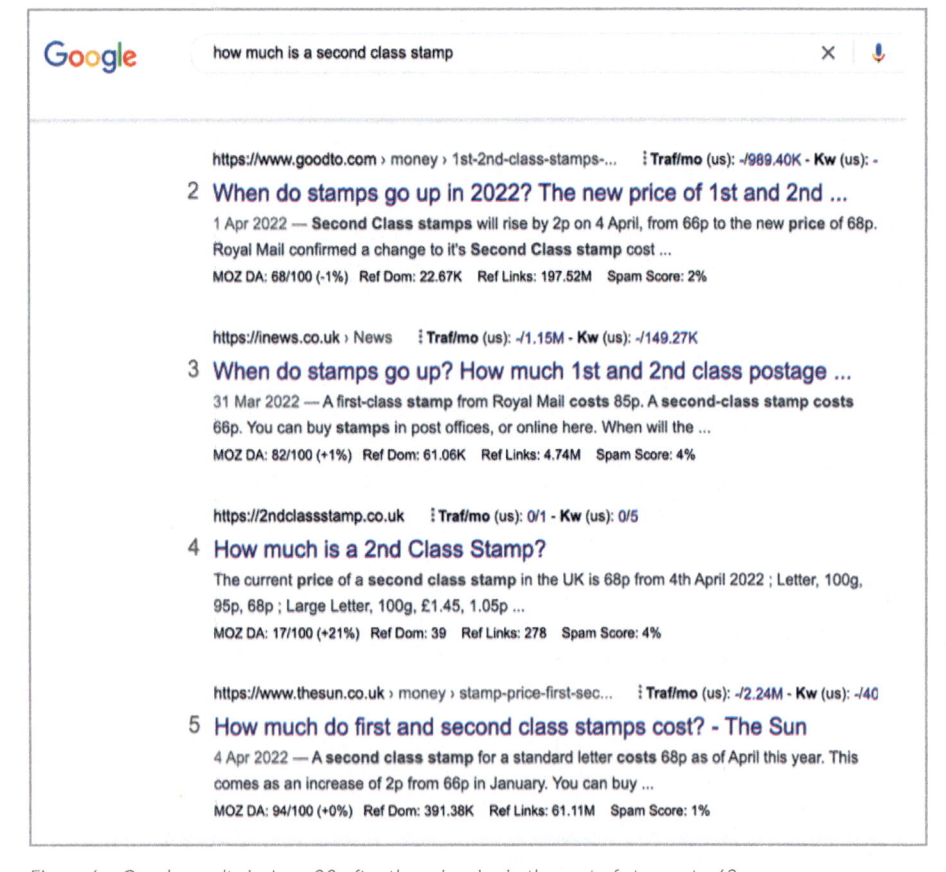

Figure 6 – Google results in June 22 after the price rise in the cost of stamps to 68p.

Google had crawled the site when the changes happened in April, and despite me removing the Google Analytics tracking code as an experiment, it still ranks me higher than other, bigger websites. It proves clearly that Google crawls everything it finds, whether we like it or not.

> **Google Analytics**
> Google Analytics tracking code is a few lines of code that acts as a unique identifier to your website. This allows Google Analytics to collect data on your website and report that data back to you as the website owner.

The crawl is constant, in that Google keeps an eye on websites regularly. For far more regularly updated or bigger websites, the crawlers come back with greater frequency. That frequency is often referred to as the 'crawl budget'. I've seen huge amounts written about what this is and isn't. The reality for most websites is, it is what it is. You can't materially change it, and unless you are a newspaper or other fast moving news outlet, you probably don't want to. The crawl budget is about how much resource Google will commit on a daily, weekly, and monthly basis, to crawling your website. Because crawling requires both time and resources to undertake. Google asks you to make it simple for it by adding in a sitemap[2] but in reality, they will crawl everything anyway, whether you help them or not and whether you like it or not. Even if you add specific instructions in the code such as 'no crawl' or 'no index', or as I did, remove the Analytics tracking code, they will still crawl your site, if only to find the instruction not to crawl it. Irrespective of any 'budget' or any instruction you might issue, Google will continue to do this as it is its *raison d'être*. If it doesn't crawl, it can't index.

If it can't index, it can't rank pages in search, and if it can't do that, it can't offer the right answer to the questions you and I ask it daily.

---

[2] A sitemap is a file where a website owner can provide information about the pages, videos, and other files on their website, and the relationships between them. I cover this in more detail later in this chapter.

So, Rule 1 still applies. It's just a machine trying to do its job.

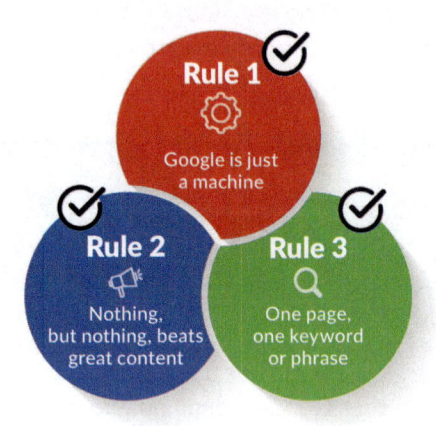

Rule 1
Google is just a machine

Rule 2
Nothing, but nothing, beats great content

Rule 3
One page, one keyword or phrase

CASE STUDY

I was approached by a firm in the legal sector who had just built and set live a new website. Two weeks after this event, one of their team noticed that when they searched on Google, the new website was not appearing, just the competitors. Further checks revealed that the regular stream of new enquiries had also dried up and they realised that they had a problem. The developers were adamant that there was nothing wrong with the new website but still, they couldn't understand why Google wasn't showing them.

When I checked, the developers had inadvertently left the <meta name="robots" content="noindex"> instruction on the home page, which meant that when Google's crawlers arrived, they found an instruction telling them not to index any of the pages they found. Egg on the face for the developers, who corrected this very quickly, and within two weeks the website was back to its old position in the search results.

Takeaway:
Rule 1 – Google is just a machine. This is why technical SEO is essential for every website.

The Three Key Areas of SEO

Which brings us to the bit it does after crawling, and that is indexing. What is indexing? Well, again Google gives the most helpful explanation, which is:

"After a page is discovered, Google tries to understand what the page is about. This process is called indexing. Google analyzes the content of the page, catalogs images and video files embedded on the page, and otherwise tries to understand the page. This information is stored in the Google index, a huge database stored in many, many (many!) computers."

This is more to do with the next area of SEO, 'on-page', so I will come to it in more detail there, but suffice to say, this is the section where Google is trying to make sense of what it has found. If you've remembered Rules 1-3, then you should be OK at this point.

Back to my website, when I added the content at the start of 2021, my hope was that I could achieve a 'position zero' knowledge box. A knowledge box is typically an answer that appears in a box at the top of a search query, as Google thinks this will help users find right answers quicker. Good examples of this include when you ask Google what the time is, or the height of the Eiffel Tower.

Ironically, the answer Google shows for the query 'What's the most valuable stamp in the world?' is not very helpful, as you can see from the following image (Figure 7). It shows a list rather than a single result – although to be fair, the

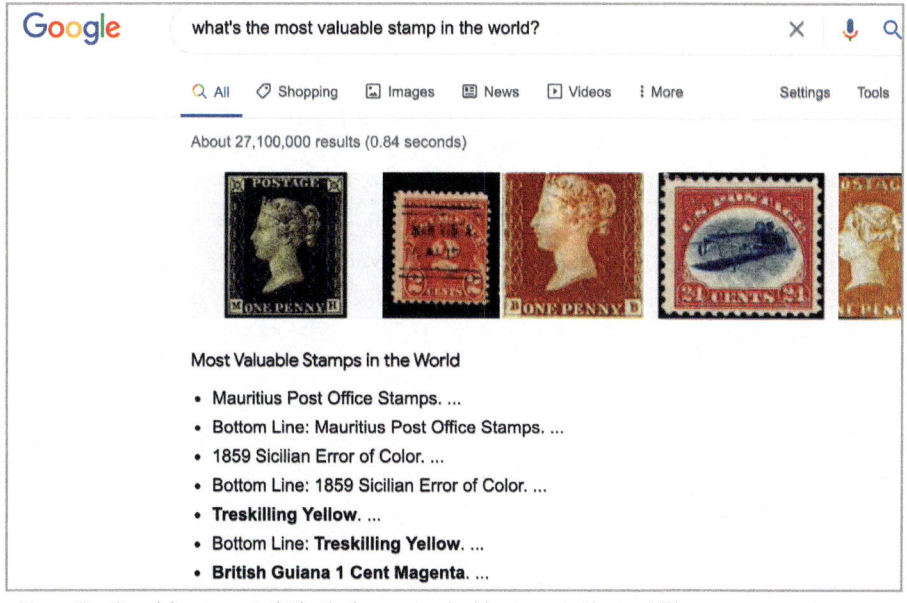

Figure 7 – Google's answer to 'What's the most valuable stamp in the world?'

51

Search Never Sleeps

correct answer is shown in the list. If you already know what the answer is, it's a doddle! And this is where Rule 1 kicks in again. Google can only show people what it has crawled and indexed and if you can't clearly mark the information you provide in a format that Google can understand, it can sometimes misinterpret what it is being shown.

In this instance, based on what you can see in the image, how many of you would think that the Penny Black, the first stamp image you can see, is the most valuable? Surprise, surprise, it's not. Not even close. Anyone can own a Penny Black and many people do. All the stamps listed underneath the images are expensive, but the prize for the most expensive goes to the British Guiana 1 Cent Magenta. The British Guiana 1 Cent Magenta currently holds the record for being the world's most expensive stamp at US$8.7 million.[3]

So why does Google not show that?

Well, that's down to how the data has been interpreted when it does stage three of its three-step process – ranking. Ranking is the most emotive part of the whole process, not only because it's the only one humans can actually see, but because it can make or break businesses, sometimes overnight. Once again, Google gives a simple explanation:

'When a user types a query, Google tries to find the most relevant answer from its index based on many factors. Google tries to determine the highest quality answers, and factor in other considerations that will provide the best user experience and most appropriate answer, by considering things such as the user's location, language, and device (desktop or phone).'

Sounds good, right? It's the machine using rules 1 and 2 to determine where your page will come in their search results. Oh, if only it were that easy. Three days after I ran the first search for the most valuable stamp, I returned to the same search in my Chrome browser history, and lo and behold, I got a different result (Figure 8).

Since my last visit, Google has clearly decided that my search was not satisfied, probably because I clicked on three or four of the search results it showed and backed out of all of them quickly, and it had revised the result. And look, it now has the correct answer, found, and displayed from the Hiscox website. Above

---

[3] In June 2022, it was sold to Stanley Gibbons for a headline figure of US$8.3m, but that figure went up once all the buyer premiums and VAT were added, to a total of US$8.7m

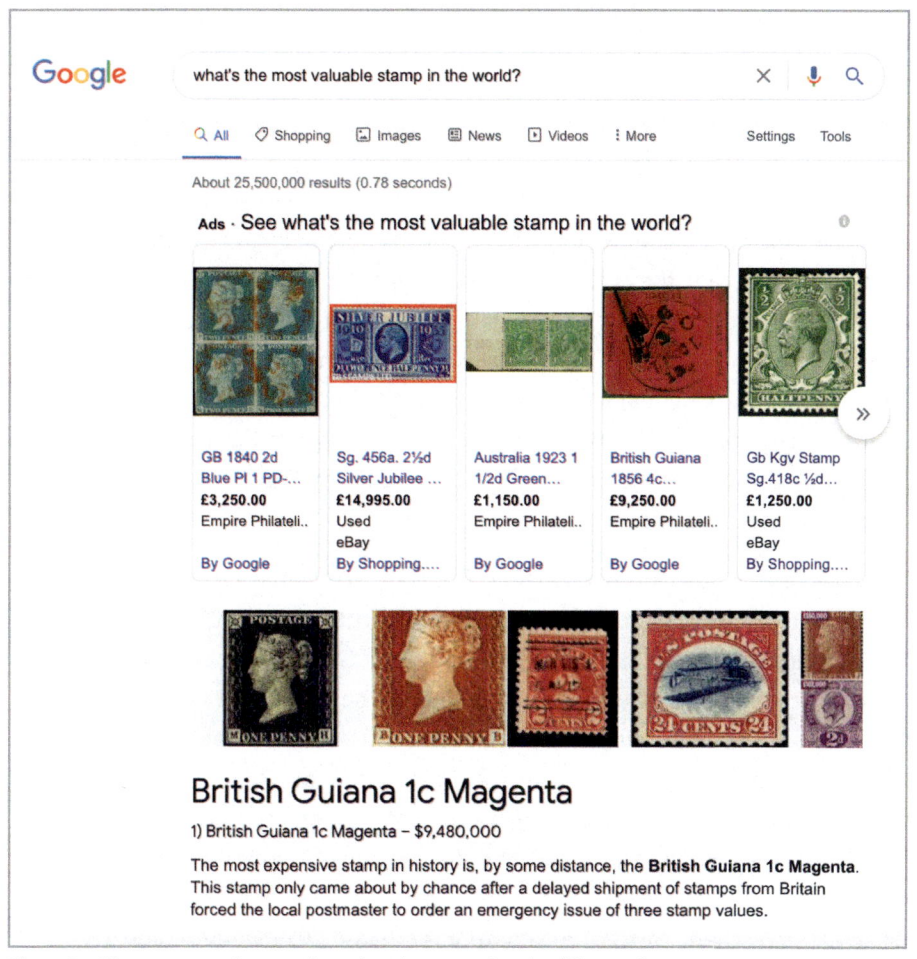

Figure 8 – The same search query three days later – notice the difference?

that, it shows me almost the same image pack, blissfully unaware that the stamp in question *still* isn't shown there anywhere, and above that, a range of shopping ads. Clearly, as I was researching around the question, it now thinks that I want to buy expensive stamps. Perhaps if this book becomes a best seller, I might be tempted…

This answer to my question being shown in plain sight is what we refer to as 'position zero', because it sits above the natural or organic listings and offers the answer without you having to visit the website. From a user perspective, this is wonderful. I can get the right answer and I don't even have to click anywhere to get it. From a website owner's perspective, this is not good at all.

First, the appearance of this answer has stopped me from clicking onto the

Hiscox website, where I'm sure they would be hoping to either reassure me of their brand or encourage me to get a quote for insurance. Secondly, it has decreased their website traffic volume. They've written the right answer to the question I have asked and almost by default, they have been penalised by Google intercepting my search before I get to their website. Thirdly, for a great many websites (and I am thinking here of websites like local newspapers, recipe websites and so on), they rely on users visiting their website and clicking on the advertising that they see there to gain revenue. If Google is placing Hiscox's content as answers in plain view, its revenue stream dries up. And this is where Google has trouble convincing people that its intentions are good. Yes, this is a better user experience, but they are piggybacking the hard work of website owners by using their material and not paying them. Right now, this works for Google but not for content creators.

However, the landscape is changing. In 2020, we began to see pushback on Google's use of information from websites, and in January 2021, Scott Morrison, the Australian Prime Minister, threatened to ban Google from Australia unless it paid for the news it was using.[4] Google's response was that it was happy to pay publishers and a deal was quickly struck in Australia, followed by a similar one in the UK and parts of Europe.[5] The business model of Google using the output of newspapers for free is clearly dysfunctional as it means the media pay for the journalism but Google uses it for free. As it stands, Google now pays for using news from these publishers, but the majority of the content on the Internet is not created by them. Most of the content is created by bloggers, companies, and online forums, and none of these get any recompense when Google shows their content without paying them. The future, I suspect, may see a very different model at work.

How should I organise my website so Google can rank me well?

If, like most website owners, you accept that Google is pretty much the only game in town (at least in large parts of the Western world currently), then you will want to ensure that what you are doing to your website will help you to rank well in Google search results. Gone are the days where you had a range of platforms on which you could advertise and expect great returns. Previously, businesses had

---

4   https://www.bbc.co.uk/news/world-australia-55760673
5   https://www.cityam.com/google-to-pay-uk-publishers-for-news-as-global-pressure-mounts/

grown by advertising in local newspapers, directories, or magazines, or in some cases, they used billboards, radio and TV. Nowadays, it's the website that is the primary advertising medium and the one that gets the biggest return. Without a website, a business is pretty much invisible, so assuming you already have one, the following are some simple ways you can configure yours so Google can crawl, index, and rank it.

Metadata — what is it and why is it important?

Meta data is one of those strange things that sounds mysterious, but in reality, is quite straightforward. Meta data (also referred to as a single word – metadata) is nothing more than a set of data that gives you information and instructions about other data.

Essentially, meta data is a summary of a set of data.

As an example, imagine walking into a car showroom. Somewhere on or near the car there will typically be a card which shows you all the information you might need, such as the make, model, engine capacity, number of seats, CO^2 emissions, etc. That card combines a range of data from different sources in a single place; it's a card of meta data.

In SEO terms, however, meta data becomes quite important, as it's the way we summarise technical information about a page in a way that both Google and people can make sense of it. This is something not often covered in other guides to SEO, as they all seem to focus on its importance to search engines and miss out the bit about human beings. Yet it is as much for people as it is for machines, and in some cases, more so.

When you are looking to optimise your website, there are four key areas of meta data that will make the most difference to your website ranking. They are:

Page Titles
Page Headers
Meta Descriptions
Image Alt Tags

Search Never Sleeps

Let's be clear though, this isn't the only meta data that is on your website, but for the purposes of this book and to make things simple, these are the four we are going to focus on. Each of these areas appear on your webpages as Meta Tags, which you can see if you examine the source code of any webpage. If you want to know more about these and how they work, I can recommend the website metatags.org[6] as a good resource.

Meta tags are part of the Hyper Text Markup Language (HTML) tags that describe the elements of your website pages and their content to both search engines and human beings. It's the coding equivalent of DNA, but instead of the building blocks of life, they are the building blocks of websites.

> **HTML**
> Hyper Text Markup Language (HTML) is the globally accepted standard markup language for any document designed to be displayed in a web browser.

You can check these for yourself if you look at the source code of any webpage (Figure 9), and to do this you need to use the correct instruction depending on which browser you are using. Here's how you do it on the four most popular browsers:

Browser	Instruction
Google Chrome	Right click on any webpage and 'View Page Source'
Firefox	Right click on any webpage and 'View Page Source'
Microsoft Edge	Right click on any webpage and 'View Page Source'
Safari	From any webpage, click on the 'Develop' menu in the top bar and click 'Show Page Source'

Figure 9 – How to examine the source code of any webpage.

Trust Apple to be different.

Before we dive into this bit, I need to give you a bit of a warning; we're about to talk code. A lot of people get uncomfortable when they see lines of code, believing that they can't understand it. This simply isn't true. Anyone can understand code; you just need to be shown what it is and how it works.

---

6   https://www.metatags.org/all-meta-tags-overview/

Once you get to the page source of a website, the meta tags will all look similar in that they start with "<meta" and they will end with "/>". Once you know what you are looking for, you'll find that it becomes quite intuitive to look for them. Best practice says that these should all be near the top of the page of code, as ideally you want the machine to read them early on in its crawl so it has an understanding and context on what it will find further down the page.

Remember, we are only focusing here on the four key areas of meta data that will make the most difference to your website:

Page Titles
Page Headers
Meta Descriptions
Image Alt Tags

To illustrate this, here's a screenshot of my personal website (Figure 10) showing the page title (shown here as 'meta property') and meta description, along with a range of other meta data that appears on my website.

```
<!-- This site is optimized with the Yoast SEO plugin v15.8 - https://yoast.com/wordpress/plugins/seo/ -->
<title>Keynote speaker on Digital Reputation Management, SEO Consultant and Chartered Marketer | Jonathan Guy
<meta name="robots" content="index, follow, max-snippet:-1, max-image-preview:large, max-video-preview:-1"
<link rel="canonical" href="https://jonathanguy.co.uk/" />
<meta property="og:locale" content="en_GB" />
<meta property="og:type" content="website" />
<meta property="og:title" content="Keynote speaker on Digital Reputation Management, SEO Consultant and Cha
<meta property="og:description" content="I came at SEO from a different angle to most; I came via the Marke
coding and site building route and many of them have awesome ninja like skills. Technically they are wizards
Keynote speaker on Digital Reputation Management, SEO Consultant and Chartered Marketer" />
<meta property="og:url" content="https://jonathanguy.co.uk/" />
<meta property="og:site_name" content="Jonathan Guy" />
<meta property="article:modified_time" content="2016-11-18T15:07:17+00:00" />
<meta name="twitter:card" content="summary_large_image" />
<meta name="twitter:label1" content="Estimated reading time">
<meta name="twitter:data1" content="2 minutes">
```

Figure 10 – Meta data on a webpage.

You can see that all the meta data starts with <meta and ends with />, shown in this image in purple type. You will also notice that at the top, in green, it says, "This site is optimised with the Yoast SEO plugin v15.8..." and this plug-in, like so many other SEO plug-ins for WordPress websites, takes care of much of the meta data that a website needs. I'll explain more on plug-ins and specifically SEO plug-ins later in this chapter, as they can be both a blessing and a curse.

> **Plug-In**
> A plug-in is something you can add onto a website to give it additional functionality.

Let's start with the first item on our list, the bit at the very top of the page, the page title, otherwise known as the title tag.

Page Titles

The page title, or meta title, is the start of the whole process. It's like the title of a chapter in a book, or the heading on a piece of paper; it tells you what's to come. A page title will be the first thing at the top of the page, which both the machine reads and that a human being can see.

When you first start to type in the domain name you are looking for, certainly when using Google's Chrome browser, it starts to autocomplete options which could match what you are typing.

> **Domain Name**
> A domain name is a unique name, comprising numbers, letters, and some special characters, that identifies your website.

In this case, as it knows I'm looking for my website, it brings up not only the remainder of the domain name but also a description of what the website is about – my Title Tag (Figure 11).

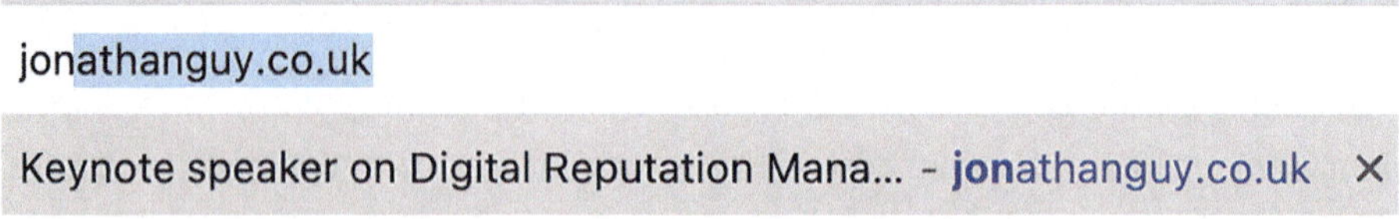

---

jonathanguy.co.uk

Keynote speaker on Digital Reputation Mana... - **jon**athanguy.co.uk ✕

Figure 11 – An example of a Title Tag.

In this case, it tells you straight away that I'm a 'Keynote speaker on Digital Reputation Management' which, as I'm often searched for under this guise, is exactly what I want people to see. So, as well as telling the machine that I'm a specialist in digital reputation management (Figure 12), Google is also telling the person typing in my domain something about me. By making sure that you have a focused and descriptive title tag, you can not only help the machine but also influence the user as to whether your webpage is the one for them.

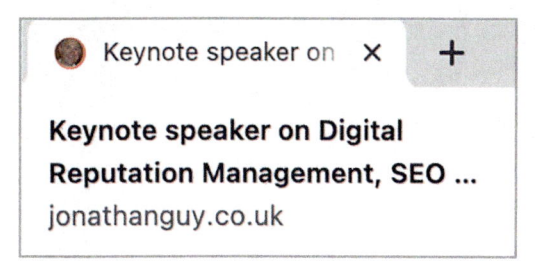

Figure 12 – Descriptive title tags help Google and users understand what the page is about.

Once the page has loaded, the title tag element is also visible for anyone who hovers the mouse over the page tab in the browser, and along with a nice favicon (the small image you can see), it gives a good user experience. The question is, what do you write as a page title if it's your website? The answer depends on which page it is.

> **Page Tab**
> A page tab is a clickable area at the top of a window that shows another page.

> **Favicon**
> A favicon is a small image that is associated with that website - often the company logo or, for personal websites, a face.

Your home page is often the most frequently visited and crawled page of your website, and if you are running a small business, it makes sense to optimise your home page for the thing you do best. If you are a builder and 80% of all the work you do is building extensions, it makes sense to ensure your home page title tag mentions that. The best way I have found to do this is to start the title tag with what you do and end with who you are, separating the two elements with a divider such as a dash or a pipe (Figure 13).

Figure 13 – The Dash and Pipe symbols on a keyboard.

As an example, if Joe's Expert Builders specialise in home extensions, I would word it like this:

Home Extension Specialists | Joe's Expert Builders

Now, if Joe has a website, and on it he has created different pages for the other building work he does, such as garden walls, loft conversions and garage conversions, then each page should have its own focused title tag. In the case of garage conversions, it could say:

Garage Conversions | Joe's Expert Builders

I have seen it suggested in some SEO literature that it's worth stuffing a lot of other things into a title tag, such as your location or the location in which you want to work, your entire range of services and even offers of discounts. Title tags are most definitely not the place for these things.

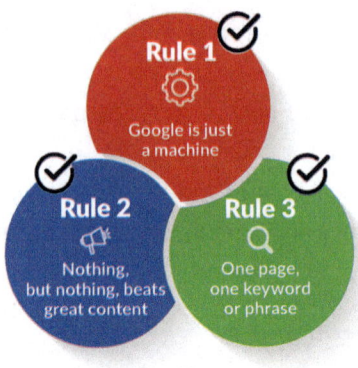

The golden rule here is Keep it Simple. If you do this along with Rule 3, you won't go wrong. If you are a more established brand and you are writing a piece about a subject area in which you are an expert, you can reverse the order and have your name first, followed by the description of what the page is about. There are no hard and fast rules on this, it's about what looks best from a human point of view, as the machine will read it the same whichever way around you put it. Think about it in terms of a human: are they looking for what you do or who you are? Create your title tag in the order you think they'll want to read it.

Typically, you get between 50-60 characters in a title tag, so within those bounds feel free to experiment with different wording to see what looks best. The reason I give a range here is that Google can display around 512 pixels of information, and different letters take up differing amounts of space. Just compare ten lowercase l's (llllllllll) with ten lowercase x's (xxxxxxxxxx) and you can see what I mean.

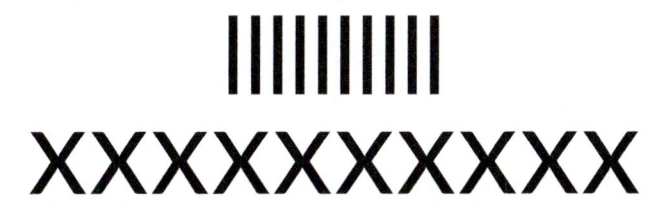

llllllllll

XXXXXXXXXX

> **Pixel**
> A pixel is a 'picture element', a tiny area of illumination on a display screen, a group of which make up an image.

Header Tags

Following directly on from the title tag comes the header tags, and these are equally important.

When I first started in SEO, I remember being told that header tags were very much like the newspaper headlines of old. Newspapers typically started with a bold headline which told you what the story was about, then within the story there were sub headlines and sub-sub headlines. In SEO, header tags are used in pretty much the same fashion, with tags being used in descending order of importance from header 1 (h1) to header 6 (h6).

You'll typically see them in the HTML code when you 'view page source' but more often you will find them in evidence when you are creating your own content, and whichever platform you are using, most of them have a heading system of some description now built into them.

The best way to think of them is in size order with h1 at the top and h6 at the bottom, like this:

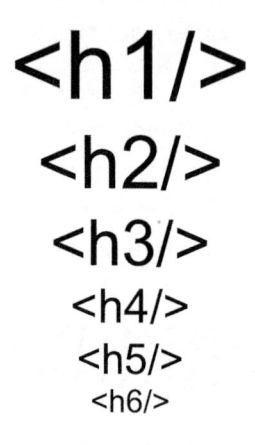

<h1/>
<h2/>
<h3/>
<h4/>
<h5/>
<h6/>

As you might imagine, the order in which you use these on the page can make a difference. Remember Rule 1? Google can't actually 'see' what you are writing and as it has no ability to understand the nuances in your written text; it needs clues to make sense of the content. This is one of those clues. If you mark your most important headline as h1 and your least important as h6, then Google knows where the emphasis should lie when interpreting your page.

Long before the Internet was in daily use, people consumed information predominantly from printed media such as newspapers and books. They relied on headlines to tell them what to expect, sub headlines to elaborate on the story and sub-sub headlines to break up the narrative. And this had worked successfully for over 100 years, so unsurprisingly, when the Internet arrived, developers copied these same principles. After all, if it ain't broke, why fix it? With such a simple system, you'd think that it would be hard to go wrong. Unfortunately, like many things in life, even the simplest things can be made difficult by laziness and a little information.

> **"A little learning is a dangerous thing."**
> *Alexander Pope*

The first place this goes wrong, sadly, is when developers are building websites, particularly WordPress websites built using a pre-designed theme. There are millions of website themes available, some free, some paid, but all of them pre-configured so that you can easily download them, add your own images and content, and set them live in no time at all. The principle is brilliant and the ultimate in mass customisation, taking just one basic framework and allowing thousands of variations from that theme. The problem is that all these pre-built themes have pre-determined styles for the h tags, from h1 to h6. Depending on the developer, these can vary greatly. Some very popular themes, for example, have an h5 tag that is a larger font than the h2 tag, which means that if you are setting out six headlines down a page, they can look like this:

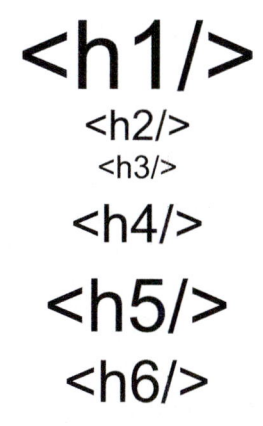

<h1/>
<h2/>
<h3/>
<h4/>
<h5/>
<h6/>

Anyone with no technical skills building a page of content, therefore, will simply use an h5 tag in place of an h2 because it looks better, and from a usability principle, that's absolutely right. But technically, it's wrong. Going back to newspaper headlines, we are saying that a small sub heading is more important than the main headline, and whilst you and I know that's not true, Rule 1 applies, and the machine may not.

I usually refer to these as 'Lazy h tags', where the developers use them for styling a website and the customer, not knowing the importance of them, thinks it looks great, oblivious to the knock-on effects. A bit like buying a car that looks like a

Ferrari but then popping the bonnet and finding a Mini 850 engine from 1978. It explains why it looks good but doesn't go quite as fast as you'd expected.

Whilst small elements like this might not seem that important (and individually they're not), collectively they can make a huge difference. And as always, we are at the mercy of the 'machine', so as long as Rule 1 applies, we should do everything we can to help it come to the right decision.

Accepting that we need to use header tags as we work down the page, the next issue is what to put into those header tags? It's not as easy as it seems. Headers are a way of breaking up a page of text and are frequently used in documents such as technical papers where researchers want to discuss different segments of their research. When it comes to the Internet, though – and particularly reading text online – headers take on an even greater importance. This is driven, in part, by our decreasing attention span, an issue highlighted in a 2019 report[7] which found that due to the density of material now demanding our attention, the time which we can dedicate to any topic diminishes.

What has this got to do with headers, you may ask? Well, the answer is that when readers have a diminished attention span, you need to find a mechanism for keeping them engaged with what you are writing, and by adding relevant headers down a page of text – particularly online – you provide two things. Firstly, you give them a signpost of something interesting to come. Secondly, you reassure readers that the time spent on the text they are currently reading will shortly be coming to an end and they can then choose to abandon reading the piece or carry on, but with a new part of the article, which may be more interesting or at the very least, different.

But what should a header contain? Clearly, it's a signpost to your reader and if you were writing a book, it may be a simple case of telling the reader what's in the next section. But online, this becomes slightly more difficult. If we remember Rule 3, we know that each page should be about just one thing, so if you are writing about something very specific, such as 'the inside of a ping pong ball', then the page is all about 'the inside of a ping pong ball'. How on earth can you break it up into sub headings?

This is where creativity comes to the fore and we need to step back for a moment and ask the question: 'What would readers of this article like to see or

---

7   https://www.eurekalert.org/pub_releases/2019-04/tuod-aoi041119.php

read?' Once you do that, you can segment your article in several different ways. However, from an SEO – and certainly a Google – point of view, you will want to ensure that each of the sub headings includes the keyword or phrase for which you are trying to rank. Remembering Rule 1, the machine is simply looking for clues as to what your page or article is about and as such, it places some store by the inclusion of the same word or words in the sub headings as appear in the page title.

If you have chosen to try and rank for 'inside of a ping pong ball' then your headings might look like this:

<h1/>What is inside a ping pong ball?</h1>

<h2/>So, there's more than just air inside a ping pong ball?</h2>

<h3/>How manufacturing affects the inside of a ping pong ball</h3>

<h4/>Is the inside of a ping pong ball the same in every country?</h4>

<h5/>What happens when we change what is inside a ping pong ball?</h5>

<h6/>Why the inside of a ping pong ball matters</h6>

Google's search includes an element of natural language understanding and as such, it can interpret different phrases to establish intent. In this instance, it recognises that there is no difference between 'inside' and 'inside of a' as it's picking up the main elements of 'inside', 'ping pong' and 'ball'.

I've deliberately used an abstract idea like the inside of a ping pong ball, particularly as this has long been the favourite of teachers across the generations as a punishment for an errant child. I certainly remember it being handed out as punishment for disruptive students in class, and woe betide any schoolboy or girl who didn't come back with a good 500 words on the subject. Because of this (and other similar punishments over the years), I know of a great many people who, faced with a blank piece of paper and the instructions to write 500 words, just freeze. But as you can see, if you have the headings to break it up, it's not that hard.

In terms of the headings, you'll notice that each one has the words 'inside of a ping pong ball' (or 'inside a ping pong ball') in them. This is deliberate on my part, and from an SEO point of view, it's the ideal scenario, in that the 'machine' sees and recognises this and it does (currently anyway) give the page a bit of a boost. From a human point of view, it might seem forced to include the same phrase time and time again, but if what is written under each heading relates directly to that heading and answers the question or elaborates on the point of the heading, currently, it works.

Whilst researching this book, I googled 'SEO Company' just to see what came up. Sure enough, on page one of the search results, there was a page from a company who had used this exact technique. The content under the headings was largely rubbish and anyone reading it would hardly be likely to be swayed by the narrative, but that wasn't a concern for them. Their concern was to get as high up on Google as possible and then when you arrive on their webpage, shove a really big pop-up advertisement in front of you with a special offer. Promoting the special offer was their primary aim and to do that they had manipulated the h tags on that page to best meet the way the machine would interpret them. Whilst h tags were not the only reason this page was ranking, they were a big contributory factor. So, when you are building your pages, pay close attention to including h tags right down to h6 if possible.

Meta Descriptions

Meta descriptions are one of those elements that are, more often than not, simply ignored. In the first instance, developers often don't want to bother with them as they are nothing to do with designing and building a website. When owners get their website for the first time, they have no idea that these are important. By the time they do, there are usually so many missing that it becomes one of those mammoth tasks that gets put off time and time again. You know the sort: important, but not urgent.

From a developer's point of view, when a website is being built, the last thing they want to do is spend time filling in a meta description for every page on the site. If by chance they do complete them, they will simply copy and paste the same meta description across every page. It's quick, it's easy and it's a tick in the box if the developer has promised to deliver an 'SEO ready' website.

What a waste!

Simply put, meta descriptions are one of the easiest ways to differentiate your webpages and one of the best ways to encourage people to click into them. In short, they can make the difference between getting traffic to your website or missing out. As a practical example, I've left the meta description on my Resources page blank to demonstrate what happens (Figure 14). Here's how it looks on Google:

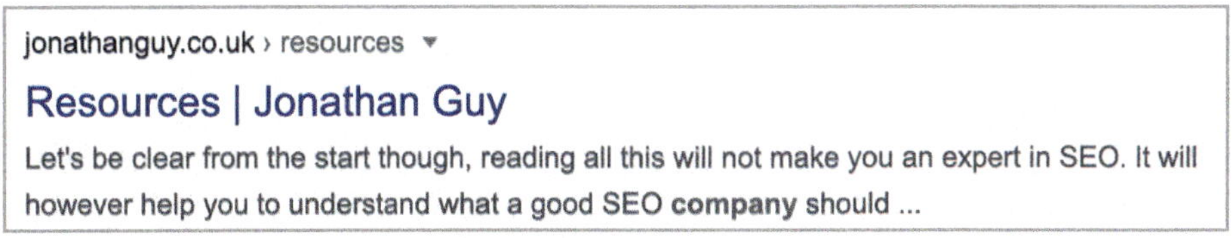

> jonathanguy.co.uk › resources ▼
> **Resources | Jonathan Guy**
> Let's be clear from the start though, reading all this will not make you an expert in SEO. It will however help you to understand what a good SEO **company** should ...

Figure 14 – Meta Descriptions are an essential part of SEO.

As you can see, Google has picked up one element of what I have written and is showing it to readers as the most relevant piece of information on that page. It's not, however, the first line of text on the page (Figure 15), it's the second paragraph:

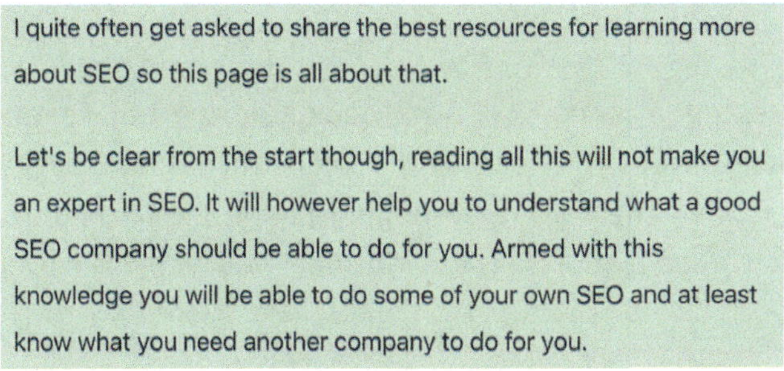

> I quite often get asked to share the best resources for learning more about SEO so this page is all about that.
>
> Let's be clear from the start though, reading all this will not make you an expert in SEO. It will however help you to understand what a good SEO company should be able to do for you. Armed with this knowledge you will be able to do some of your own SEO and at least know what you need another company to do for you.

Figure 15 – Google may pick something different to show as your meta description.

This is one of the myths that needs busting apart, as some people believe that Google will just pick up the first line of text. Sometimes it does, sometimes it doesn't. More often these days, with more of the algorithm being driven by artificial intelligence, it picks the bits it finds relevant to the search query that has been requested, rather than just the first line of text.

As a test, I rewrote the meta description (Figure 16) to see how long it would take for Google to pick it up, if indeed it would pick it up at all.

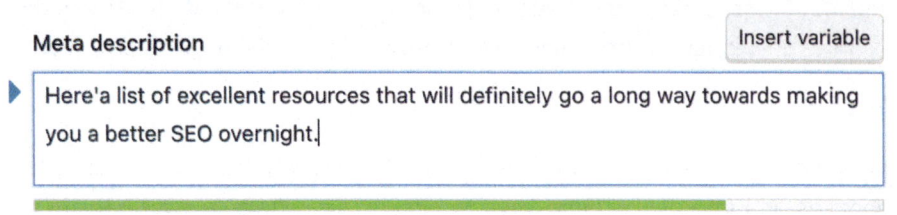

Figure 16 – Revising a meta description.

Of course, there's no guarantee that Google will show this as it may consider that it knows better and will continue to show something else from the page instead of my meta description. In fact, for a lot of queries now, Google is tending to show what it thinks is the most relevant information, based on whatever query the searcher has entered.

Fast forward a year, and in July 2022, Google is now showing a completely different meta description (Figure 17) to both the previous one and the one I wrote:

Figure 17 – Proof that Google decides what to show in your meta description.

It's instead picked out a sentence about a book I recommend, as it feels that is the most relevant part of the page. This demonstrates that Google will show what it considers to be the most relevant information, based on the search that is made. Your job in the first place is to write what you would like users to know about that page.

If Google isn't showing the correct meta description, you can push it in the right

The Three Key Areas of SEO

direction by using one of its free tools for website owners. Google provides Google Analytics free for any website owner and alongside that, it also offers Google Search Console, which helps owners to measure their traffic, performance and to identify errors so they can fix issues. Search Console can also be used for URL inspection (Figure 18). This allows you to put in a URL – for example http://jonathanguy.co.uk/resources/ – and then ask Google to test that page and report if it can find any issues on the page. If you've made a change, then using this tool, you can simply click on the 'Request Indexing' wording in the bottom right corner of the display box, and Google will re-crawl that page for you.

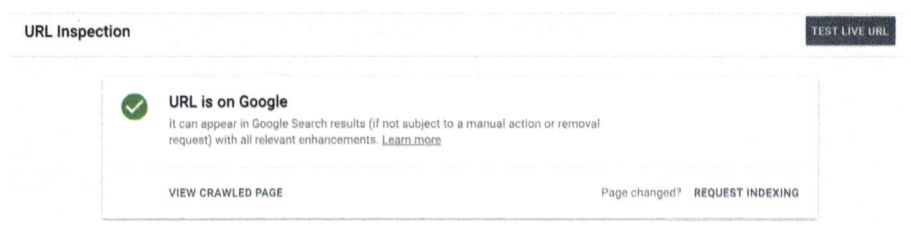

Figure 18 – Testing a url has been indexed.

But Google isn't the only search engine around and Bing, its major competitor, still typically picks up the first content on the page like this (Figure 19):

Resources | Jonathan Guy
https://jonathanguy.co.uk/resources ▾
I quite often get asked to share the best resources for learning more about SEO so this page is all about that. Let's be clear from the start though, reading all this will not make you an expert in SEO. It will however help you to understand what a good SEO company should be able to [...]

Figure 19 – Bing's Meta Description.

From a content point of view, it makes sense that the first thing you write on the page should be the main selling point of that page. The problem that most people have is that they don't know how to sell, let alone how to write compelling sales copy. Moreover, being asked to write a killer 'call to action' in 160 characters or less for a meta description is an even bigger challenge. Meta descriptions are, in essence, tiny advertisements and every page needs to have one. They need to be clear, concise, have punch, convey what a searcher will find on that page and give them a reason to click into that page. No wonder so many are so bad.

Alternatively, if you don't want people to click into your page, but you want them to take action just from looking at the list of search results, you can put something like 'For your free quote call us today on 0800 XXXXXXX' or something similar. In other words, you can use it as a call to action. This works particularly well when you are faced with stiff competition in classifications, such as plumbing or insurance. Generally, however, meta descriptions are better when they offer a benefit or a promise of something to come. Phrases such as 'Find out more about...' or 'All the help you need with...' often work a lot better than 'we are specialists in...' Which frankly leaves most readers cold.

I don't intend to teach you how to write a meta description as part of this book; there are far too many other resources available online[8] which do that already. What I will say is that where you have the opportunity to write a meta description for a page, do it. You might not be a trained copywriter nor an advertising professional, but you have one thing that neither of those professions have: knowledge of your own business. You know what you are selling and why people should buy it. Make those factors part of your meta description and you can easily stand out from the crowd.

Image Alt Tags (or Alternative Text)

This is a really quick win for most websites and probably the best example of Rule 1 in action.

Let's start by saying that, in reality, there's no such thing as 'Image Alt Tags', although everyone seems to refer to them in this way. Technically, it's 'alternative Text' and it is used to describe the image that is being shown in such a way that anyone (or anything) attempting to understand the image, without the benefit of sight, can be clear about what is shown in the image. In short, it's for blind and partially sighted people, and machines like Google.

One of my favourite examples of why alternative text is important is this image (Figure 20).

Without thinking too much about it, try describing what you can see.

Figure 20 - How would you describe what's in this picture?

---

8   I've included some links for this in the Resources chapter.

The Three Key Areas of SEO

What was your answer? Would that answer make sense if you said it to someone who'd never seen the image before?

Whenever I show this image as part of a talk, I ask people this question and the most common answers include:

A Portakabin
A school
A clinic
An office

The key point here is that no matter what people shout out, they always have different answers. I've never given a talk where everybody simultaneously agreed on a single description. This is the issue that Google faces. If we remember Rule 1, Google is just a machine, it has no eyes and cannot therefore make a visual assessment of this image. It can make a judgement based on what it thinks it might be, but it can't use intuition to give it a precise answer.

To test this, I uploaded the image you can see to Google's Image Search (Figure 21), to see what it came up with. The file name was random, with a series of numbers and letters typical of a photograph that you might include in your website. In other words, there were no clues as to what it might be.

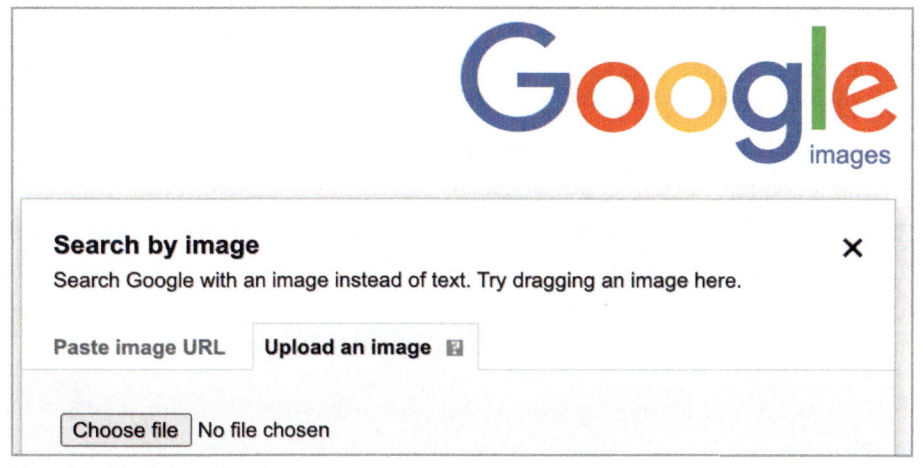

Figure 21 – Google Image Search.

Search Never Sleeps

What Google returned as a search result was that it thought it was 'grassland' (Figure 22). This is not what I expected. Clearly, as humans we can see that the focus of the image is the building, not the grass, but Google can't see that.

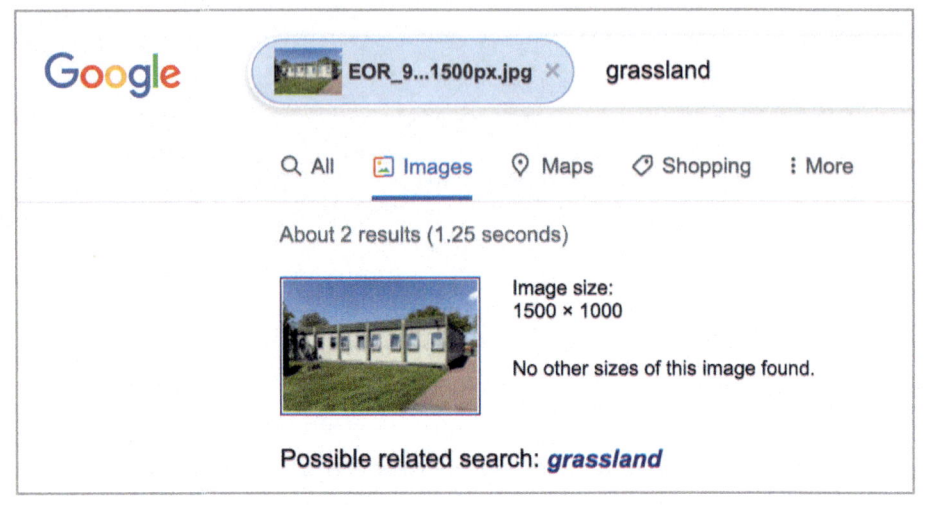

Figure 22 - This is what Google thinks my picture shows.

Even if it could classify it as a building, it would also struggle with the fact that the top answer I normally get, that of Portakabin, is actually a trademark-protected brand name.

Herein lies the problem. First of all, Google cannot correctly classify it as a building as it simply sees grassland, and even if it could identify that we are uploading a building, it can't call it a Portakabin because it doesn't have enough information to know if it is a Portakabin. Secondly, it's an almost impossible task for the machine, as there's no single answer to the question, 'What is in this picture?' It could be any of the answers I'm normally given, as well as a modular building, a portable building, or a portable modular building. It could also be a site hut, a clinic, a classroom – the list goes on. In fact, it could be any of a hundred different descriptions, so how is Google supposed to know?

The answer is that it can't possibly know, so it needs your help to classify the image.

The Three Key Areas of SEO

CASE STUDY

Working with a company in the hobby market, their target was people who collected specific types of their product. As an example, if they sold baseball cards, people wanted to collect those of a specific team only, or in some cases, just the individual players. I discovered that their customers were making some very precise searches and so they needed to be seen in those search results. The problem was, they were up against some heavyweight competitors.

The solution was to focus on the images and to create specifically named image alt tags for each one of their products. By ensuring Google could crawl, understand, and index their images, it started to show an image pack right at the top of the search results. This meant that the images appeared above the normal organic listings and people simply clicked on the images rather than the listings below. They managed to steal a great deal of traffic and customers from their bigger competitors before they caught up to them.

Takeaway:
Use a clear naming convention on every image you load onto your pages as this could significantly improve your chances of attracting visitors to your website.

Whenever you upload an image to your website you will find that most website systems offer you the opportunity to provide some extra information about the picture you are using. WordPress does this quite simply as you can see in the image (Figure 23), offering four boxes

Alternative Text
Title
Caption
Description

The more information you can include in these boxes, the more opportunity you will have to rank in search for that image.

Search Never Sleeps

The top box is Alternative Text, and this is principally for better web accessibility. Anyone using a screen reader, including the visually impaired, will be read out whatever you type in this box. Try closing your eyes and saying what you've put; does it make sense? Could you guess what the image is from your description? As well as helping the visually impaired, whatever you type will be shown on screen if the image cannot be loaded, and importantly, it's the first clue for any search engines as to what the image shows.

The next box is Title, and this gives you a chance to describe succinctly what you would put if you had to summarise what the image is about. Don't worry about it being a short description as the next two boxes will allow you to elaborate.

The Caption box is next, and this gives you the chance to write something that will be shown underneath the image whenever it appears on a page of your website. But beware, as whatever you write will appear every time the image is shown, so not ideal if you intend reusing the same picture in a range of situations on your website.

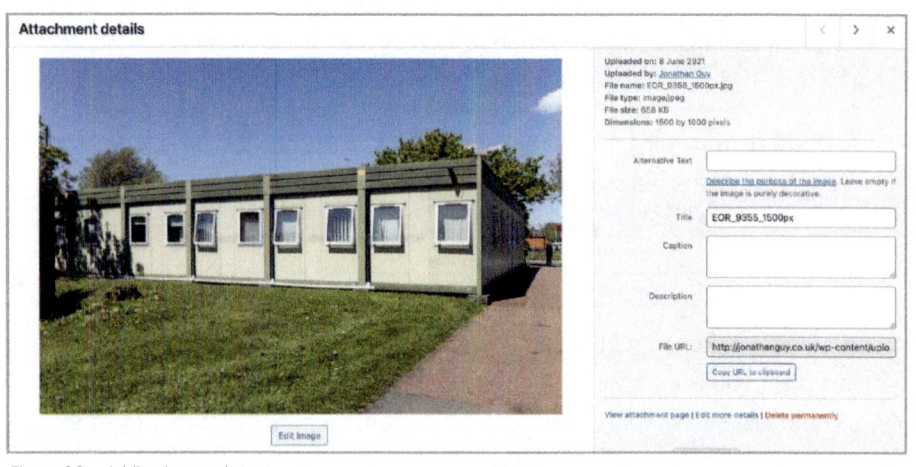

Figure 23 – Adding image alt text.

Finally, there is the Description box, and this is your chance to write a fuller description of the image, what you can see and what you want people to know about the image. This is the part where you can say that it's a modular building being used as a clinic extension, if that's what it is. Whatever you do though, please don't be tempted to use these boxes to include lots of different keywords. I've seen them stuffed with things like 'portable building, modular building, Portakabin, portable modular building, temporary office accommodation…' Not

The Three Key Areas of SEO

only is this regarded as keyword stuffing (the overuse of keywords to try and manipulate where something appears in search) but it simply won't help your image rank for anything.

To illustrate how Google uses the information you provide with a photograph to position it in the search results, a number of years ago I uploaded a range of photographs I'd taken to my website and gave them a variety of alternative text. Each of them was tagged with something relating to SEO and some of them still, to this day, persist on Google. Despite removing the tags over a year ago, Google is still showing photographs like this one (Figure 24), which appears in a search for 'SEO Walsall'.

SEO Walsall | Aqueous Digital
aqueous-digital.co.uk

Figure 24 – Google relies on you to tell it what each picture shows.

The bottom line is that Google needs your help to know what images mean. Don't miss the opportunity to help it – and your users – by including relevant alternative text.

Takeaways:

The right content will mean your website ranks, irrespective of its size or age.

Give Google the information it needs in the format it prefers.

Rule 1 applies — Google is just a machine.

On-page

On-page SEO is something that has always interested me. It's the part where you get to think about and understand what people might actually want to see when they visit your website. Most people consider this to be the easy bit as it's seemingly about how shiny a website looks. Yet it's not just about appearance. Pictures can only get you halfway there, and to fully engage with and convince your audience, you are going to need words. Good words, and lots of them. Essentially, it's about substance and as such, it's the part most often neglected by website owners.

Part of the problem lies in the fact that when a business gets a website built, it is prepared to spend money – sometimes a lot of money – on something that looks great, but it rarely spends any time or money on content. Why this should be the case is something of a mystery, as normally rational business owners seem transfixed by the appearance and forget that it has to be about more than that. You often see the same effect when people have built their own website; the site may look fabulous with some wonderful imagery that they have spent hours arranging, but there's virtually no substance beyond it looking good.

Retailers would hardly spend good money on securing a prime high street plot without considering how the shop will look and feel when customers walk in. There's no point in spending money on window dressing if people simply can't find what they want when they walk into the shop. Yet when it comes to a new website, more often than not it's left to either the designer and developer to produce the content, or they rely on the customer to produce the content.

Herein lies the problem. Neither of these are copywriters.

Most developers are interested in developing, and whilst they are happy writing code, they are disinterested in content. Likewise with designers; it's just not their thing. And whilst the business owner is ultimately the one person who knows more about their business than anyone else, they simply won't have the time to create the content needed for their website. Moreover, they (like the designers and developers) are not copywriters. Most business owners are busy every day doing things like running their business. Finding time to create not just content, but the right content, simply isn't going to happen.

Next time you find yourself talking to a developer about building a new website, ask them the most frequent reason website build projects run behind schedule. They'll tell you it's waiting for either sign off of the design, or content from the client, with content being the biggest brake on a project.

Faced with a blank piece of paper and the instruction to write a thousand words about a subject, even if it's about their own businesses, far too many business owners are transported back to their school days where they were forced to write essays. It's a chore, it's not what they are good at and it's not what they are used to doing. I've had conversations with people in this situation, frightened because they can't overcome writer's block and have difficulty in writing even a single word. This doesn't mean, however, that you can't do it – you can. You just need to know how to start, and as you are the one person who knows more about your business than anyone else, the information you need is already in your head. It's about getting it out and putting it in order.

Frankly, we find ourselves in a situation which is not sustainable. Everyone is now expected to be an expert in the technical aspects of websites and to understand what makes good content, and this is driven by Google. Read their Webmasters Guidelines[9] and see for yourself. Unless you have any training in advertising, marketing and content writing, you're going to struggle. It's for this reason that point seven in their 'basic' list says, 'consider hiring a professional'.

CASE STUDY

Back in 2013 I received an email from a company in the IT sector. They had used two different SEO firms but were stuck at #2 for the main keyword they were after. One of the directors emailed me and asked if I could make any suggestions.

The other SEO firms had done lots of link building to the home page, which was the page they were using to target this keyword. I realised after a quick check that the competitor above them mentioned the keyword more often on its home page than they did. I wrote a quick paragraph, including the keyword three times, and sent it back to them with instructions to put it on the home page.

Three weeks later I received another email from them confirming that they had risen to #1 and asking me if I'd like to come and talk to them about a long-term contract. We went on to work with them until they sold the business five years later.

Takeaway:
Mentioning the keyword you are targeting on the page is important.

---

9   https://developers.google.com/search/docs/basics/optimize-your-site

If we accept that on-page SEO and the creation of compelling content is the part which engages directly with the consumer, shouldn't it be part of building a website? After all, what's the point in building something that looks great but won't convince anyone or sell anything? Accepting that it's not currently part of the website build process and that very few developers have any idea on how to create something that sells, what are the key areas that you should be looking at on your own website to make sure that when it goes live, it's fit for purpose?

It's all about Rule 3

Rule 3, you will recall, is all about one page, one keyword or phrase, and this is at the heart of what you need to create for your website.

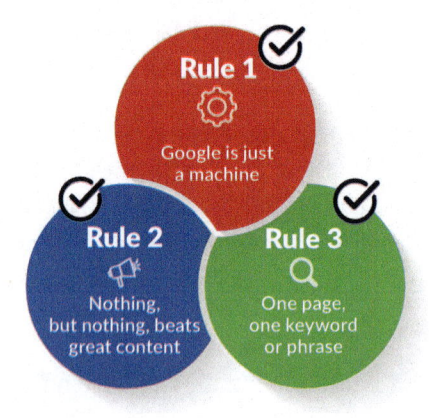

Let's look at what Google says in its page on 'how search works':[10]

"The most basic signal that information is relevant is when a **webpage contains the same keywords as your search query.** If those **keywords appear on the page**, or if they appear in the headings or body of the text, the information is more likely to be relevant."

You'll remember that we covered titles, heading tags and meta descriptions earlier in this chapter, so at this point I'm assuming that you understand the importance of these and that they will also need to contain the keyword or phrase for which you want to rank. What this nugget of information from Google shows, however, is that it's important to include the word you want to rank for in the content on the page you are building.

---

10 https://www.google.com/search/howsearchworks/algorithms/

I know this sounds basic, but you'd be astonished how often people miss this simple point. And if you want to check this yourself, take a look at any one of your current webpages that doesn't rank for a keyword, despite you thinking it should. Then, using the 'find' option (Control 'F' on a PC, Command 'F' on a Mac), see how many times the word or phrase you want to rank for appears on the page. Warning: in most cases it will be fewer than you think.

This is such a fundamental part of creating a great webpage that you'd think there would be more warnings about this, but in practice we are lured by the shiny pictures and the snazzy layout, or perhaps the way the developer has made elements of the page move around in a clever way and we think that this will be enough to impress users. Of course, users might be impressed by some or all of this, but a key point is being missed here – users need to find it in the first place. To do that, you need to rank well in search and to do that you need to ensure the page is ranked well by the search engines. Remember Rule 1 – Google can't see any of these wonderful images, it can't infer from the elements on the page what your intention is (or was) and it certainly can't make the mental leaps that we can.

Think for a moment about car number plates. Lots of people nowadays have personalised car number plates which, when the letters and numbers are spaced in a certain way, make a person's name. As one example, what do you see when you read this number plate (Figure 25)?

MA 71 ORY

Figure 25 – What does this number plate say?

The number plate doesn't *actually* contain a word, but our brains do a remarkable thing, and fill in the blanks. So much so, that most people reading this will see the word MALLORY, even though it's not there. Whilst this kind of mental agility is commonplace amongst human beings, its noticeably absent in machines, including search engines. Google and all the other search engines will read this exactly as it is, MA17 ORY. In short, if we want to ensure a search engine knows what we mean, we need to spell it out as simply as possible.

How often should the word I want to rank for appear on the page?

If we know that it's important for a page to include the keyword for which it's trying to rank, the next obvious question is how many times should it appear? Unfortunately, there's no simple answer for this, nor a formula by which you can calculate this. Some SEO plug-ins will try and do this for you, telling you what they consider to be a suitable word density for the page, but sadly, despite being built on solid research and with the best intentions, they are often wrong.

If you ask Google the question, 'What is the ideal page keyword density?' you will see a range of articles, all of which try to answer the question. As I write this, the top answer, which Google has highlighted in a featured snippet, states

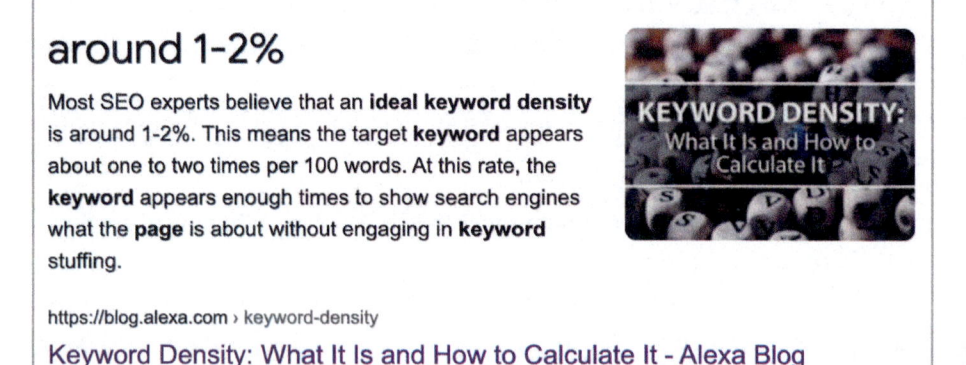

Figure 26 - Keyword Density.

that the 'ideal keyword density is around 1-2%' (Figure 26), but crucially, there is no reference for this. As with many of the articles that talk about keyword density, there is no science to back up the 1-2% claim, nor any reference to where this has come from. As such, I would urge you to treat all numbers like this as apocryphal and that unless someone can clearly evidence where they have sourced the statistic, everything should be treated with extreme caution.

> **"Over 85% of all statistics are made up on the spot."**
>
> *David Mitchell – Number 9 Dream*

The Yoast SEO plug-in uses a number of 3% (or 3.5% with their premium version – I've no ideas why paying them money increases your ability to include words on a page!?) but again, there doesn't appear to be any scientific research to back this up.

As a case in point, on my business website at Aqueous Digital, there is a service page where I describe our SEO service[11] offering. Including every word you can see on the page, from top to bottom, there are 1,782 words a human can read. Of those words, 25 are 'SEO', which is 1.4%. Did I deliberately set out to have a keyword density of between 1-2%? No, of course not. What I did was to create a page that I felt might be helpful for a reader looking for information on SEO, what it was and wasn't, and my hope was that anyone reading it would find it informative. Could I have included the term 'SEO' more frequently on the page? Yes, I'm sure I could have shoehorned it in a few more times and increased the density, but frankly, there was no need. There are enough clues already on the page for both humans and search engines without me desperately trying to mention SEO a few more times. The key here is to ensure that whatever you write, it means something to a reader and a search engine can also make sense of it.

If I include the keyword too often, will I get penalised for 'keyword stuffing'?

One of the great myths of SEO that seems to persist is that website owners can get penalised by Google for 'keyword stuffing' – the process of including the keyword you are trying to rank for lots of times on a single page. In mid-2021, I undertook a small study to see if I could find any evidence of a keyword stuffing penalty. Despite being someone who has spent over a decade in SEO – and having seen a range of ideas, fads and urban myths come and go – I've never seen a customer website with a penalty for keyword stuffing. As I have no first-hand experience in this, I realised that perhaps this lack of experience might have coloured my view. I did some research to establish whether this is a real issue or simply a mythical 'bogeyman' designed to scare people into doing the right thing.

The problem is that there are several issues here, all intertwined, beginning with what exactly is considered keyword stuffing and ending with can it get you a Google penalty? I therefore started by trying to establish 'What is keyword stuffing?'

---

11 https://aqueous-digital.co.uk/services/seo/

As already established, keyword stuffing is, quite simply, the overuse of a keyword (or phrase) on a single webpage with the aim of manipulating the search results. Historically, this had been used to help websites rank in search, but the advantage of this pretty much disappeared in the early 2000s.

Google gives a good description of this on their developers' page:

"Examples of keyword stuffing include:
Lists of phone numbers without substantial added value

Blocks of text that list cities and states that a webpage is trying to rank for

Repeating the same words or phrases so often that it sounds unnatural, for example:

We sell custom cigar humidors. Our custom cigar humidors are handmade. If you're thinking of buying a custom cigar humidor, please contact our custom cigar humidor specialists at custom.cigar.humidors@example.com."

What isn't clear though, is how much is too much? And does the keyword have to appear on the page (which is what we are talking about here), or does it include the text in the source code (the on site elements), which a search engine would be reading? Is it based on the way a person is likely to react to it, or is there some kind of algorithm behind the scenes monitoring this?

On all these good questions, I came up short. Despite extensive searches, I was unable to find a single conclusive answer to any of them. Of course, there is a lot of speculation online, but very little in the way of hard evidence. Partly this is because Google will not publish this type of information. If they told people that seventeen mentions of a keyword on a page were fine but eighteen were too many, then every website owner would put seventeen mentions on the page, irrespective of whether it warranted or needed it.

Some SEO websites have decided that there is a figure, which they express as a percentage typically ranging from 2-5%, but even though they state this is the correct figure, it's not sourced so we have no way of establishing where this figure comes from nor why it is correct. In truth, trying to nail it down to a single figure is pointless, as it will vary site by site and page by page. The other issue is that there are so many places you can put keywords that it's hard to know where to stop counting. When you create a new page, you can easily insert the keyword you want in the following places:

- Page Title
- Header tags
- Meta description
- Content
- Image alt tags
- Website menu
- Website footer
- Schema data
- Page tags
- Meta keywords

This is not a complete list, as there are far more places keywords can be included, such as the url's and the stylesheet (code which describes how the website will display). Whilst many of these are on-site elements rather than on-page, a search engine will read all of them equally.

Take as an example the home page of another website I own and run. The word for which I want to rank appears 32 times on this page. More importantly, if I look at the source code (the on site elements), I can find it a staggering 377 times as it's in every single url. This website currently ranks number one for pretty much every variation on this keyword I am targeting and is an authority website in its field. I have used the website as a testbed for many years, to establish what does and doesn't work in SEO terms. As it ranks top for this keyword, despite 377 mentions on the page, I think that we can discount the notion of it being a simple count.

Having established that it is not just a simple count of the number of times a keyword appears, the next logical area is context – does the keyword appear contextually correct to a user?

As we can see from the earlier Google example about humidors, stuffing the same word repeatedly into sentences is not good from a user perspective. It was precisely this type of content which persuaded Google to act back in 2011 when it introduced the Panda update.[12] The bottom line was that poor, low quality

---

[12] Panda was Google's first attempt at ensuring that high quality content ranked better than low quality content stuffed with keywords. If you want a history lesson on what the Panda update was and is and how it changed search, Search Engine journal have produced a very good guide that explains everything - https://www.searchenginejournal.com/google-algorithm-history/panda-update/

content, including content that simply repeated the keyword over and over, was diminished, and their value in ranking for certain keywords disappeared overnight. This new quality control mechanism meant that sites producing low quality content, including articles with high keyword repetition, were devalued and dropped from search. A great many of the websites that relied on this sort of poor quality writing with keyword stuffing complained bitterly at the time that they had been 'penalised' by Google, but in reality, they hadn't. They may have lost most of their traffic but what they were doing was pointless, irrelevant, and diminishing the value of search, rather than helping it. Panda was not about penalties, more about rewarding good quality content over poor.

I had yet to nail what could cause a keyword stuffing penalty, and by this stage of my research I was starting to think that it might not exist. Could it be an urban myth?

In searching Google for answers to this, the top and most authoritative articles all fail to give a concrete example of a website that has received a specific 'keyword stuffing' penalty. The nearest I could see is a list of all the likely Google penalties from *Search Engine Journal*,[13] but even they didn't give an example of a keyword stuffing penalty. Their example is bundled in with 'hidden text', which was an old trick of, for example, placing white text on a white background (or black on black) so that search engines would read it as part of the code but visually, a user would not be able to see it. Forbidden from the start, this was something Google made clear in early Webmaster Guidelines that sites deliberately using this technique to manipulate search results would be penalised (though not for keyword stuffing).

Today, in Webmaster Guidelines, Google lists a range of things you should avoid. Although not a definitive list, it does include (Figure 27):

Term	Meaning
Automatically generated content	Content created by a programme but makes no sense.
Sneaky redirects	Sending people to a different page than the one they thought they were going to.

[13] https://www.searchenginejournal.com/the-complete-list-of-google-penalties-and-how-to-recover/201510/

The Three Key Areas of SEO

Link schemes	Buying or selling links to try and improve rankings.
Paid Links	Links purchased for advertising but not disclosed as such.
Cloaking	Presenting a different set of content to users and search engines.
Hidden text and links	e.g. white text on a white background or hiding a link in a full stop.
Doorway pages	Pages designed only to rank in search but then lead a user to a different final destination
Scraped content	Copying or republishing content from other websites without permission.
Affiliate programmes	Sites designed entirely to send links to other websites (larger online retailers) but with little or no useful content themselves.
Irrelevant keywords	This is what Google considers to be keyword stuffing.
Creating pages with malicious behaviour	A page that injects malware or performs an unexpected behaviour.
Automated queries	A programme that automatically interrogates Google without first asking permission.
User generated spam	Typically, a good website that has allowed users to add new accounts or comments without any restrictions.

Figure 27 – Things Google says you should NOT do.

Any or all of these can be responsible for triggering a Manual Action, which is Google's term for penalties, but nowhere does it specifically mention a keyword stuffing penalty.

In the past decade, I can honestly say I only recall seeing a handful of these manual actions and none of them through work I had done. Most were on websites whose owners approached me to help them recover from a penalty, usually around poor backlinks, not content.

If you search Google today for examples of keyword stuffing penalties, the top results that are served are all from 2012 and 2013, and none of them show concrete examples. It does look like keyword stuffing penalties don't actually exist. The lack of examples suggests that what may have started out as a threat has ended up as an urban myth.

It's not that Google wouldn't act on this, it is probably more that no one bothers with stuffing keywords onto a page these days, as most people know and understand that it won't help their website or page rank in search.

Certain website tools, like the Yoast SEO plugin for WordPress, include a keyword density checker to let you know, when you are writing an article, just how many times a word or phrase appears on the page. They all have different upper limits for keyword density, but in truth, as Google won't rank irrelevant content any more, this is largely redundant.

The reality of search today is that it doesn't appear to matter how many times a keyword appears, it's more about how users read and react with that page. On that basis, virtually no one is keyword stuffing as it serves no purpose.

How do I create a great website page?

The trick to creating a great page of content for your website is to write something that means something to your reader. I appreciate that this might sound self-evident – after all, why bother writing a page that means nothing and turns them away? Is this not just simply stating the obvious? Unfortunately not.

As I said earlier, one of the biggest issues with websites is that neither the website developer nor the business owners are specialist copywriters. Typically, neither have the skills needed to create outstanding, compelling content which resonates with every reader and persuades them to take action. If they did, then there would be no need for advertising agencies.

With most developers relying on the customer to provide the content, it's a sad fact that the majority of websites end up with poorly written, ill-thought-through content, which serves no real purpose other than filling up a page. In some cases I've seen, they would have been better off leaving the 'Lorum Ipsum' in place.

The Three Key Areas of SEO

> **Lorem Ipsum**
> Lorem Ipsum is dummy text, historically used in the printing and typesetting industries and latterly, included automatically as a placeholder on all new templated websites. The idea is that website owners can replace this with something meaningful, but some fail to do this.

As a case in point, take a much-used phrase in the building industry:

'WE SPECIALISE IN ALL TYPES OF BUILDING WORK'

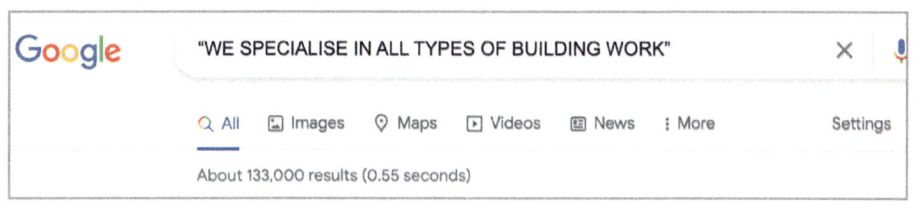

Figure 28 – Does your website include this well-used phrase?

As you can see from the image (Figure 28), an exact match search for this phrase reveals that Google has found 133,000 results for this term. Quite apart from the fact that this is an oxymoron (you can't be an expert in every type of anything), in what way is this line supposed to reassure potential customers of your ability to help them? As someone reading this, would it make you think that a firm saying this is in any way reliable? Does it instil you with a sense of confidence that they could handle any building job, or do you feel that they appear a bit 'jack of all trades'? Also, if they are that good, why are they not telling you about it instead of hiding behind a coverall statement, claiming to be specialists in everything?

> **Exact Match Search**
> An 'exact match search' is one where you use double quotation marks at the start and end of the phrase you are searching for. Most search engines will only return results which match exactly what you have typed between the quotation marks.

Let's take a look at another well-worn (some might say hackneyed) phrase, 'no job too small' (Figure 29).

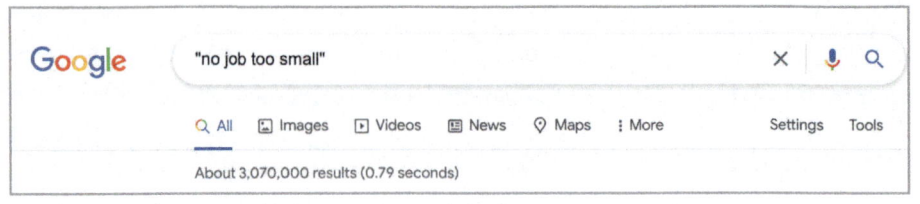

Figure 29 – Phrases such as this are not unique or helpful to users.

Google can find this on over 3 million webpages, so whilst it might accurately reflect what your business offers, in what way does it differentiate you from the competition? Moreover, if I were to ring the top ten results on that search result and ask all of them to come around to my house and hang a picture, how many of them would want the job? Particularly if I only chose those with no call-out charge?

You see, when you start to pick apart some of the most frequently used statements in general advertising you find that they don't actually mean anything at all, they are simply words, taking up space on a page but delivering nothing of value.

The good news, however, is that there is a way for you to create something meaningful for your website without it costing a fortune. You are already an expert in your business and you have all the information needed for this task inside your head. You can definitely do this as long as you have a structure, so this chapter will give you that structure.

The starting point for creating a great page has to be deciding what that page is to be about. Deciding a page's purpose is one of the most important decisions you can make, as without it the temptation is to write enough to fill the available space, even if what you put is irrelevant. By doing that you are in danger of not only losing a reader, but also distracting the search engines as well.

Now is the time when we can start to link together some of the elements we've discussed in this and earlier chapters, with the concept of creating a page. Earlier, under on site elements, we talked about writing a page title, including the correct header tags, and writing a compelling meta description. All of these elements are now going to come together when you create your page.

The Three Key Areas of SEO

First, you need to decide what is going in your page, and more importantly, what you are leaving out. In the case of our builder's example, they will need to decide which of the aspects of building they are really good at and focus on one of them at a time. I often find it helpful thinking of this in terms of a hierarchy or a pyramid, with the top of the pyramid being the home page of your website and underneath that, pages for each of your products or services you sell. In the case of our builders, the pyramid could look like this (Figure 30):

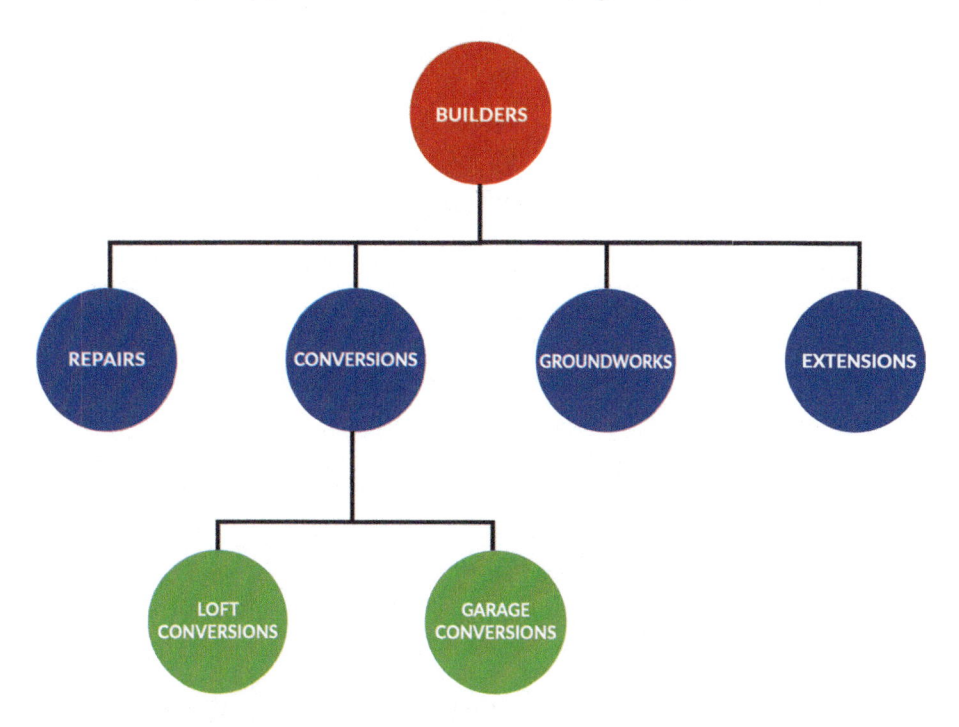

Figure 30 - Example website hierarchy.

At the very top is a home page for 'Builders'. This is the page on which they can say how fabulous they are, that they are great builders, have been helping customers for over twenty years and they are members of various trade bodies. They could also include testimonials from people they have helped over that period. Underneath that, however, they will need to break down their service offering. In this example, it's into four areas of repairs, conversions, groundworks, and extensions. Some of these break down even further, such as conversions which could break into loft conversions, garage conversions, etc. Each of these aspects of building all need their own, separate pages.

Search Never Sleeps

If you were running a website selling shoes, for example, one of your top level pages could be Men's Shoes and underneath that, Men's Trainers, Men's Loafers, Men's Brogues. In the Brogues section, you could have individual pages for Black Brogues, Brown Brogues, etc. The principles are the same no matter what your website is about.

Once you have a hierarchy, you can then start to create the elements you need for a great page. Typically, you are looking to answer six questions on every page, and these are:

Who?
What?
Why?
When?
Where?
How?

These six questions are considered essential in any problem solving exercise and are regularly used in journalism, police work and many other aspects of life. If you can answer all of these, then your page should contain the essential ingredients for customers looking for your product or service.

> **"I keep six honest serving-men**
> **(They taught me all I knew);**
> **Their names are What and Why and When**
> **And How and Where and Who."**
>
> Rudyard Kipling — The Elephant's Child

The order in which these appear is more important that it seems, as your customers (or potential customers) will probably already know what you do when they arrive on your website. If we've got the technical aspects of the page in place and the search engines have indexed the page correctly, then ideally someone looking for a garage conversion will have arrived on the garage conversion page.

Assuming this to be the case, what do you think is the most important thing you could put first on this page? Is it how to contact your firm? Where you are based? Technical details of a garage conversion? The answer is something which you already know. It's the one thing which subliminally you always need when you are faced with making a decision of any type; it's why should you do it.

Why?

The 'why' question is by far the most important in this instance, as it's the trigger which will mean the difference between someone contacting you or not.

Think about it for a moment. Anyone getting a garage conversion, no matter who they choose, is likely to get the same or a very similar job. The materials used won't differ much, the time needed will be similar and the end result should look similar. So, if everyone is going to use the same materials and labour hours to get a similar result, what's the differentiation other than price? And why would anyone choose anything other than the lowest price?

Often, it's the small things that make the biggest difference. On a job like this, the homeowners are going to have to invite a team of builders into their house, where they are definitely going to make a mess. The builders are likely to be there for some time and naturally, the customer might be concerned. They are likely to have worries around noise, mess, security, and the behaviour of the workers, as well as the normal concerns about the quality of the work, keeping to the completion date and after sales care. Faced with this, you can see why starting the page with 'we specialise in all types of building work' is unlikely to influence customers to choose you.

The starting point is to tell people 'why' they should choose you, rather than any of the other bits of information. It's about selling your differences first, convincing people that there's something about your business that's worth more than your competitors.

It might be that your team of builders all wear overshoes at any time they are in the customers' houses, that they tidy up at the end of every work day, that all materials are kept neat whilst on-site, that they adhere to a 'considerate constructors' code or any of a thousand other variables. Whatever it is, the reassurance that you can give a potential customer, in advance of seeing the job, is worth an enormous amount. In many cases, it's the differentiator that will ensure you are one of the firms chosen to quote, as opposed to someone who simply says that 'no job is too small'.

Once you've told people why they should choose you, then it's about proving that what you have written is not just meaningless words. We all want to be reassured, particularly if we are about to make a fairly sizeable purchase, that we are making the correct decision. We all use a range of cues to help us decide, including intangible factors such as our trust in the brand, the 'look' of a website and even the font which has been used. The single biggest factor, however, is another of these intangibles – it's trust.

> ### CASE STUDY
>
> After working for several years with a firm in the legal sector, we had created a great deal of content built around a solid content strategy. People often research answers to legal problems online before they go on to contact a solicitor, so having the correct answers (or with complex issues, at least having sound advice that they need to speak to a solicitor) is important. A crucial factor in choosing a legal firm is that you believe that they will be someone you can trust to help with your problem. I was delighted to receive an email from them letting me know that they had just landed a major customer who had gone online to research their problem, saw they could trust them as they provided the correct advice, and then rang the firm directly from one of the articles. The profit on the job more than paid for all the SEO services over the previous three years.
>
> ### Takeaway:
> Rule 2 – Nothing but nothing beats great content.

We want to believe that we can trust what we are being told, and that we can trust the company we are about to use to deliver what they say they will. On the webpage you are creating, that can take a variety of forms, but two things which typically work well are testimonials or quotes from former customers, and cases studies of jobs that went well. Both help to cement in our minds that we are: not alone in trusting the company; that others have gone before and found them to be a reliable business; and that the type of work we are going to ask them to do is well within their capabilities. Of course, it goes without saying that the company may have hundreds of dissatisfied customers, none of whom are likely to feature on their website, but at this point we dismiss that fear in the face of sufficient overwhelming evidence that they are capable.

Another element that often helps to cement trust is the use of imagery. Photographs of the work previously completed, before and after comparisons, and shots of the team working on a job all help to increase trust in a company. If the business you are looking to use is one where personal service is an important element and you are likely to be dealing with the business owner (such as a chiropractor, dentist, or builder), then including an image of the person who runs the business often helps. People like to know who they are dealing with and if we can see a smiling face on the page then it helps to reassure us that we are making the correct decision. Today, that can also be supplemented by video, which is far more widely used than in the early days of websites. With mobile phone ownership virtually universal, everyone seems to have access to a camera these days. In May 2019, YouTube users were uploading 500 hours of new, fresh content every single minute.[14] This figure only seems set to rise and today, video is consumed widely on social media channels such as TikTok, Facebook and Twitter.

The use of a video on the page does have some technical drawbacks, namely that it increases the amount of information a page has to load and therefore slows down the load speed. Given that page speed is one of Google's key metrics, there is clearly a balance to be struck here.

The good news is that there are lots of different ways of making a website technically fast, even with video, and one of the best ways is not to host the video on your own website. Technically, this means that instead of the video existing only on your website and being loaded as part of the page, the video sits instead on a third party video hosting website, such as YouTube or Vimeo, and a small amount of code (known as embedding the video) is added to your webpage. What this does is to pre-load a static frame of the video when someone loads your webpage, but only loads the rest if someone clicks to watch it. Developers can now also take advantage of developments in coding to use something called 'lazy loading', which defers the loading of elements that are not immediately visible on the initial screen that loads. What this means is that the phone or desktop browser focuses on getting as much of the page to show to a user as quickly as possible, so they can be satisfied that they have reached the webpage. Clever use of technical elements like this can make your webpage appear to load quickly and that improves customer trust in a website.

---

14   https://www.statista.com/statistics/259477/hours-of-video-uploaded-to-youtube-every-minute/

What?

After you've written the 'why' part of the page, the rest of the job should be fairly simple. People need information. Some of it comes logically after they have been convinced that they want to deal with you. The order of the remaining elements can be adjusted to suit; however, I prefer thinking of them in a sequence as it ensures we get the priorities that a customer may have in the correct order.

Logically, the 'what' element comes next. If we assume that customers have searched for what they want (garage extension) and arrived at the correct webpage on your website, your first job is to convince them that you are a trustworthy business and can do the job well. After that (assuming they are convinced), then you need to explain to them what you actually do. This may involve a list of the things you do for that particular piece of work, a description of the completeness of your service or just a broad overview. Whatever you choose, it should be enough to answer the typical questions you might be asked by a prospective customer.

To extend the garage conversion example, if a customer typically asks you 'Do I need planning permission for this work?' then you should try to answer that as part of the description of your services by putting something like 'We arrange for all relevant planning permissions before starting work.'

Telling people what you do should be straightforward; after all, it's quite literally, what you do.

When?

Next on the list is to explain the 'when' to people. This can take a range of forms as the importance of 'when' depends on what you are selling. If you are a builder, there's probably very little requirement for an urgent garage conversion, but if you are an emergency plumber, time is very much of the essence.

'When' can also come in different forms, such as when is the best time to call your business (your opening hours), when your business was founded and most importantly, when people should take action to contact you. This final 'when' is often referred to as the 'call to action', something to motivate a potential buyer to get in touch with you immediately.

Where?

Location matters. In all my years in business, I've visited thousands of small-and medium-sized businesses across the UK. In almost every case they tell the same story, namely that the majority of their business comes from their local market. Clearly, if you are looking for a gardener, plumber, garage, or any other service where you need to visit them or they need to visit you, most people will choose a local service. This is borne out by the numbers, with Google stating that 30% of all mobile searches are related to location.[15] Of course, if your business is solely online, then the numbers will be different, as location won't be as much of an issue for the majority of your buyers.

Given that we know people choose local businesses in a great many cases, it makes sense to be clear about your location on your website. Far too often, people obscure this information, or in some cases, simply omit it altogether. Whilst there can be a case for privacy, particularly if you operate from home, the inclusion of a legitimate address sends a positive signal to a potential buyer that they can trust you and that you are near their location. When it's a selling point, make a virtue of your location.

Who?

To this point we've assumed that people who arrive on the correct page on your website will know who you are and what you do, as we're assuming that your SEO has been effective. But how can they be sure that they are the right kind of customer for your business? The process of defining 'who' is therefore quite important and there are certain cues you can use in the wording and images that can help people to decide to use your business, or not.

As an example, if you are a builder and only want to do extensions, a picture of a large extension and lots of narrative about extensions will tell people the kind of work you are looking for. Subliminally, this is likely to deter a buyer that only wants a dozen bricks replacing in a garden wall or a sticking door fixed.

'Who' is about defining who your customers are as well as letting them know who you are.

---

15   https://www.thinkwithgoogle.com/marketing-strategies/app-and-mobile/mobile-search-trends-consumers-to-stores/

How?

This is all about how people can contact your business. Ideally, you need to make it as easy as possible for someone to contact you by phone, email, chat or instant message.

Whichever options you choose, it will do no harm to include a simple line such as 'contact us now', 'call now for immediate help' or 'ring today for immediate service'. You'll be surprised just how effective a line like this can be and how often people forget to put it on their website.

What makes great content?

The answer to this question depends, I suppose, on which angle you are approaching it. If you think about it from a search engine point of view, great content is any content that correctly answers the query that it has been asked. In this way, almost any content can be 'great', even if it's old and poorly written. As search engines become more intelligent and rely on Artificial Intelligence (AI) and machine learning to help them answer queries, more often than not, great content becomes defined as content with which users engage and have their needs satisfied.

From a website owner's point of view, great content is anything that your visitors like, read and that ultimately encourages them to take the action that you want. You might want them to buy something, call you, sign up for a newsletter or just read more content. Whatever your aim, great content is anything that achieves your aim.

We've seen earlier in this chapter that there is no magic trick to content. There's no perfect number of times something has to be mentioned on a page, there's no substitute for doing a good job by filling in all the meta data you can and there's no magic formula that works for every website every time. Doing the basics and doing them well is a great starting point, as is remembering that the secret formula to unlocking the magic that brings customers to your business is inherent within you. You already know why people should use your business, so take the opportunity to tell them. Be real. Be yourself and be honest. If you start with honesty, you won't go far wrong.

Having said that, let's take a look at how you can create, from scratch, a page or a blog that has everything a reader and search engine might need. To do this we need to look at:

Content Quality and Length
Keywords and Phrases
Meta Data
Images
Internal and External Links
E.A.T.

One of the most frequently asked questions when I do a presentation is 'How long should my blog posts be?' Time and again, I'm asked the same thing in different forms and the answer is always the same – as long as it needs to be. Just focusing on the length of your writing is always going to lead to disappointment, as any author will tell you. It's not about how much you write, but which words you are using. To paraphrase a very old saying, "I'm writing all the right words, but not necessarily in the right order."[16]

Simply focusing on word count will lead to disaster as without the right quality, readers will switch off long before they get to the end of what you have written. But there is a proven correlation between the length of content on a page and the position in search, though it is inextricably linked with the quality of the content on a page.

> **"I would have written a shorter letter, but I did not have the time."**
>
> *Blaise Pascal*

If you are writing a blog, whatever you write will be fine. A blog is typically a short, hopefully pithy piece, where you get to share your view on something. Some people will read it, some won't. If it's an opinion on something, it will simply add to the millions of other opinions that exist in the ether on any given day. But if you are writing the correct answer to a specific question, such as 'What it the ideal water pH for keeping Koi Carp?', or 'How to correctly measure your garden for turf', as long as you have the correct answer, it doesn't matter how many words you use. What matters is getting your point across clearly, succinctly, and accurately. The number of words you use to do this is entirely up to you.

---

[16] The original quote was, of course, Eric Morecambe with the infamous line delivered to Andre Previn: "I'm playing all the right notes, but not necessarily in the right order."

Back in April 2012, there was blog on an SEO website with a graph showing a correlation between content length and position in the search result. Whilst the company who wrote this and their website have long since gone, the graph and opinions on its conclusions are still widely available online. Many writers refer to this at some point and will tell you that you need to write thousands of words to rank in search. This simply isn't true.

What they are all missing is that this research was a one-off piece, the data was never publicly available for scrutiny, and we are now ten years on from its first appearance. Today, Google offers the following advice on their Webmaster Guidelines:

"A frequently updated site encourages people to return – as long as your content remains relevant and engaging. A useful post once a week is better than low-quality content published daily."

You will notice that there is nothing here about content length; in fact, Google doesn't mention content length anywhere in its guidance for website owners. For Google, it's about frequency and quality. In other words, fresh and relevant.

So, write the very best articles you can and make sure that readers will engage with it and read to the end.

There are, however, other considerations when writing, which make longer articles slightly more appealing. There is some evidence that longer articles do rank higher (though this is not scientifically correlated by research) but there is clear evidence that bigger articles gather more backlinks (websites that have links to yours) and get shared more frequently on social media. There's also some evidence that there is a loose correlation between content length and organic traffic, though this could be a secondary correlation if we accept that longer content is likely to be more comprehensive and therefore rank well in search.

As websites respond to changes in Google, so does the behaviour of website owners. Faced with losing search rankings or improving their offerings, most website owners opted to improve their content. In doing so, they created better and longer content, and not only do they rank well in the search results, but it also satisfies users. It's something of a virtuous circle and a continual focus on quality will inevitably lead to better results.

> **CASE STUDY**
>
> We were working with a customer on a new website and identified, through keyword research, that there was one topic which their prospective customers were searching for on Google. When we checked, it seemed that no one had written a comprehensive answer on this topic, so we set about doing this.
>
> Within days of launch, the page went to number one and doubled their entire website traffic as no one else was correctly answering that question. The page was not designed to sell to customers, but to inform. However, the more people that arrived on site, the more enquiries started appearing as people had found someone who was knowledgeable and had expertise in this field and felt reassured that they could answer their query.
>
> **Takeaway:**
>
> Not every page has to sell; some pages are simply there to inform. People will be reassured by finding a knowledgeable answer to their query, and if they need the product or service, they may be reassured enough to make an enquiry. If not, then at least they go away with a positive feel about your brand and website.

Keywords and phrases

What is a keyword and what is a key phrase? Why the difference? Is it important and if so, why? These are a few of the questions I get asked regularly and we should start with the difference between keywords and phrases.

At its inception, Google was driven by keywords. Websites were built around keywords and to this day there is still a field in the meta descriptions of some websites called 'meta keywords'. In its simplest form (and I am oversimplifying here to make the point), keywords were the way of telling search engines which word was important on a page, and therefore, which search results you wanted to appear in.

In 2010, however, it became clear that Google wanted to shift away from this. Webmasters had become obsessed with keywords, to the detriment of creating great content, hence the examples earlier of stuffing a page with thousands of repetitions of the same keyword in white text, hidden on a white page. Slowly, Google began to push people towards a better user experience. First, they reduced the access people had to keyword data.

Having hidden large parts of this data in its Google Ads dashboard, it then started to encourage to people to think in terms of search phrases, something that continues to this day. If you look in Google Search Console now you won't find any mention of keywords, just search phrases (Figure 31), and whilst you can see paid and organic keywords in Google Analytics (Figure 32), much of the data is redacted and appears as *(not provided)* or *(not set)*.

Top queries	Clicks	Impressions
how much is a second class stamp 2021	42	3,222
how much is a second class stamp	26	13,595
2nd class stamp cost	18	12,471
second class stamp cost 2021	15	4,326
2nd class stamp 2021	14	1,899
how much is a first class stamp 2021	13	4,237

Figure 31 – Search phrases, not keywords, in Google Search Console.

Quite simply, (not provided) means that Google knows what these keywords are, they have just chosen not to share them with you. It's almost like you can't be trusted with this information so like a parent shielding a child from harm, you can't see them. Data that is (not set) is slightly different and is a case of machines not talking to each other. According to Google, it is "a placeholder name that Analytics uses when it hasn't received any information for the dimension you have selected." In short, it doesn't know.

Google doesn't want you to obsess over keywords, they want you to concentrate on user experience. They have invested so much over so long in improving the

The Three Key Areas of SEO

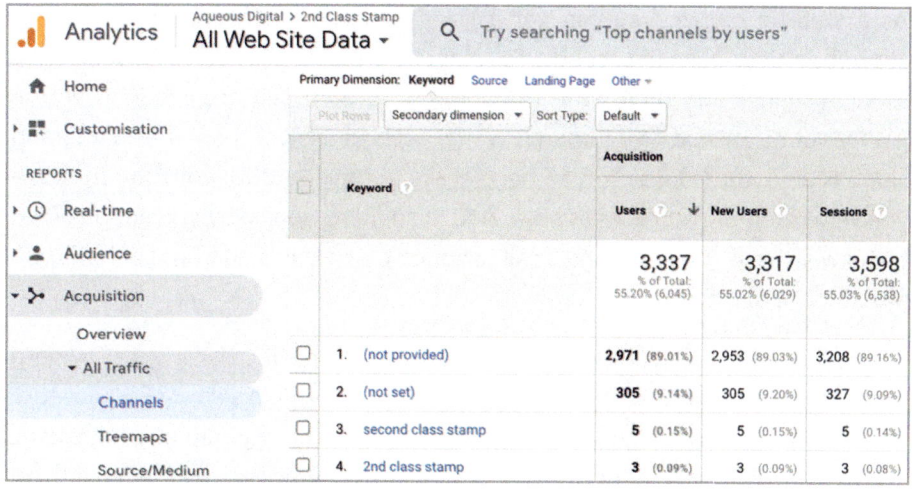

		Users	New Users	Sessions
	Keyword	3,337 % of Total: 55.20% (6,045)	3,317 % of Total: 55.02% (6,029)	3,598 % of Total: 55.03% (6,538)
1.	(not provided)	2,971 (89.01%)	2,953 (89.03%)	3,208 (89.16%)
2.	(not set)	305 (9.14%)	305 (9.20%)	327 (9.09%)
3.	second class stamp	5 (0.15%)	5 (0.15%)	5 (0.14%)
4.	2nd class stamp	3 (0.09%)	3 (0.09%)	3 (0.08%)

Figure 32 – (not provided) and (not set) in Google Analytics.

quality of the search results, that currently, the search engines (using Machine Learning and AI to continually improve) can now make sense of so much more of the content available on the Internet. Yet so much of it is still poor. Their advice is now 'write better content', knowing full well that they have the ability to crawl, index and make sense of whatever you write.

When it comes to writing your page, the best advice is to start with the main purpose of that page. If you are a solicitor and writing about 'divorce settlements', then use that phrase and write a great page about 'divorce settlements'. You are not trying to write about 'divorce', 'divorces', 'divorcing', 'divorced' or any other variation on a single word. You are writing about the topic of divorce settlements and for this you can write anything you like.

To help, start by putting the phrase you want to write about into a free website called Answer The Public.[17] The website allows you to enter any search phrase and it will tell you, in seconds, which are the most frequently asked questions about your chosen topic. In this case, it tells me that the questions people want answering are:

- How divorce settlement is calculated?
- What divorce settlement am I entitled to?
- When is divorce settlement final?
- Are divorce settlement payments tax deductible?
- Can divorce settlements be changed?

---

[17] https://answerthepublic.com/

As a website owner, you can get a list of the main questions you need to answer on your page in seconds. So, start by creating each of these questions as subheadings and then write the answers. Even if you are succinct, you've got five questions, at two hundred words each to answer them (this paragraph alone is 107 words long) so you have easily got over 1,000 words by the time you've written the correct answers. Add in some reasons why you are qualified to answer these questions and a call to action at the end, and lo and behold, you have a page of content.

You will notice that to this point, I've not talked specifically about 'Keyword Research' as a separate item, even though it is prominent in all the SEO literature you will read. There's a good reason for this; I'm not a huge fan of what exists. There are so many different keyword research tools out there and some of them are really quite good, but they all miss one of the fundamentals, and that is Rule 1 – Google is just a machine.

All these tools do the same thing. They all interrogate what's already out there and try to bring back enormous lists of words and phrases that the machine can already see. In other words, they are machines interrogating a machine, and despite differences in all the tools, they will all arrive at broadly the same result. But what about the 25% of search queries that are brand new to Google each year? Where are they in these lists? The answer is that, of course, they are absent, and this brings us neatly back to 'What makes great content?'. Great content, as I said previously, is both the correct answers to the questions that people ask Google and anything that your visitors like, read and that ultimately encourages them to take the action that you want.

If you want to find out more about keyword research and the tools that are available to help, they are included in the Resources chapter at the back of the book. By all means read about this area of SEO, try it yourself and see what kind of results you get. Then take a step back and remember that the main aim of your website is to engage with human beings and see if the work you have done really chimes with your audience or has just been created to satisfy the machine. Once you've done that you will see that some of the tools, like Answer The Public, are the next best thing to having some real intelligence on your audience as they provide real insights into what human beings search for on Google.

CASE STUDY

We were working with a customer who was in the scientific instruments field and was convinced that writing for their niche was hard, and that their potential audience would not like anything other than seriously scientific content. We managed to convince them that not everyone coming to their website would be the buyer; there would be more junior people told to research before purchasing an expensive piece of scientific machinery.

Because of this, we launched pieces of content that were 'explainers'; a more basic form of the information needed about the machinery. These pieces got lots of traffic and readers included people who then went on to buy from them. It turned out that not all their customers were as knowledgeable about their product as they thought. In fact, some had been put off previously by the technical and jargon-led approach and had been scared to speak to them for fear of looking stupid.

Takeaway:
Explaining your product or service in simple terms will rarely be of detriment. Content should be written in the simplest form possible to make it as accessible as possible to everyone.

Meta Data

We talked at length in the 'on-site' section about what meta data is and how you use it to construct a page that search engines (and humans) can understand. Now is the time to put it to good use by making sure you include a clear title for the page, making sure you have relevant headings throughout your article (h1, h2, h3, etc.) and that you have a well-written meta description. You should also make sure you include an image or images if possible and that they are correctly described for both readers and search engines.

If you have forgotten, skip back to the earlier section and remind yourself how this works.

Images

Remember, a picture paints a thousand words. If you are going to use images on your website, then you would be well advised to choose them carefully. Far too often people simply stick any old picture up, hoping that it will suffice. If you are writing your blog and it's about you, then by all means use a photo taken on your phone. People will happily accept it's not perfect as, after all, this is your blog. But if you are a professional offering a professional service, such as a solicitor, accountant or dentist, just think for a second before you upload a picture.

Problems with images tend to occur in one of three areas:
- Copyright
- Relevance
- Quality

Whether you realise it or not, copyright is a big issue and image rights infringements on the Internet are not without penalty. Certain companies who provide images have been known to pursue small business owners in court for showing a thumbnail of one of their images without permission. In this case, permission comes at a cost as all the larger picture agencies charge significant amounts of money for using their images. The golden rule is don't, under any circumstances, just lift an image from the Internet for use on your website. Even if you use Google filters to find something which is free for re-use, you can still fall foul of the law.

There are several very good websites where you can get high quality images, free of charge, for use and reuse. Often, all they ask is that you credit the photographer in your blog or article and provide a link back to them. If you don't have any of your own images you can use, try Pexels[18] or Pixabay[19] for free images. If you do this, however, make sure that you choose something relevant. There's no point in using a great shot of a landscape if you are talking about skateboards on your page, as no matter how much you like the photograph, it won't add value.

---

18 https://www.pexels.com/
19 https://pixabay.com/

The Three Key Areas of SEO

Finally, whatever you decide to use, remember that quality is important. Far too often I see websites from professional businesses, some of them highly regarded, and the imagery is both poor quality and from a stock image website. When you are starting out in business it's unlikely that you will be able to access high quality photographs, unless you happen to own a decent camera and the other equipment needed. In this case, using stock imagery is fine. But as your business grows, consider using a professional photographer. There are a lot of good professional photographers who don't charge the earth and can provide some stunning imagery for you to use. Quite apart from the fact that it looks good, it's yours to use and no one else can use it, meaning your website can stand out from the crowd. I've used the same photographer for almost ten years and as he's got to know me and my business, he now comes to us with great ideas of how we can best use his photography to enhance our website. It's more than just hiring a photographer; you are enlisting someone to help you with your image and marketing.

Just before we leave images, remember the meta data. Make sure you've completed all the relevant data behind the images, so the search engines know what the picture is, what it represents and how it links with the content on your page.

Internal and External links

This is such a quick win, but so often missed by people. And it's so effective it can make the difference between a page ranking on the top of the search results and not ranking at all.

When I talk about linking, I'm talking about providing a connection between two pages, either within the same website, or between different websites. This is achieved by providing a hyperlink – a small line of code that contains an instruction to open a different page to the one you are on when it is clicked. As an example, if you are creating a page about fire extinguishers and you want to create a link to your fire alarms page, you can add a link to the words 'fire alarms' which, when clicked, will open the fire alarms page. Alternatively, if you wanted to link out to another website which has a page about the importance of fire extinguishers, you could also do this with a hyperlink.

Linking is so important. Thinking back to the beginning of the book, you'll remember that the reason Google became the preeminent search engine is because it identified and codified the value of the links that existed between websites, embedding the knowledge into a search algorithm. Before then, search results were patchy at best. Since the launch of Google, links have been the currency of the Internet. In pretty much every poll of SEOs over the last twenty years, the number one item for getting a website ranking is links.

I'll talk in more detail about links and linking in the next part of the book, but for now, the most important thing to remember is that you need them. For your page to be successful, you will need links, and these may be internal, external or most powerfully, a combination of the two.

Let's start with external links, as these are the links that most people regard as important for ranking. Ideally, you will need links coming into your page from external sources as signs of validation of your content. But when you are creating a new page or a blog, how do you get these links? Despite their importance, no one can actually link to your page yet, because it doesn't exist, so instead of thinking about getting people to link to you, why not include some links on the page which go out to other websites?

This might sound counterintuitive; why would you want to include a link to another website that contains similar material to that which you have written? It's a good question but the question betrays a mindset that affects most website owners and indeed, a lot of the web industry. The question assumes that this is a competition, that you have to be the best, appear at the top of Google and be the pre-eminent player in your field. This is ironic, as when the Internet was created, it was designed as a tool to facilitate sharing ideas and knowledge between people no matter where they were. Here's a quote from Tim Berners-Lee (as mentioned previously, author of *Weaving the Web* and inventor of the Internet) on how he saw it working:

"...a vision encompassing the decentralised, organic growth of ideas, technology and society. The vision I have for the Web is about anything being potentially connected with anything...Suppose all the information stored on computers everywhere were linked. Suppose I could program my computer to create a space in which anything could be linked to anything. All the bits of information in every computer...on the planet, would be available to me and to anyone else. There would be a single, global information space."

In short, ideas can occur anywhere and for us to grow as a society, they need to be shared. So, when you are creating your webpage, consider whether you could include some links out to other 'authority' websites which, if your reader went there, would lead them to a deeper understanding of your product or service. In some cases, this might be a link to Wikipedia.

> **'Authority' Website**
> An 'authority' website is one which Google (and users) find to be reliable, reputable and a source of good information.

To continue the example of fire extinguishers, you might send them to the Wikipedia page[20] which explains all about the history and development of fire extinguishers. As someone selling extinguishers, you probably have neither the time nor the inclination to create a page about their history and development, and in this case, there's no need, as a perfectly good page already exists, so link to it. The key question to ask yourself when creating these links is 'If my reader follows this link, will it add value to them?' If the answer is yes, then include a link; if the answer is no, then it simply isn't worth it.

Having created your page and adding some external links, you should next consider your internal links. Most people miss this, but it can make a significant difference to how well your website performs in the search results. As an example, I regularly write about SEO and other digital marketing matters. On our website, I have articles going back ten years. These days, when I write a new article about e-commerce, I can include links back to previous articles I have written which a reader might find useful. This linking not only helps a reader navigate around the subject, but also sends a powerful signal to search engines about your authority on a topic. If you are writing about fire extinguishers and have written dozens of other articles about them, then include the links to those which are relevant. If your new page is about why extinguishers are different colours, link back to the page where you explain how to use each one of these different coloured extinguishers safely.

In the next part of the book, we will cover links in more detail and why they became the dirty secret of the SEO industry in the early 2000s.

---

20   https://en.wikipedia.org/wiki/Fire_extinguisher

E.A.T.

The first, and most obvious question to answer here is 'What is E.A.T. and why is it important?'

E.A.T stands for Expertise, Authoritativeness and Trustworthiness, and these are three elements that make up a large part of the Google Quality Raters Guidelines work. Quality Raters are real people, employed by Google to check and verify that the search results that are being shown on Google meet users' requirements.

As Google says:

"We constantly experiment with ideas to improve the results you see. One of the ways we evaluate those experiments is by getting feedback from third-party Search Quality Raters. Quality Raters are spread out all over the world and are highly trained using our extensive guidelines. Their feedback helps us understand which changes make Search more useful."

The Guidelines are available online[21] and if you want to read the 175-page document, you will be far better informed as to what these are. For those who prefer the TL;DR version (Too Long; Don't Read), these guidelines are about ensuring that the answers that appear on the websites in Google search results are the best they can be. The guidelines revolve around two key concepts: YMYL and EAT.

Your Money or Your Life (YMYL) websites are described by Google as:

"Some types of pages or topics could potentially impact a person's future happiness, health, financial stability, or safety. We call such pages 'Your Money or Your Life' pages, or YMYL."

In essence, this means that if your website is in any of the health, finance or safety categories, you need to pay very close attention to the Quality Guidelines. However, if you are in a business which is nothing to do with health, finance or safety – such as beekeeping or jewellery – don't immediately dismiss the guidelines. Much of the advice Google offers for the health, finance and safety sectors could equally apply to others. I have started to notice that by applying EAT factors to websites which are not in these three targeted sectors, I am getting improvements in search positions.

---

21   https://static.googleusercontent.com/media/guidelines.raterhub.com/en/searchqualityevaluatorguidelines.pdf

The Three Key Areas of SEO

Some of this is just common sense: for example, Google suggests that if you run a website lending money to people, you should have a clear address which they can visit. It sounds obvious, but as the Internet opened up, many companies decided that they'd rather deal online and simply omitted their address. Brands have built huge online presences without the necessity of a physical location people can visit. But if the transaction involves people parting with money, then Google is looking at it with a careful eye. A jeweller thinking they are not impacted by these rules would be wrong. A brand new Rolex wristwatch could set you back anywhere between £3,000 and £250,000 and that's definitely YMYL territory. So, what can a purely online business selling Rolex watches do to get around this?

The answer sits in the second acronym, EAT.

Google accepts that not everyone is a high street brand and in fact, the majority of businesses these days exist online rather than in a physical high street location. If people are unable to visit these businesses, there should be other ways of validating their credentials, these being Expertise, Authoritativeness and Trustworthiness.

If I wanted to buy a £10,000 watch, I'd want to be assured that firstly, I was buying a genuine product, and secondly, that if I bought through a website, that I would actually receive that product. I'd also quite like to know that the people I was buying from knew a bit about the subject. When I check the Google results today for 'Rolex watches' I can see that the top result is an online only brand. The page I'm sent to has over 68,000 results, all clearly showing prices and photographs of what I assume to be the original products. They have written over 4,000 words, all about Rolex watches, that supports the idea that this page is not only relevant but shows expertise. On top of this, it turns out that they are a middle man, so have watches from private and professional sellers, and that all transactions go through an escrow account which protects my money. They offer a guarantee of authenticity, a simple returns policy and a phone number at which I can speak to a real human being. They also offer payment by credit card, which means that if I'm buying in the UK I can get free Section 75 protection, meaning that under Section 75 of the UK Consumer Credit Act (1974), the credit card company is jointly and severally liable for any breach of contract or misrepresentation by the retailer or trader. In other words, if the dealer or website disappears, I can get my money back, in full, from the credit card company.

The summary of this is that you need to think about your website and pages in a slightly different way; think of it as if you were a customer. What would you expect to see – or like to see – about a business selling whatever it is you sell, to make you feel comfortable enough to buy from them? Whatever it is, that's the minimum that you should put on your website and pages.

Should I add or make changes to the information already on my website?

By the time you've read through all the information in this and the previous chapters, if you already have a website, you're probably wondering whether your existing content is good enough (hint: it's probably not). Which leads to the next question: 'Should I change it?' usually followed swiftly by 'But what if I lose my existing rankings?'

There's both an art and a science to making changes to an existing website, but as long as you approach it in a methodical way, you can improve what you already have without throwing away any gains your site may already have achieved.

The art side of it is very much about how the page looks, feels and how a reader will interpret it, and no amount of fancy programming has ever yet been able to replicate that feeling. If you are unsure whether your webpage really does cut the mustard, try asking people – but not your friends. Friends will rarely tell you what you need to hear, and more often than not, will only tell you what they think you want to hear. What you need for this process is people who are independent of your business yet who might offer a valid input. This could either be your existing customers, prospective customers, or someone who, in a professional capacity, might have some knowledge of this subject. This latter category is quite important to get right, as I have some friends who are highly regarded professional people, responsible for running multi-million pound businesses, yet who would not be able to tell you the first thing about what makes a good webpage. This is not to suggest that these people lack intelligence – far from it. They are highly regarded individuals who have made careers and names for themselves in a particular field. They just know nothing about websites, webpages and how to market to your prospective customers. The people who will know something about this are, amongst others, specialists in website optimisation, other successful small business owners, and professional copywriters.

The science side of this process is very much about measuring what you change. Too often, people make changes and fail to note what they did and when. What this means is if something works spectacularly, they have no way of replicating it as, in most cases, they cannot remember what it was that they changed. Many professional SEO businesses will make a point of logging not only what they changed, but when it changed and how they changed it so they can then report progress. Change, measure and analyse then becomes a recurring loop by which they can continually improve the way your website performs.

If you are worried about making too many changes all at once, you should try and break down the changes you plan to make, and do them over time. This typically applies to pages that already rank well for a particular keyword, but if your page ranks for nothing, then feel free to make wholesale changes in one go.

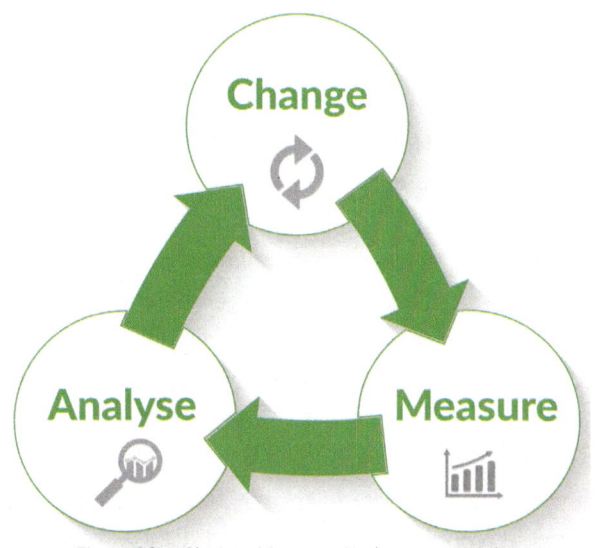

Figure 33 – Change, Measure, Analyse recurring loop.

To see the keywords that your pages already rank for, you will need to ensure that you have Google Analytics installed and that you have access to Google Search Console. Search Console will show you the search phrases for which your pages have been seen in search results over the past period, from thirty days to sixteen months.

As well as the elements that you can measure via Google Analytics and Search Console, there is also a range of other tools you can use to measure other variables, such as keyword position on Google, the number of keywords for which you rank, and gains or losses in those keyword positions. These are also extremely important metrics and I'll cover the various tools available in a later chapter on Resources.

When you are making your changes, the things that you can measure and those that you should measure are two different beasts entirely. Analytics will allow you to measure an enormous number of variables, but that doesn't mean that you should. In fact, most of the things you can measure will be no use to you at all. Before you start, you will need to decide what makes the most difference to your website. Will it be the number of visitors to your page, the number who return, the amount of time they spend on a particular page, how far down the page they scroll, whether they visit more than one page, bounce rate (more of that in a bit), whether they fill in a form, ask for a download, give you their email address or buy something? As I said, a lot of different things you can measure, so decide what you need, not what you want.

To understand how any changes you make to your website are having an impact, once you decide what to measure, fix a point in time and take a reading. It might be that on yesterday's date you ascertain that your website received 275 visitors. That's a good starting point. Ideally, if after making the changes, you record 375 visitors to your website, it would seem that the changes did some good. But beware, as SEO is always measured over a longer timeframe than you might imagine. Be careful of attributing positive (or negative) results to the wrong thing. Remember, correlation and causation are two separate things and proving the link between the two is often harder than you might imagine. Just because something happens after an event, it does not mean that the event caused that thing to happen. As an example, you may record a rise of 100 visitors to your website between mid-October and mid-November after you've made some changes, but if you sell fireworks, attributing the uplift in traffic to your changes could be incorrect. Seasonality, time of the month, time of the week and even which day it is can lead to unrelated changes in traffic. If you are an office-based business, such as a solicitor, accountant or surveyor, you may well see website traffic drop significantly every weekend, whilst if you are a nightclub, it might be reversed. Understanding your existing traffic is essential before you measure change.

Typically, if you take a three-month snapshot of your website and measure before and after on a rolling three-month basis, that will eliminate most of the

The Three Key Areas of SEO

daily, weekly and some of the monthly variability. Often, I will measure year on year, month for month, and therefore like for like to get a true comparison.

If you have decided what you want to change and made a note of how much traffic the page (or website) gets and which keywords currently rank, you have made a great start to improving the viability of your website in the search results.

Bounce Rate

Bounce rate is one of those things that really annoy me. Not the metric itself, but the nonsense people attach to it. As an example, coincidentally on the day I am writing this piece, I received the following in an email:

"First, monitor your bounce rate like a hawk. This number reveals how many people click away from your site almost instantly after landing on it. Taking steps to lower your bounce rate (like making sure you're showing up in the right search results or that you have a killer landing page) will greatly improve on-site conversion rates."

I need to start by saying that this is dangerously misleading.

I'm not challenging the idea that you could improve your on-site conversion by looking at your bounce rate, more the fact of its importance. The opening sentence imploring you to "monitor like a hawk" is, in my opinion, a complete waste of time and resources. Invest your time in doing this and it will tell you nothing.

As an example, if I told you today that the bounce rate on one of my websites is currently 83%, what would you conclude? Is that good or bad? And why? And if it dropped to 70%, would that be good or bad? And why?

Exactly.

Yet bounce rates get talked about so much in SEO, in my experience, for all the wrong reasons.

To understand why this is such a dividing issue, let's start with what bounce rate is. Google describes it unhelpfully in semi technical language:

"A bounce is a single-page session on your site. In Analytics, a bounce is calculated specifically as a session that triggers only a single request to the

Analytics server, such as when a user opens a single page on your site and then exits without triggering any other requests to the Analytics server during that session."

I appreciate that if you are like me, you may need to read that a couple of times to get the sense of what it is saying. So, let me try and explain this in simpler terms.

Bounce rate is when someone visits your website, lands on a page, and then leaves your website without visiting any other pages. And on the face of it, this is a useful piece of information to have. After all, if you are spending time and money sending visitors to your website (particularly if you are using paid advertising to do this) then you'd want to know if they were arriving and then leaving immediately without looking around or buying anything. This is why so many people talk so much about lowering bounce rates – to the point of fixation in some cases. They truly believe that there is a direct correlation between bounce rate and money made online. This is partly driven by articles and emails such as the one I received today. As a reminder, it said, "taking steps to lower your bounce rate...will greatly improve on-site conversion rates." This is said with such conviction you'd be hard pressed to challenge the logic. What this statement misses, however, is context.

Having worked with a variety of websites in a variety of sectors over the course of the last ten years, I can say with certainty that bounce rate alone is NOT the key determinant of whether people will buy from you. It might be part of the puzzle, but it's definitely not the one thing you should focus on. High bounce rates are not an issue for a great many pages. On my example website where I discussed Google Crawl, you'll remember that I said that at the turn of the new year I had added some content which answered a specific question about postage costs. That question is one where there is only one right answer – and my website has it. When people land there, their search is entirely satisfied and there is absolutely no need for them to go onto any other page. In fact, I'd argue that this page is probably one of the most effective I have on all my websites because it answers completely and quickly the question people are asking. The bounce rate on that page is always around 90%.

Meanwhile, we also work with a number of e-commerce websites, and they too have pages with a high bounce rate. As an example, look at the sample data I've

The Three Key Areas of SEO

Default Channel Grouping	Acquisition			Behaviour			Conversions E-commerce		
	Users	New Users	Sessions	Bounce Rate	Pages/Session	Avg. Session Duration	E-commerce Conversion Rate	Transactions	Revenue
	56,089 % of Total 100.00% (56,089)	55,857 % of Total 100.07% (55,819)	70,220 % of Total 100.00% (70,220)	71.34% Avg for View 71.34% (0.00%)	2.27 Avg for View 2.27 (0.00%)	00:01:07 Avg for View 00:01:07 (0.00%)	2.43% Avg for View 2.43% (0.00%)	1,704 % of Total 100.00% (1,704)	£38,526.87 % of Total 100.00% (£38,526.87)
1. Organic Search	46,135 (80.19%)	45,164 (80.86%)	54,861 (78.13%)	82.55%	1.76	00:00:58	1.08%	592 (34.74%)	£14,122.11 (36.66%)
2. Paid Search	4,667 (8.11%)	4,188 (7.50%)	6,658 (9.48%)	2.04%	5.19	00:01:47	9.51%	633 (37.15%)	£13,321.67 (34.58%)
3. Direct	4,630 (8.05%)	4,543 (8.13%)	6,370 (9.07%)	50.97%	3.47	00:01:44	6.06%	386 (22.65%)	£8,910.39 (23.13%)
4. Social	1,606 (2.79%)	1,565 (2.80%)	1,692 (2.41%)	67.55%	2.06	00:00:46	1.18%	20 (1.17%)	£414.14 (1.07%)
5. Referral	482 (0.84%)	385 (0.69%)	624 (0.89%)	43.91%	4.46	00:02:12	11.70%	73 (4.28%)	£1,758.56 (4.56%)
6. (Other)	14 (0.02%)	12 (0.02%)	15 (0.02%)	53.33%	4.53	00:02:46	0.00%	0 (0.00%)	£0.00 (0.00%)

Figure 34 – High bounce rate does not automatically mean user dissatisfaction.

extracted from one of them in Figure 34, a company who sell clothing. The first thing you can see from this is that their bounce rate overall is just over 71%. That's seven out of ten visitors to their website arriving and leaving without ever visiting another page. How can that be effective? Surely, they should focus on their bounce rate to improve this?

Actually, no. And it's to do with what their website is set up to do.

Take a look at the bounce rate for their Paid Search, on row two. Just 2% of visitors bounce off without visiting another page. They visit an average of five pages every visit and spend nearly two minutes on the site on average. And in the timeframe we are looking at here, they bought £13,000 of goods from the shop. Those who fixate on bounce rates will tell you that this is exactly why you need to 'watch like a hawk' as by driving the bounce rate down to 2%, the remaining 98% are going on to visit other pages and buy stuff. Which of course, is true. They are doing exactly that and to the tune of £13,000, which given their average order value is around £30, is pretty good going.

But the more observant of you will also have spotted row one, Organic Search, which in the same timeframe delivered £14,000 of sales with a bounce rate of 82%. If you truly believe bounce rate to be the main driver for sales, how on earth do you reconcile this data?

The reality is that you are missing a vital piece of information, and as I said earlier, this is all about context. Without context you can make dangerous assumptions and even more dangerous decisions about changing your website, only to see your bounce rate and your sales drop simultaneously.

The context with this website is that they have spent the best part of ten years building up a superb online resource for people looking for advice on a subject. If you need advice on this subject and search online around any of the issues you might be facing, you will find their website. When you get to the website it will offer you the help and advice you need and as a by-product, you will also see their £10 item offered for sale, which will probably resolve the problem you have. But not everybody will buy it straight away. Most people, in fact, read the article then go back to Google and search for a different problem or symptoms they might be facing. Whatever the search though, the chances are they will arrive back at this website.

By the time you've found the same website offering you answers to two or three questions you have asked, you're going to have built up some trust in the brand. After all, they are appearing highly in Google searches, they are offering free impartial advice, even offering to send you to competitor websites (yes, they do link to them) and they sell a solution to your problem which is at pocket money prices. This is the point at which people buy from them.

So, given that context, you can see that fixating on bounce rates is not a healthy way to optimise your website. You need to look at it as just one of the metrics which is useful and not the panacea to all your ills.

UI/UX – you what?

Along with my passion for exposing people in our industry who try to focus you on the wrong things, my other *bête noire*[22] is jargon. My word, isn't the digital space just awash with it? You need to check where you are in the SERPS, watch the CPC on your PPC and of course, focus on your UI/UX. All of which might be true, but how is the average business owner supposed to make sense of this? Why should a business owner who specialises in a particular trade be forced to learn the language of our trade, just to have a website? I'm not required to understand the niceties of the laws of the land, nor know how a push fit joint works, just to run my website, so why are we insisting that everyone becomes a website specialist before they can run a business?

One of the worst abbreviations of the last few years has been the emergence of

---

22 Translates to 'a person or thing that one particularly dislikes.' And yes, I'm being ironic including it in a section about jargon!

The Three Key Areas of SEO

UI/UX and its rapid ascent into the daily lexicon of website jargon. Even Google's autocomplete feature recognises this and offers a choice of searches, none of which (other than the top one) explains what the heck it is.

Figure 35 – What is UI/UX?

The abbreviation stands for User Interface and User eXperience, and both elements have become another niche digital area over which there is a shroud of mystery for most people. Hopefully, the following will lift the veil a bit for you and give you some idea of what it is and why it is important.

To start with, User Interface is quite simply anything that your customer is faced with when dealing with your business. In the context of a website, it's about every image, button, clickable element and how they work when someone uses them. It can be anything to do with any interface between a user and your business, not just a website, so it could be an app, a digital device (such as a fridge connected to the Internet) or even wearable tech such as watches. User Interface can play an enormous role in reassuring and engaging customers, so much so that Apple (who pioneered a lot of this work) gained many users and advocates in the early days of both their iPod and iPhone, simply because of how they looked and felt in your hand. Their chief designer, Sir Jony Ive,[23] was responsible for so much of what users today take for granted. Smooth, seamless products which are not just functional, with their ground breaking 'app' layout, but also a delight to hold.

---

23 https://en.wikipedia.org/wiki/Jony_Ive

User eXperience, on the other hand, normally comes after user interface. It reflects how users feel about your product or service once they've been given a way to interface with them. Again, Apple take credit here as the term 'user experience' is often credited to Don Norman, a Cognitive Scientist who worked for Apple in the early 1990s. He had authored an article back in 1981 entitled 'The truth about Unix: The user interface is horrid', in which he argued that for all the wonderful abilities of Unix (an early computer operating system), it was extremely hard for a human being to use. Within this paper lie the seeds of what became UX. User eXperience is more about how you or I will feel once we've interacted with a business, often through their website, and from there, how likely we are to be satisfied with that interaction.

To help distinguish between UI and UX, I'll defer back to Don Norman again, who said:

"I like the restaurant analogy I've heard others use: UI is the table, chair, plate, glass, and utensils. UX is everything from the food, to the service, parking, lighting and music."

In other words, you will need both UI and UX for your restaurant to be successful, and they are two different things. In pure marketing terms, these almost translate to two of the '7 P's of Marketing', the two being Process and Physical evidence.

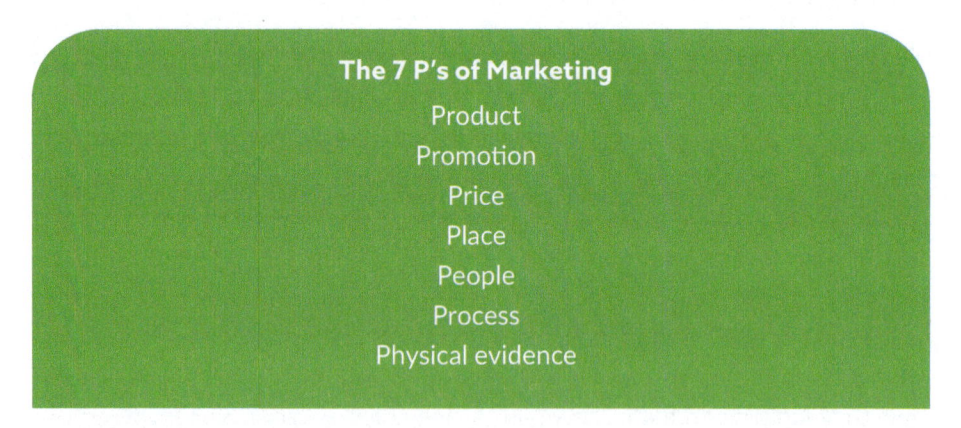

> **The 7 P's of Marketing**
> Product
> Promotion
> Price
> Place
> People
> Process
> Physical evidence

Whilst not directly comparable, it's close enough to suggest that Process equates to User Interface and Physical Evidence equates to User eXperience. I know that the truth is it's a lot more nuanced than that, but in the interests of simplicity, if you've ever had to do any marketing for your business, you will understand what this means.

Now, let's translate this to your website.

Often your User Interface is pre-determined for you in that your website may have been built by someone who has used a pre-built theme or framework. These can be great for building websites that look good, but not so good when it comes to interfacing with the customer. As an example, when you search on your mobile phone for a product or service, you expect that the website you arrive on will allow you to buy what you want, or at least to contact the company. Simple things like having the telephone number at the top of the page and making it clickable, so that when a user taps on it, their phone offers to connect the call. Even today, people build websites with the phone numbers hidden at the bottom of the page and they fail to make it clickable, meaning you have to write it down or copy it, then tap it into your phone again to make the call. It's simply too hard for most people, who will go elsewhere before they do that.

A great many of the ready templated solutions provided by some of the bigger providers (such as Go Daddy, Ionos, Wix and Weebly), whilst providing a low-cost entry point for a small business, can suffer in this regard. Not only do they sometimes provide a poor UI/UX but they are also too inflexible and therefore cannot be changed or adapted to improve this situation. Whilst these platforms have, over recent years, invested in improving their basic offering, to many in our industry, these still leave a lot to be desired.

If you accept that it's important for your website to be both functional and accessible, we are back to the 'Should I add or make changes?' argument from earlier. Again, the best resource to determine this is the people who are likely to be your biggest critics. If you really want to know how good your website is, try buying from yourself. Get your website up on your mobile phone right now and try to see if you can buy a product, request a sample, or simply call yourself. How easy is it to do? How many clicks did you need to make before you could do this? Is the site easy to read? Could you find the information you were looking for? Can you easily navigate not only forwards and backwards, but to other areas of interest on the site? These, and questions like these, should help inform your decision as to whether you think your website is currently fit for purpose.

Summary

This chapter has all been about Rule 2: 'Nothing, but nothing beats great content'. All of the elements discussed come back to just one thing: write some great content for your website. Of course, you need to think about accessibility, about how users will view and interact with your website and how Google and other search engines make sense of your website. But the bottom line is that if what you create on your website is great, you are halfway towards getting your website to work the way you want.

> **Takeaways:**
> Content is King.
> Write for your intended audience, not Google.
> Rule 3 applies – make each page unique.

Off-site

Let me say upfront that this is quite a long section, and for that, I make no apology. Links and link building are amongst the hardest parts of SEO and possibly the most misunderstood. Having spent some time reading a range of other books people have published on the subject, this is the one bit that they all skip. They either give it a light touch and offer nothing in the way of help, or they try to tell you all the different techniques you can use for link building, which involves simply copying and pasting what's already on the Internet. Frankly, that's simply not good enough. As things currently stand, link building is an essential part of getting your website to rank on Google, but bewildering you with hundreds of techniques doesn't really help.

This part is different. I will show you what you need to consider when building links, but more importantly, I will question why we should be doing this at all. And that is the elephant in the room.

Link building and the voice of the crowd

As we learned in Chapter 1, Google's breakthrough – and the differentiator that helped it conquer the search market in such a short time – was the accuracy of its results. Instead of just relying on what it could crawl on each webpage it

The Three Key Areas of SEO

visited, it also measured the number and quality of the links that were pointing to that page from other websites. The combination of these two elements made the Google search results the most accurate and powerful in the world.

For those of you who were using computers in the late 1990s, the rise of Google seemed to be an almost overnight phenomenon. I recall sitting at my desk in 1999 and searching on Yahoo[24] (the default search engine at the time) for a local tyre dealer. I was working in a town called Sale, which is a few miles outside Manchester and quite a busy place. So, I searched for 'tyres sale'. And as you might imagine, the results were awful. The front page was full of garages offering tyres for sale, or who had a tyre sale at that time, but crucially, not one of the results were local to me, with most of them being in London or the South East of England, around 200 miles away. This was not a good user experience.

Figure 36 – How Yahoo's home page looked in 1999.

---

24 https://web.archive.org/web/19980630072557/http://www.yahoo.com/

I'd heard of Google but not yet tried it and at that moment I was so disappointed with the results I'd got from Yahoo, I reasoned that I had nothing to lose. So, I typed in google.co.uk and was surprised to see an almost clear, white page with a single search box in the middle. At the time, the Yahoo search on its home page was a busy page, trying desperately to group your searches into different classifications and offering news snippets as well as local guides, like a combination of a local newspaper and the Yellow Pages directory.

Figure 37 – Google's home page in 1999.

By contrast, Google was nothing more than a small box on a page with two buttons beneath it: 'Google Search' and 'I'm feeling lucky'. I typed 'tyres sale' into the box and clicked on the Google Search button. Within half a second I had a page full of the search results, and to my astonishment, all of them were relevant. There were local garages and tyre dealers, and in a few moments, I had called to get their prices and availability.

Remember, at the time, the way to get the best deal for tyres was to get a Yellow Pages or other local directory and ring around a number of advertisers until you found what you were looking for. To switch to a different way of searching, the results would have to be good enough to replicate or improve on that user journey. And with Google, it was.

How did Google manage to do this? I was intrigued about how it could be so accurate, not just with this search result, but with so many others I tried. The other search engines were so poor that I have to confess, initially, I had no idea how Google seemed to 'know' what I was looking for. Over time though, I learned that it was a combination of what it could read on the page (like the other search engines) but crucially including signals that it took from other sources, including links that came into the website. What this meant in practice was that in the example of my local tyre dealers, Google had figured out that, amongst other things, as the tyre dealer had links to their website from other local Sale-based businesses, it had correctly inferred that they were based in Sale. Google had used the 'voice of the crowd' to better inform the search results. This is an oversimplification of how it works but I tell the story to make the point that the number and relevance of the links pointing to a website was so powerful that it helped propel Google from a small start-up company to the largest search engine in the world in just a few years.

Google, however, still had a long way to go before it became the default search engine of the country, but with a strong start like this it didn't take long before people were recommending it to work colleagues and friends and the country switched *en masse* to make it the new search engine of choice.

What exactly is a 'backlink'?

If you have spent any time working to get your website to rank in the search results, you will know that backlinks are the holy grail, the almost unachievable goal for any website owner. Why do I say that? Simply, because they are so hard to acquire. Any basic overview of search engine optimisation that you read will tell you that you need to get backlinks to your website. Some of them will go into great detail about how you can do this, but most treat it with a cursory mention. The reason their advice is so perfunctory is often because they don't know how to tell you that this is the most difficult part of the job. But make no mistake, it really is the hardest part of optimising a website.

Which brings us to the key question, what is a backlink?

In simple terms, backlinks are links between two websites, where one site provides a bridge or link back to another website. This is based on a simple piece of html code (the computer language that makes the Internet work) that exists on all websites. On your website, when you click on anything that takes you to another element of your site, such a page or an image, you are clicking on a hyperlink. When this hyperlink is on another website and clicking on it takes it to a page on your website, that becomes a backlink. It really is as simple as a link back to your website.

The links all look very similar in that they are all written in the same format, which is:

<a href="https://aqueous-digital.co.uk/articles/ever-changing-world-link-building/">Link Building</a>

The breakdown of this is that the first bit – the '<a' – is simply an instruction to start a link tag. The next part – which is 'https://aqueous-digital.co.uk/articles/ever-changing-world-link-building/' – is the location of the page you are linking to, the '>Link Building<' is the anchor text (more of that in a bit) and finally, the instruction that we've finished telling anyone what the link is and where it is on the Internet is made using the closing tag of '/a>'.

When you start looking closely at websites, you can find clickable links everywhere. Most of these links will be internal, in that when you click on them, they will take the user to somewhere else within your website. But occasionally, they will take you to somewhere else on the Internet and that is a backlink.

As an example, on my website I have a Resources[25] section and in that, I list some of the best resources for anyone trying to understand SEO. Within that section on 'Websites about SEO', there is a backlink, although it's not immediately obvious when you look at the page (Figure 38).

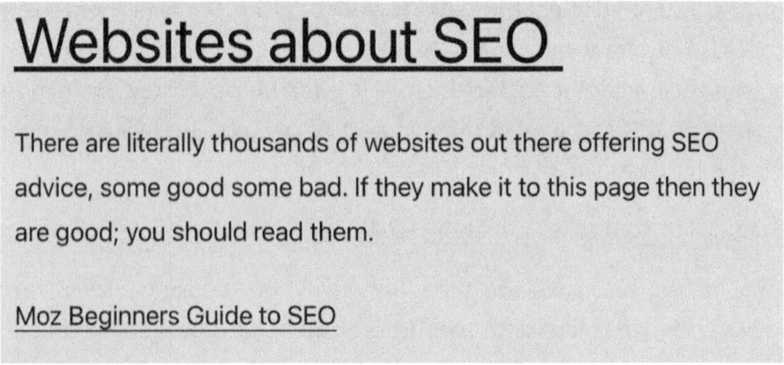

Websites about SEO

There are literally thousands of websites out there offering SEO advice, some good some bad. If they make it to this page then they are good; you should read them.

Moz Beginners Guide to SEO

Figure 38 – A snapshot of the Resources page on my website.

---

25   https://jonathanguy.co.uk/resources/

The link is contained with the phrase 'Moz Beginners Guide to SEO' highlighted in blue (Figure 39).

Websites about SEO

There are literally thousands of websites out there offering SEO advice, some good some bad. If they make it to this page then they are good; you should read them.

Moz Beginners Guide to SEO

Figure 39 – The link on that page, highlighted in blue.

If you click on that link, it will take you directly from my website to the page on Moz that contains the *Beginners Guide to SEO*. There are several reasons why I have constructed the link in this fashion, including the value of linking out to another site – in this case, a website which is an authority on SEO. Also of importance are the exact words I have used in the link and whether it is a 'follow' or 'no follow' link (more of that in bit). The main reason the link is there is that it is relevant and helps my readers. It is within a section about SEO, on a website that tells you the owner works within SEO. The link is both relevant and contextual. Of course, my website is far from being important and therefore the value of that link to Moz is minimal, but what it does do is send a positive signal to search engines that I find this page valuable; so valuable that I'm happy to direct my readers to it.

Figure 40 – Moz Beginners Guide to SEO.

Links play a vital part in how the Internet works and as we learned earlier, are integral to Google's earliest patent and the algorithm that followed. As links are important, so acquiring links to your website is important. Take it from me though, this is the hardest part of the job and the part that goes wrong most frequently. There are so many articles about link building, so much advice and so many different types of links you can acquire, that knowing where to start is a real challenge. Many website owners decide not to bother with them and instead focus on the easy bits, like making sure the images look nice or the content tells everyone how good they are. Ironically, doing this is unlikely to help you acquire any links at all, as it adds little or no value to other users. Links, therefore, remain a conundrum to most website owners.

How do I know who is linking to my website?

As a starting point, you need to know whether your website has acquired any links from any other websites. To do that, the simplest tool is Google Search Console. Whilst fairly basic, Search Console does have the advantage of being free and as a 'starter for ten' it will give you some data. Visit Search Console and look at the left hand sidebar.

About two thirds of the way down you will see a heading for 'Links' (Figure 41). Click on this and it will show you a range of items, including the one thing you want – a list of the websites that link to you (Figure 42). Alongside this information it also shows which pages these

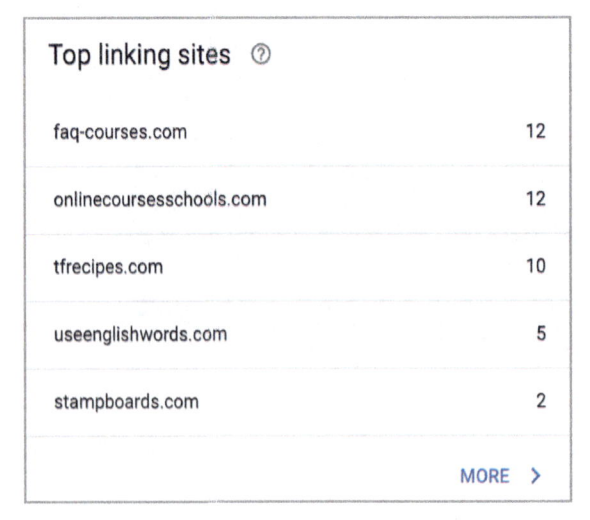

Figure 42 - Google Search Console showing which websites link to your website.

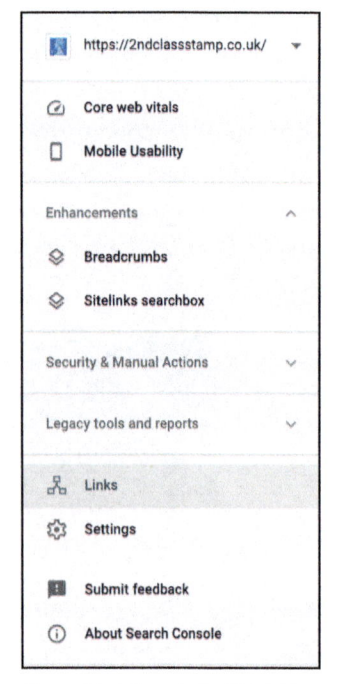

Figure 41 - Where to find 'Links' in Google Search Console.

The Three Key Areas of SEO

websites link to on your website and what anchor text they have used to link to you. We will cover this in more detail later in this chapter.

There are dozens of other SEO tools on the market, such as Majestic or Ahrefs, and some are free but most these days most are paid. There's a list in the Resources chapter to help you decide which is best for you. Most of these tools will give you a more detailed insight into the backlinks pointing to your website. As you progress you will probably find that one or more of these will be better suited to your needs as they give you far more information, such as the reputability of these sites and whether they are considered to be spammy or not. Be warned though, no two tools will show you the same data. As an example, here's the full list of backlinks that Google tells me I have pointing to my website:

Total external links		
47		

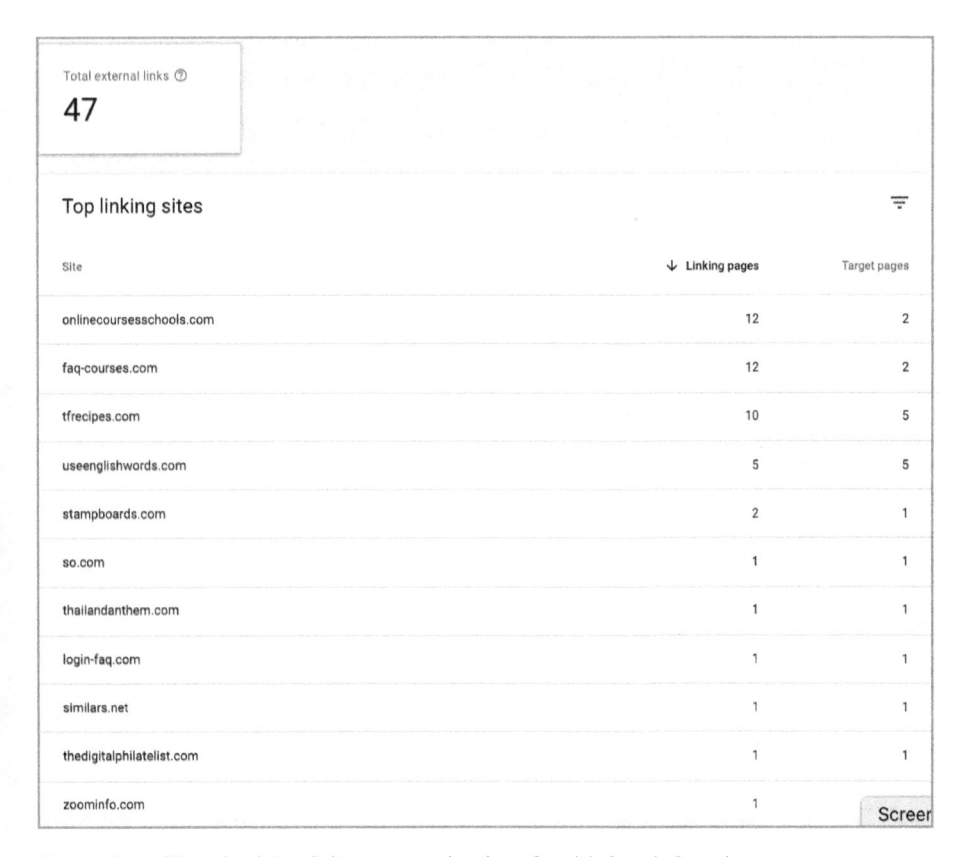

Top linking sites

Site	Linking pages	Target pages
onlinecoursesschools.com	12	2
faq-courses.com	12	2
tfrecipes.com	10	5
useenglishwords.com	5	5
stampboards.com	2	1
so.com	1	1
thailandanthem.com	1	1
login-faq.com	1	1
similars.net	1	1
thedigitalphilatelist.com	1	1
zoominfo.com	1	

Figure 43 – Full list of websites linking to me, taken from Google's Search Console.

Google shows me I have 47 external links from 11 different websites, almost none of which I know or recognise. This is important, as the act of simply having a website which people can access means that you will acquire links from a variety of random sources. In the example in Figure 43, I don't recognise FAQ Courses but I'm guessing that my website answers a question which is frequently asked, hence the link.

By contrast, however, Ahrefs, which is one of the professional tools I use on a daily basis, shows me that I currently have 142 backlinks from 73 referring domains and that historically the number of backlinks was once as high as 144.

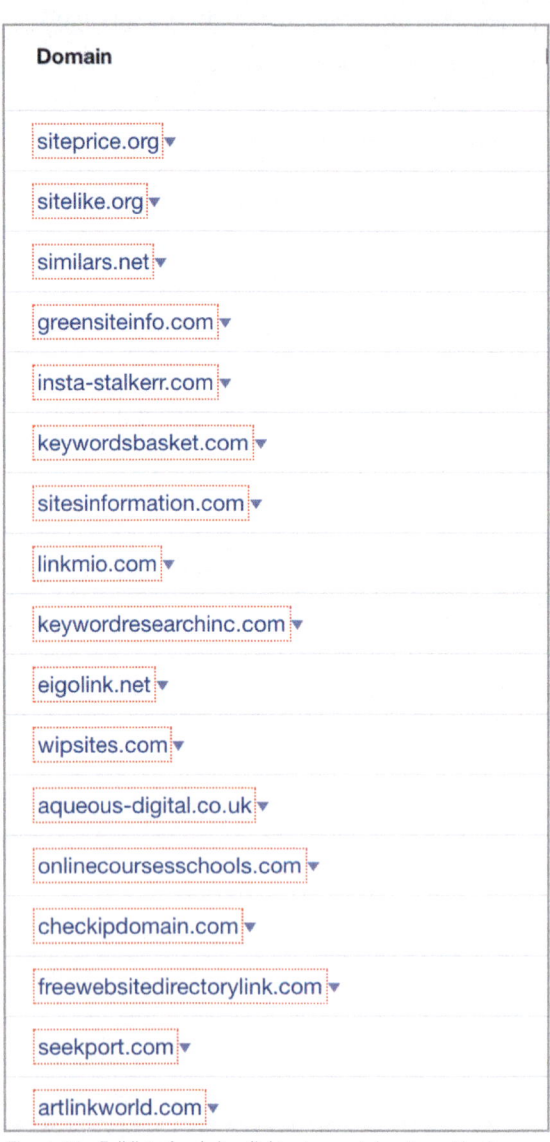

Domain
siteprice.org
sitelike.org
similars.net
greensiteinfo.com
insta-stalkerr.com
keywordsbasket.com
sitesinformation.com
linkmio.com
keywordresearchinc.com
eigolink.net
wipsites.com
aqueous-digital.co.uk
onlinecoursesschools.com
checkipdomain.com
freewebsitedirectorylink.com
seekport.com
artlinkworld.com

Figure 44 - Full list of websites linking to me, taken from Ahrefs.

The lists of websites Ahrefs is showing me is in Figure 44. As you can see, a completely different list of websites with only one in common with Google. Moreover, other than one from my company website, I've not built any of these backlinks; they have chosen to link to my website either because I am showing something of value that they want to share, or they have been created automatically by bots (there are tools on websites that will allow you to do this, though I don't recommend it). So, how do you choose which to believe or indeed, which to use? Over time I've discovered that no one tool completely fits the bill so it's best to try out a few and then choose two or three that you like and that give you what you need, so you get a better picture. If you are running a small website, you probably need to weigh up the time (and money) spent versus the benefit you can get. For most small business or hobby websites, Google Search Console is perfectly adequate. Larger websites, on the other hand, are far more likely to see a benefit from using these tools.

The bottom line is that the entire Internet is a web held together by links. They will happen whether you want them to or not, but the challenge is to get more and (most importantly) better links to your website than your competitors. If, having reviewed the links you currently have, you don't like what you see, don't despair. There are things you can do about this, and I'll cover that later in the chapter.

How do I get people to link to my website?

Having established the importance of links and that they are essentially votes of confidence in your website by another website, the next step is to get some of them pointing to your website. But how do you do that? How can you get people to link from their website to yours?

There are many different ways to build links to your website, but before you do this, it's important that you understand what you should, and more importantly, should not be doing. Back in the early 2000s, when webmasters realised that links caused their websites to rank so highly in Google, they started link building in earnest and this practice has continued to this day. Google makes it clear in its Webmaster Guidelines what is and isn't acceptable (which we covered in Chapter 1) but in the early days, these guidelines were not as comprehensive as today, so people were spending an inordinate amount of time looking for ways to cheat the system. They did this because the potential rewards were huge. Early adopter websites that appeared at the top of Google search results found that the amount of traffic they generated and sales they made from this activity was breathtaking. It quite literally made some website owners millionaires almost overnight.

What these early adopters also discovered was that not all links are created equal. When Larry Page (one of the co-founders of Google) registered one of their original patents in 1997, he included something called PageRank.[26] Not as you might think, something that helps to rank pages, but named after himself. In

---

26 https://en.wikipedia.org/wiki/PageRank

Search Never Sleeps

essence, what PageRank measured was the relative importance of the link based on the size, strength and credibility of the website from which it came.

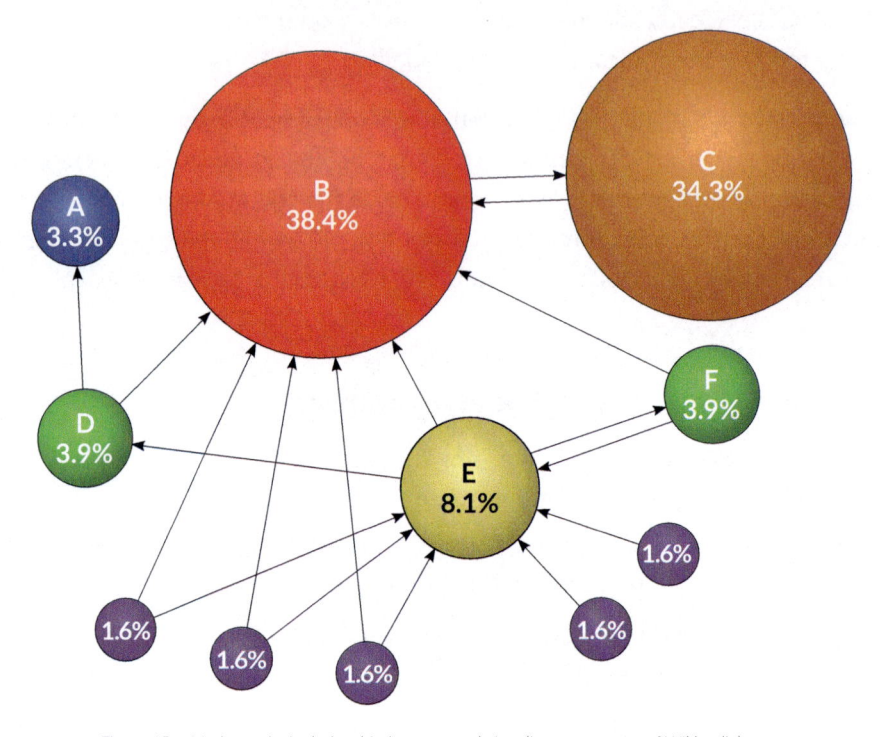

Figure 45 – Mathematical relationship between websites (Image courtesy of Wikipedia).

As an example, Figure 45 shows the mathematical relationship between each website (represented by the coloured circles) and the links that they share between them. In simple terms, it shows that even though website E has more links coming into it, website C has a higher Page Rank as the single link it has comes from a higher value website.

Or to put it another way, it's very much based on a hierarchical structure. In Page's early research, he noticed that not only did certain websites have more authority, but those more authoritative websites often tended to link to each other. This meant that in practice, the Federal Reserve website might link to the *The Wall Street Journal* website and vice versa, but it was highly unlikely to link to a Ma & Pa shop in Boise, Idaho. Similarly, the Ma & Pa shop might link to a local bicycle repair shop but was unlikely to link to the Federal reserve. There were, however, examples where these links between higher and lower tier websites existed and in almost every example they found, they linked because there was something of relevance on the receiving website. So, if the *The Wall Street Journal* did link to the Ma & Pa shop in Boise, it was because it was the subject of an article in the paper and a link was relevant. Likewise, if the Ma & Pa shop did link to the *The Wall Street Journal*, it was usually because they were posting out a relevant article to readers of their blog. With this as a base, the understanding that the value of a website or webpage is based on the number and quality of the links became part of the algorithm.

Back to the original question of 'How do I get people to link to my website?' There is now another and probably more relevant question, which is 'How do I get the right people to link to my website?' From what we can see in the diagram, it's clearly more important to get one really good link from a high authority website than a hundred from low authority websites. But what is a high authority website and what would make them link to you?

The value of backlinks

If you are going to attract valuable links to your website, then you are going to have to create something worth linking to. We've already talked in Chapter 3 about how you should approach the creation of compelling content. If you've taken that on board and created the ultimate piece of content for your website, what sort of links should you be looking for?

There are three main types of links that you want to attract to your website, and they are:

1. Authority Links
2. Relevant Links
3. Anchored Links

Let's go through these one at a time.

Authority Links

An authority link is a link from a website that clearly has a higher authority than your website. There are a number of ways of measuring this and most of the available SEO tools have their own version to help. Typically, you will see it referred to as Domain Authority (DA) or Domain Rating (DR) and all of them work on a similar 100-point scale, with the very best websites ranking 90+. Most websites typically rank anywhere from 20-40, so if your website score is in that range, don't worry, you're in good company. Domain authority is summarised nicely by Wikipedia[27] as:

> **Four Dimensions of Domain Authority**
> 1. Prestige of the website and its authors
> 2. Quality of the information presented
> 3. Information and website centrality
> 4. Competitive situation around a subject

In essence, it's about how reliable a website is likely to be, how good its content is, how authoritative its authors are and how it is perceived by others in both the wider web and specifically in the market in which it operates. What you are looking for is a link back to your website from another website which is regarded highly by other people.

Relevant links

Relevance is key when it comes to link building. If you run a law firm and you write a blog about the legal issues around child custody, it's great to get a link back to your article from a website that talks about child issues, or legal matters, or both if you can! Not only is the link you receive a relevant link but, if your article is a good one, you may find you get links from higher authority websites as well. In fact, the better the quality of your website content, the more likely you are to attract high quality links.

When I talk about relevance of links in the context of link building, I often find that people are concerned about generating or receiving links back to their website that are 'irrelevant'. Whilst an understandable concern, given the importance of relevance, it simply is not an issue. The reason for this is back to the way people use the Internet; in short, you can't control who likes your page, content

---

[27] https://en.wikipedia.org/wiki/Domain_authority

or website any more than you can change the weather. If on social media, you write a post that strikes a chord and gets widely shared and linked to, you have no control over who likes or dislikes it. With link building, you can't control who will like your page or post. The good news is that you don't need to worry about this, as the search engines already know that good content will attract links, and many from places that you would not expect.

Search engines understand that links can and will arise from any website and link to anywhere on the Internet. They don't need to be relevant, contextual or even have any special anchor text (see next section). This is precisely why relevance has such a premium; links which have relevance to the page, post or article to which they link demonstrate that what you have written on your website is of value. These, search engines will reward, more than all the other links that you might have arriving on that page, post or website.

We saw an example of a relevant link earlier with the one I had placed on my website to the Moz *Beginner's Guide to SEO*. The link is relevant to them as I write about SEO. Sadly for them, however, my website is a relative minnow and as such, the link has very little domain authority, so it won't necessarily boost their own page or domain authority. The good news is that the relevance, in this case, adds a lot more to their article than if it was from an irrelevant website. This is because relevant links, in my opinion, add more to the value of a webpage, blog or article than authority links. I appreciate that this may be considered controversial by some of my colleagues in the SEO space, so let me explain my thinking here.

Imagine two websites, both writing an excellent article on the same topic. One of them receives 100 links back from other websites, all of which are relevant. The other receives just one backlink but from Wikipedia. Which website would you rank first in the search results?

This is the kind of problem that Google has to solve millions of times a day. In reality, it presents both, sometimes at position one and sometimes at position two, and assesses what users do when they arrive on the page. Do they stay and read it, or do they go back and look for another article? User behaviour drives a lot of the algorithm as Google is, as we have seen, constantly trying to solve our problems. The site or page which achieves the best user response generally gets the highest search position. In the case of our theoretical question, Google is faced with a choice. In the absence of any user behaviour data, it needs to decide which webpage it should put first. I would argue that based purely on the question of which would rank first, it should (and probably would) put the page with 100 backlinks higher in the search results. Why? Because even though the PageRank diagram earlier showed that the higher value link would confer more authority, in this case, relevance clearly outweighs that value. When Google was launched, relevance was not specified, principally because at that time, almost all links were relevant. In the days before people started link building, a link from one website to another typically signified that there was value in the page they were directing you to. Today, relevance plays a huge part in what Google does, as to answer our incessant questions, it needs to provide relevant answers.

Interestingly, when you search Google for 'the importance of link relevance' it returns an odd mix of articles. None that I could see were anything more than cursory treatments of the subject. One of the top results was published in 2002, making it twenty years out of date. Other than that, there is very little recent relevant material. The remaining articles in the top ten were all from digital agencies or link builders and none of them gave this topic any serious discussion. This suggests that whilst we continue to parrot the Google advice to 'make links relevant', there has been little or no testing of this belief to truly understand the difference it makes. In the absence of any empirical data, we need to continue to believe and trust that relevance is important.

Relevance remains one of the cornerstones of link building, although not, it seems, at this stage empirically tested by anyone outside of Google.

Anchored Links

This section is all about the importance of anchor text, which has been referenced a number of times already. To start, we need to understand what is meant by anchor text. In simple terms, anchor text is the word or words that forms the clickable link on one website to another; it quite literally anchors two points on the Internet together. You can spot these quite easily on any website as the accepted format for a link is that any anchored text will be underlined, and the text is usually in blue. In the example of the link from my website to Moz's Guide, the anchor text is 'Moz Beginners Guide to SEO'. Of course, I could just as easily have anchored on the word 'Moz' or 'SEO' or 'Beginners Guide'; there is nothing stopping me or anyone else choosing any type of anchor text for the link being created. Therefore, if I can choose any anchor text, why is it important?

Anchor text informs both the search engines and users of the context of the link, and as we saw from the previous section, context will help to infer relevance, which we know to be essential.

As an example, if I had chosen to link to the Moz guide using the anchor text 'to' (as the word does appear in the phrase), on its own it would give no context as to what a user could expect to find at the end of that link. In isolation, any search engine would be hard pressed to make a determination as well. Fortunately, search engines have adapted and now routinely read the words around any anchor text, so in this case because the words 'Moz Beginners Guide' and 'SEO' surround the word 'to', it would be able to piece together the context of the link even if I just anchored on the word 'to'.

From a user point of view, correctly naming links makes it an awful lot easier to navigate around the Internet. Take these two sentences as an example and, assuming that they both link to the same page on another website, consider which of these makes it clear what is at the end of the link?

Option 1
To find out more about this subject click here

Option 2
To find out more about Giraffe Conservation visit the Giraffe World website

Users are far more likely to understand what they can expect to find at the end of the link in option 2 as the context is clear. Moreover, some people are nervous about clicking on a link when they don't know where it will take them so adding context gives a reassurance that it's a good link.

Anchor text plays a vital role in helping search engines make sense of the links they find and in helping users to navigate from place to place. But what difference does anchor text make to your website ranking?

There is an extraordinarily large amount of literature available on the importance of anchor text in link building and a simple search for 'the importance of anchor text' today returns over 67 million results on Google. That's a lot of opinions!

Figure 46 - A Google search for 'the importance of anchor text'.

But does anchor text make a difference? If so, what is the best anchor text and how can you create it on your website?

Before I talk further about this, let me say up front that in my opinion, far too much importance is placed on the relevance of anchor text by too many commentators. In most cases, they simply parrot the opinions of others and fail to challenge the narrative. After all, it's easier to echo someone else's point of view than to develop your own.

Personally, having dealt with this over the past decade, I can say with some confidence that anchor text is becoming less relevant for search engines and more relevant for users. Users need help with navigation; you should be aiming to make everything as simple for a visitor to your website as you possibly can. Search engines, however, have enough sophistication to understand the larger patterns and will make their own decisions on relevance, almost despite whatever you do.

In the earlier example about giraffes, if both articles were about giraffe conservation, whilst the second option makes it easier for users, search engines would find both links equally valid and are unlikely to rate one higher than the other. Why? Because they understand links at the macro scale.

SEMRush (one of the online marketing software providers — see Resources chapter for details) has categorised all the different anchor text into ten different types, which they explain quite nicely on their blog.[28] When you get time, I suggest you read it in detail.

---

28 https://www.semrush.com/blog/what-is-anchor-text-and-how-can-i-optimize-it/

The Three Key Areas of SEO

For now, these are the ten types:

Type	Description	Example
Generic Anchor Text	Any generic words such as link, here, click, etc	To find out more click here
Branded Anchor Text	Linking on your brand or company name	Aqueous Digital
Partial Match keywords	The exact words you want along with other generic or random words	Buy cat food here
Brand plus keyword anchor text	Your brand or company plus what you want to sell	SEO from Aqueous Digital
Random anchor text	Any random words from the text	Interesting viewpoint
Long tail anchor text	The keyword you want but not the exact phrase	Is link building essential in SEO?
Exact match anchor text	The precise words you want to rank for	Family Law or Central Heating Repairs
Related anchor text	Use a variation of the keyword to link to the page	Boiler Repairs (when your page targets Central Heating Installations)
Naked Link Text	Any clickable link with the full address visible	https://jonathanguy.co.uk/
Image anchor links	The image 'alt text' is what Google reads as the anchor for images	On a picture of a new boiler, you might have alt text of 'Professional boiler installation by Joe's Plumbers'

Figure 47 – 10 different types of anchor text.

As you can see, there are a huge number of ways to anchor your links, which of course begs the question, which is best?

Historically, the prevailing belief was that *exact match* anchor text was the very best you could get and indeed, creating links like this used to work very well. I recall people desperately trying to create as many backlinks as they could with the exact match anchor text in them as this used to work. Websites with this type of backlink often found themselves much higher up the search results than their competitors and often you could find websites with millions of backlinks, all with the same exact match anchor text. But Google also realised that this was happening and made a concerted effort to discourage people from doing this. Ultimately, it culminated in Google introducing the Penguin update, starting in 2012, which was principally designed to stop this kind of link spam. This evolved and was folded into the main Google algorithm in 2015. Today, the algorithm can look for unnatural patterns of links and if necessary, issue a Google manual action (or penalty) to a website for breaching these rules.

Current received wisdom is that you need to create a 'natural' backlink profile, with a range of anchor text, so that when anyone looks at your website backlink profile it appears to be natural rather than an artificial construct in an attempt to rank for one or more keywords.

What does a natural link profile look like?

If a 'natural' backlink profile is the holy grail here, we should take some time to consider what that looks like. It's very easy to say that it should look natural, but does anyone know what this means?

Perhaps if we take a large step back for a moment and consider what links might look like at the macro scale, we might see that there are patterns which emerge. These patterns are probably the best way to determine what 'natural' looks like in this context. One of the best tools to do this is supplied by the team at Majestic,[29] who are able to graph the distribution of links for any website in a simple-to-use format and to show you what anchor text has been used in those links. I often use these images in presentations on link building as they are the most effective way of explaining what a search engine will see, and by definition, what natural might look like.

The starting point is to look at some large and well-known websites and see what their backlink profiles look like. Take a look at these examples of some well-known UK websites including eBay, Next, The *Telegraph* and BBC, all taken in 2015. For this example, I used their 'Historic Index' which contains every backlink that Majestic have ever noted pointing to these websites. In each case,

---

[29] https://majestic.com/

The Three Key Areas of SEO

this numbers over 1,000,000 links and gives us sufficient data to ensure a reliable aggregate result. The most strikingly obvious thing about these profiles is that all of them conform to the same basic pattern. In the images shown, the X axis refers to Citation Flow, which Majestic describe as "a score which reflects the **quantity** of links that point to any given website." Bear in mind that this has zero relevance to **quality**, it simply looks at the absolute number of links. The Y axis represents Trust Flow, which again they describe as "the quality of links that point to URLs and websites". Logically, the aim is to get the higher Trust Flow links to point to your website and if possible, as many of them as you can.

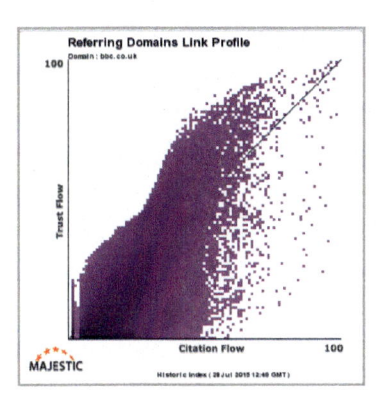

Figure 48 - bbc.co.uk

Figure 49 - eBay.co.uk

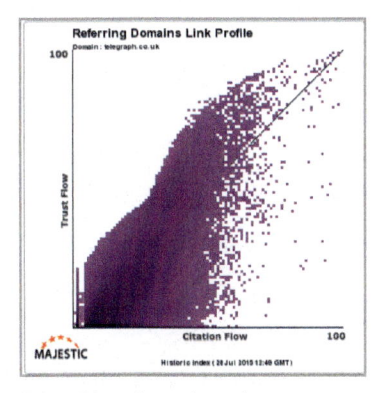

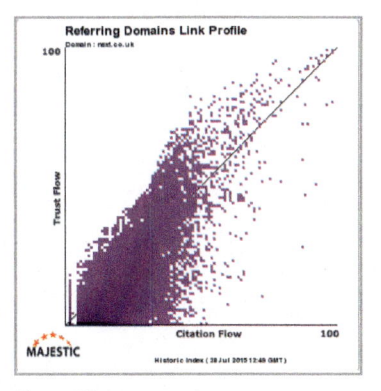

Figure 50 - telegraph.co.uk

Figure 51 - next.co.uk

The examples shown here all share the same basic pattern, similar shapes and, because each of them has a significant number of backlinks pointing to them, these can be said to represent a 'natural' link distribution. Given that Google and the other search engines crawl billions of links every day, I think it's safe to assume that they too can see this pattern. So, when it comes to assessing your website, they will already have in mind a 'template' of what natural looks like. That's not to say that your website must always conform to this, far from it. Bear in mind that these profiles are based on years of data with no indication as to which link arrived when. It could be that each of them first attracted lots of low value links from sites with high Citation Flow but low Trust Flow. What we do know is that over time, each website will attract a link profile conforming to these basic patterns if they are acquiring links naturally.

Majestic also helpfully shows you the top anchor text for each of these websites. If you take a closer look at these in the images (Figures 52 and 53) you can see that for larger websites, the anchor text is generally not an issue. The top ten anchor text for the BBC doesn't feature anything other than their own brand name, yet the BBC website ranks highly for a huge range of topics. You could, however, argue that 'it's the BBC' and they will always rank highly, but what about websites that are selling things. In which case, let's take a look at Next, who as a clothing retailer with a significant online presence, must be looking to rank for a whole range of keywords other than their brand?

#	Anchor Text
1	bbc
2	www.bbc.co.uk
3	Empty Anchor Text
4	bbc.co.uk
5	http://www.bbc.co.uk
6	http://www.bbc.co.uk/
7	bbc news
8	the bbc
9	BBC
10	英国bbc

#	Anchor Text
1	next
2	Empty Anchor Text
3	next.co.uk
4	https://www.next.co.uk/
5	www.next.co.uk
6	next official site: online fashion, k...
7	https://www.next.co.uk
8	go now
9	website
10	shop the latest women's, men's and ch...

Figure 52 – BBC anchor text.   *Figure 53 – Next anchor text.*

Once again, we can see that whilst they may rank highly in search for a huge range of fashion terms including 'dresses' and 'men's suits' (for which they are currently number one organically), these terms don't appear in the anchor text top ten. In fact, anyone looking at this data without context could easily assume that the best anchor text for any website to rank for any product or service would be its name.

Ironically, despite being the wrong conclusion based on the data, in many respects it's the right thing to do. Sure, there are times when it would be natural to create a backlink to a website which is focused entirely on the product they are selling, but in most cases, most people would use the website name.

Here's an example where you can decide on the placement of the link. Either is fine but as you are not linking to a single item, surely most people would just anchor the link on the brand name?

You can get *cheap fashion* on eBay

You can get cheap fashion on eBay

In reality, most people creating a link will either put the naked link text or they will anchor on the name of the website to which they are linking. Few people are going to specifically choose to create a link on 'cheap Nike Airmax' when they could simply link to the store selling them.

A 'natural' link profile is a profile that looks natural according to Google. As Google doesn't give you any idea what this is, other than to list the things you shouldn't do,[30] then what is 'natural' continues to be open to interpretation.

A quick guide to link building strategies

I've called this a quick guide and I have absolutely no desire to simply recreate what is already freely available online and in most other books written on SEO. I've provided links to some of the best resources at the back of the book so for now, here's a potted version of how to build links.

Let's start with the basics; first you are supposed to create some amazing content. Yes, I know, this is the challenge we covered earlier in this chapter and at this point I'm assuming you've managed to create something that people might feel

---

30 https://developers.google.com/search/docs/advanced/guidelines/link-schemes

is worthy of linking to. The next step is to help people find your amazing content and to do this you might choose to do some or all of the following.

Social media activity

Probably one of the easiest ways to get your content to a wider audience is to share it on social media. Of course, this depends on you having social media channels set up for your business and that you already have some people following you on these channels. If you don't have them set up for your business, consider using your personal accounts for now whilst you establish your business accounts, but be careful as Facebook are quite particular about ensuring personal accounts remain personal.

Historically, this form of promotion was a lot easier as there were few restrictions, particularly on Twitter and Facebook in the early days. Now, however, every social platform is looking to monetise your efforts and most of them will push you towards paying to promote your content. Ideally, you don't want to pay for this promotion as organic reach is far and away the best, but without paying, you will find the reach is limited, particularly on Facebook, who deliberately choke the number of your followers to whom it will show your organic posts.

Those of you familiar with link building might, at this point, be asking why the first thing I'm talking about is social media, when Google has made it clear that links from social media don't have an impact on where your content, webpage or website appears in the search results. As far back as 2014, Matt Cutts (who at the time was Head of Webspam for Google) stated that signals from social media were not a ranking factor for Google. Yet here I am suggesting that you should share your content on social channels. Whilst it might seem counterintuitive, the fact is that indirectly, social activity could help your ranking after all.

As an example, if you've created a fabulous blog about giraffe conservation and you share it on social media, it will appear as a link on each of the channels on which you share the content. Google will be crawling these platforms and will find the link back to your website. What it won't do is credit you with a link back from any of them, so the value of your page will not increase because it has appeared on the social media websites. What it will do is track what happens when people click on that link. When people click a link on social media, it takes them to your giraffe content and as soon as people arrive on your website,

Google tracks what they do, where they go and how long they stay. If it finds that people are reading all your content, sharing it themselves on social media and interacting with it – whilst the fact that it is popular on social media counts for nothing, the fact that people are engaging with it on your website does – it is more likely to push you up the search results for giraffe conservation as it is clear from user activity that you have written something that resonates with people. They like it, they are engaged with it, and they are sharing it. The social interactions are not the ranking factor here, but how people behave when they are on your website and reading the content are the ranking factor. Your content is fresh (always a good thing), relevant and people like it. Why wouldn't a search engine want to place this highly in its index for other people to find?

Social media is not a great place to start if you are looking to create backlinks, but it is a good place to start if you want to make noise, get people to your website, and establish yourself as an expert voice in your field.

Outreach

This is definitely one you'll be encouraged to have a go at to try and get your content noticed by everyone who talks about link building. But I have a confession to make – I hate it.

Outreach is the polite term used for sending emails to people you don't know, asking them if they'll include a link to your wonderful content from their website. There are lots of different forms of outreach but if you've run a website for any time, you've undoubtedly received one of these cold outreach emails in your inbox by now. I get them all the time, including an astonishing one last year which led me to send quite a curt email response. I'm going to include it here as an example of what not to do if you are planning on asking people to link to your website.

The original email was headed 'Website update request', which struck me as odd as I couldn't immediately see why someone I didn't know might need me to update my website. The email then read like this (and I've redacted the bits which might identify who they were {a travel company}, but you will get the gist of it).

Hi,

I came across your 'links' landing page at https://www.mywebsite.co.uk/resources/useful-links/ and noted you've put a comprehensive list of useful travel resources.

We believe [Redacted] is a perfect addition. We've got bucketloads of deals to suit every kind of budget, with everything from family breaks to adults-only options and once-in-a-lifetime getaways in our catalogue. You'll find holidays that are just the ticket if you want a one-click package that takes care of everything.

Or, if you're the type of person who wants to fine-tune every detail – like your break's duration, the airport you fly from and the board basis – we've got tonnes of options for you to get your mitts on, too.

It would be great if you would consider linking to our page https://www.ourwebsite.co.uk with the anchor text "[Redacted]".

Thank you for your support, we're extremely grateful.

Please let me know if you have any questions.

Kind Regards,

Kate

As someone involved in SEO and link building for a long time, this email struck me as odd. Not only did it sound like a sales pitch, but they were also telling me what anchor text they wanted me to use. As you might imagine, despite the initial temptation to react, I simply ignored this first email. The problem with outreach though, is that those doing it at scale use tools to help them manage it and those tools always include a follow up email for people who don't respond the first time. You have probably guessed what happened next; the inevitable follow up email arrived, this time asking me if I'd had time to consider their request but crucially adding "*I would be grateful for any feedback*". With that kind of offer, how could I resist?

My reply read as follows:

Hi Kate (I'm assuming this is your name, though it could be your outreach persona),

You say you'd welcome feedback and I've held off until now as I wanted to make sure I was not too abrupt, but following this second email I'll happily share my thoughts.

When your first email arrived, it came, as most of the outreach emails do these days, in my junk mail. I always read them though, in case I'm missing something.

In your case, what struck me was the unusual nature of the request. We've never met, you have no ideas who I am and yet you wanted me to insert a pretty specific link into my website. Not only was it for a company I've never booked with and therefore am unlikely to promote, the narrative beforehand was pretty much a sales pitch, lifted, no doubt, from one of your sales brochures. Naturally, this struck me as unlikely to succeed and in truth, made it feel less like an outreach request and more like a sales pitch.

Not only do I run the website as a 'free' resource for people specifically looking for [Redacted], but as you can tell if you've bothered going through the website, other than a handful of holiday snaps, we're not about promoting [Redacted] tourism, and definitely not with a specific partner. Ironically, the thing that made me read your first email was that it was from [Redacted], a company my sister worked for over a number of years.

So, apart from the fact that I don't add links to my website unless they relate specifically to [Redacted], the other thing I should disclose is I run a digital marketing agency, and we do our own outreach. In fact, I teach the people in our business how to do it properly. You might expect therefore that I am likely to be ever so slightly critical of your efforts.

As you have asked for feedback, I'm happy to offer a few ideas which might help you going forwards. I hope these are received in the spirit they are intended.

1. Don't do outreach through 'Contact' forms on websites. If the email address isn't readily available, then it probably means the website aren't looking for you to contact them.

2. If you wanted to find this email address, it's readily available elsewhere on the website (https://www.mywebsite.co.uk/privacy-policy/). The fact that you didn't find it suggests that you've used scraping software to do this and as such, you're more likely to get rejected or ignored.

3. Personalise your outreach. If you'd approached me with some photographs to add to this page https://www.mywebsite.co.uk/resources/photos-of-thelocation/ and suggested that in return for using them I could credit you, there might have been a different outcome, which leads me to....

4. Offer something of benefit to the outreach partner. Running a website costs money and anything that offsets that will help a small website owner. It doesn't have to be money, it could be, for example, a link. Why not offer link partners the chance to

write something for the [Redacted] website? Any decent articles get included with a link back. It's not a reciprocal link programme, as there is a hurdle to overcome (the content needs to be worthy of inclusion) and the value of a link from you to me is greater than from me to you. As an example, I have postcards from [Redacted location] from the 1970s – they make fascinating reading and it wouldn't be hard to create a backstory around the message on the card.

5. Mention your affiliate programme. Anyone who provides a link can be entered into the affiliate programme and I can see from your website that it pays commission on a booking within 30 days of a visit. But only if they don't copy/paste what you sent them. Already some have (do some Google searches and you will see) and of course, Google will recognise this as link building and devalue those links automatically.

6. Get creative. Why not create a 'postcard from [Redacted location]' competition whereby any visitors to the island can send a 'postcard from [Redacted location]' to [Redacted] within a specific time window, and the winning postcard could be the one with the most inventive reason for visiting the island? As a [specialist] website, I would promote that, particularly if you approached me and said I could have all the postcards afterwards, as this is an area I collect. I appreciate there might be GDPR issues but at least it's creative.

7. Run your own competition and ask people with websites that relate to [Redacted location] if they'd mind promoting it. If you are giving away a free holiday I'd be tempted to enter and include the link in a blog post.

I could go on, but I hope that this has given you a little food for thought?

I appreciate that you might be faced with an uphill challenge, generating links at scale for a website and an industry that has had a torrid year. Which is all the more reason to get inventive with your outreach. There's no limits to creativity...

Wishing you all the very best with your endeavours.

Kind Regards,

Jonathan

Now as I re-read this, I still think that, on balance, I got the tone right. This was during 2020 and the travel industry was on its knees so asking people for links might have seemed a fair thing to do. But as I said in the reply, there are better

The Three Key Areas of SEO

ways to do this than simply asking me cold to cut and paste your text into my website, giving the impression that I both support and recommend you.

I've included this because for me, it summed up everything I dislike about outreach in the way it is currently promoted. It is cold, impersonal and annoying. It offers me no value for doing what you want and moreover, it adds no value to your website. In this instance, asking everyone who received the email to add the same anchor text means you are creating an unnatural number of links with the same text, which isn't good.

> **Scraper software**
> Scraper software — an automated programme that scours the Internet looking for email addresses to add to their contact list.

Having said this, some outreach *is* good. Sometimes (rarely) I get great emails from people who have taken the time to look at my website rather than using scraping software, know a bit about who I am, what I do and what I might like, and in even rarer situations, they tell me why adding a link on my website, directing people to their website, might be a benefit to me. So, if you do want to use outreach to get people to create links back to your website, do some homework first. Create an email which might be received well and the best way to do that is to read it first and imagine how you would react if it landed in your inbox.

> Things to include in your outreach email:
>
> - **The name of the website owner (if available)**
> - **Something about the website that you like**
> - A reason why you think your website and their website might be a good fit (e.g. we are both in the same sector)
> - A reason why you think adding a link to your page, article or image would help their readers
> - A really polite thank you

How not to do it

As I was writing this chapter, this appeared in my inbox. It's a clear case of what not to do and is included here so you can see what your email shouldn't look like! It's not personalised, it wants a 'do follow' link with no benefit to me, and it wants to pay me for including a link, which is against Google's Webmaster guidelines.

Hello,

Greetings of the day!

While hunting the web I came across your website and was interested in posting guest articles (with a Do-follow link) on it.

As yours is a very quality website, please let me know the cost price for the same?

Also, please let us know the possibility of an advertisement banner insertion on your website's home page and in the existing posts.

The banner would be relevant and in line with your homepage or article content. Also, the banner/image that we want to insert in your existing posts would have a link inserted with it.

Please let us know the scope of this work and the fee that you would charge for the same?

Looking forward in anticipation.

Regards & Thanks

Directory Backlinks

These are fairly simple to do, and the principle is fine; submit your company details to a website that lists companies. It's no different to the good old fashioned 'Yellow Pages' which had a fairly comprehensive list of every business in the country, whichever country you were in. The idea of producing a list of businesses for people to search has been around for over 100 years so it was inevitable that this would be extended to the online environment, as it was also inevitable that it would be abused.

I've long held that if you are going to add your company details to any directory website, you should first ask yourself the question, 'Would I use this website to find a list of reputable companies?' If the answer is yes, then go ahead and list your business. In the UK, websites like yell.com and thomsonlocal.com have a long history of being reputable directory lists as they have evolved from a printed product. In the USA, there are websites like the Better Business Bureau, who are a trusted source of local business information. There are also pure online brands such as Bing, Yelp and of course, Google My Business, which are useful websites on which to submit your details. If, on the other hand, you are offered a link from something like seolinkdirectory.com, then can I suggest that you simply don't bother? Not only has no one ever heard of it, the name is also something of an issue as it is clearly not designed for humans to provide a trusted list of businesses but has been created with the express purpose of manipulating Google's search results.

There are a number of firms who are currently advertising a directory listings product which they typically badge as being a way of ensuring your company name is consistent across the Internet. They often cite the need for your business information to be accurate across the Internet and that if you don't have that then Google may rank your company name lower. This idea gained traction a number of years ago, and even today is still touted as a critical element of any marketing strategy. On the back of this they might sell a 'package' that contains over thirty (or forty, or fifty or as many as they want) directories in which they 'guarantee' that your details will be accurate – as long as you keep paying them annually for the privilege. The reality is that you simply don't need this. True, it's important that you ensure your company details are consistent wherever they appear online, but honestly, Google can spot the difference between 'road' and 'rd' or 'street' and 'st' and understands that these are interchangeable. I've used some of the online 'tools' and they have told me that my reputation is in danger because of these differences. Nonsense, it simply doesn't work that way.

The trick with business directories is to only use them if they are reputable or relevant. Don't pay a company to do this for you either, just do it once yourself and then leave them alone – unless, of course, your details change. For that reason, you should keep a record of what you have completed so you can revise it later if needed. The value of directory links these days is basically zero and if you think about it, the reason is obvious. They are essentially free of charge;

anyone can have one and if everyone can have one, then why would a search engine attach much value to it?

You will see some writers extolling their virtues as part of a consistent EAT strategy (remember — Expertise, Authoritativeness and Trustworthiness), adding that unless your name, address and phone number (NAP) are consistent, then search engines won't trust you. Sure, if in one listing you are Joe Bloggs with a business address of 20 Bolton Gardens, Basingstoke, and in the next, Bloggs Builders, Head office, Bolton Gardens, Basingstoke, then that might be considered untrustworthy. When you read these two different descriptions it seems obvious to a human being that they are probably the same company, but it also sends up a bit of a red flag as the second address is trying to hide where they are. We ask ourselves: 'Would I trust a building company that hides where to find them?' Search engines are programmed as best they can, to behave the same way, and it would take issue with these two listings as being inconsistent. As I said though, making sure the listings are exact down to the last letter is not important and neither is it something worth paying for. Even if it did make a difference to your SEO, the percentage difference it would make is so small as to be negligible.

So, list yourself in as many directories as you like. Keep the company name and address details as consistent as you can but don't think it will make a bit of difference to your overall SEO.

Video on YouTube and Vimeo

Creating video can be fun, if time consuming, but don't think that you can just rock up with the latest iPhone and create amazing content for your business that will fly – you can't. Don't get me wrong, if you want to use your mobile phone to create content for your website and YouTube or Vimeo channel then go ahead and do it, but before you publish it online, ask yourself the question 'Does this accurately reflect my business?'

From a link building perspective, video content is useful because it can be hosted on YouTube, Vimeo, or other online video hosting platforms and these will provide links back to your website, specifically to the page in which you have inserted the video. Whatever you do, don't be tempted to simply host the video on your own website as not only does it take up server space, but it also slows down your website, which is a negative signal to Google. Given that anyone can create video nowadays, the value of these links is limited so the trick is to make content that people will want to share and link back to. In the b2b environment, videos that get the most traction are those which are creative, in that they do something different from everyone else, or they offer value to the viewer. If you create a video explaining the correct way to safely erect scaffolding, that may well be of interest to some people. On the other hand, a video of the business owner standing in front of some scaffolding telling you how great his business is doesn't have the same sort of cut through. In the b2c environment, creativity is key – as demonstrated by the very best brands out there. Not only do you remember their videos, but they are cross platform and cover website, social media and TV. You probably won't have the budget to compete with these so focus on what you can do differently. Find something unique about your business and make it your 'go-to' in your videos.

The aim of video is to create something that proves useful for a potential customer. By including it on your social channels and in your blog or even your newsletter, you can get people to watch your key message about a product or service that you offer. The aim is to get people to visit your website and hopefully they can watch your video in full. Getting them to your website creates traffic, which we know the search engines watch. Keeping people on your website whilst they watch the video creates a good dwell time; they stay on your site for longer. Finally, if they like what they see, there's a chance they may become customers and that, after all, is the holy grail. In the meantime, search engines measure what traffic arrives on your site and what that traffic does. A good engaging video means more engaged visitors, which in turn means that Google is likely to rank you higher in the search results. And that is where video can really help with SEO.

Press and PR Activity

This is currently one of the best and most consistently rewarding link building strategies in terms of generating great natural backlinks to your website. The concept is simple: create a press release around a story about your business and send it out into the ether. The media will latch onto it, everyone will be talking about you, and it will create lots of links back to your websites from other websites which discuss your press release. Meanwhile, back in the real world, it doesn't happen like that. For most businesses, they don't even get as far as finding an interesting story, so there's only a small proportion of businesses who will even attempt a press release. Even those who are brave enough to create a press release and get one written in a professional format will find that doing so – and sending it directly to the newspapers and magazines in which you wish to feature, or using a mass distribution service – will rarely get you any traction. In most cases, the best backlink you get is from the press distribution service website and no one is interested in what you have to say.

The sad truth is that most business stories are dull. Whatever you may think about your own business, few people will be interested. Sure, you may have poured your heart and soul into it over many years and the news that it's your business' birthday, or that you've just landed a big deal, or that you have taken on a new member of staff might be momentous in your world, but to the world of journalism, it's nothing. Journalists are more likely to report that you've gone bust than expanded and there's nothing the media like more than a bad news story. It's the old adage: bad news sells.

So, with that in mind, how on earth can you get people to sit up and take notice of you?

The starting point is to figure out what your target newspaper or magazine is currently writing about. Look through the past issues and see if you can figure out what they like about business stories. In our local paper, they like reporting record turnover and expansion and anything that includes a million pound or more investment. Knowing that, my best bet for a story in our local newspaper is that we've just been given £1.5m investment capital to fuel our expansion plans, which are to create thirty new local jobs over the next five years and float the business on the stock market. OK, so this might not be entirely true but if I were to write this as a press release it would get their attention. Am I suggesting that you make up stories to get press coverage? Of course not. What I am suggesting is that you should think carefully about what message you are trying to convey and try and understand what would resonate with their readership.

Unless you are already a major brand and a significant employer in the local area, most newspapers will not pay much attention to you.

How to create links from your website

Having spent the best part of a decade link building, I must confess that I sometimes take for granted the knowledge I have. Despite regularly offering advice to my team on aspects of link building, I still have an in-built 'blind spot' to certain questions. One of them, which rather caught me by surprise a while back, was being asked by a website owner how they should create links out of their website. They had a number of genuine concerns that if they created links out from their site, they might cause some harm, or in some way diminish the value of the website. Nothing could be further from the truth. When I dug deeper, it seems that some of the anxiety came from the research they had done and an article they had read on Google which suggested that by linking out to another website, they could lose 'link juice'.

Let's be clear, the Internet is founded on links. If websites didn't link to each other, then the value of the information available would be lost, as information sitting in silos would be incredibly hard to find and access. So, linking from your site to another valuable website (that you feel your readers would benefit from seeing) is a good thing to do. And the short answer is that there is no 'wrong' way to do it, but lots of different ways you can do it.

As we saw earlier in this chapter, the relationship between websites and the value of the links helped Google to originally create 'page rank', and in so doing, they created a formula which passes a fraction of the value of the sending website to the receiving website. From this, some early commentators conflated this into the idea that linking out from your website means you lost link juice (today referred to as link equity) every time, and the more outbound links you had, the worse it was. Of course, if this is true, then it destroys the very thing that makes the Internet of value and simply reinforces the creation of information silos. The truth is somewhat different and as you might expect, bears only a passing relationship to the scare stories.

When you create a link from your website to another website, it simply creates a bridge which a reader of your page or a search engine can follow. To a search engine, it can and does interpret the link juice or link equity of the sending page and confers some of that value to the receiving page, but it is a very small part of the equation. What's more important is that the link is relevant, has authority and adds value to a reader. Today's algorithm is more concerned with whether the link is 'on topic' than the relative importance of both websites.

When you create links, you should aim to consider the following points:

1. **Does the link add value to your reader?** If they follow the link, are they going to find something that will help add to the knowledge that your page is offering them?

2. **Is the link relevant?** If you are writing about giraffe conservation and decide to link out to another page which is all about shoe repairs, Google will understand that the link is nonsense. A link to a zoo, or a Wikipedia page about giraffes, or a page about giraffes on the WWT website would be relevant.

3. **What type of link do you want to create?** Today, on WordPress, when you create a link it offers you a choice of four options which are (Figure 54):

Open link in a new tab
Add rel="nofollow" to link
Add ref="sponsored" to link
Add rel="UGC" to link

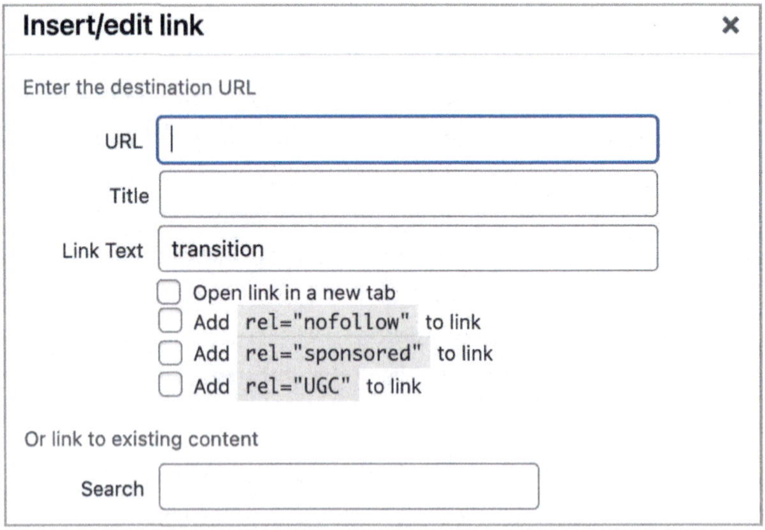

Figure 54 - The options to create different types of links in WordPress.

I'll cover these different types shortly.

4. **Where on the page are you placing the link?** Search engines place more value on links that appear early on in an article than those further down a page. They also place more value if the link is within an article and anchored on relevant text (as we talked about earlier) than if they are in a sidebar or in the footer.

5. **How many links are there on the page?** All search engines will view a page with hundreds of links as spammy unless there is a really good reason for them being there. As an example, an e-commerce website may have over 100 links on a page and as long as they link to relevant and contextual pages, that is fine, but 100 links in an article about, for example, giraffe conservation, going to lots of other websites which have nothing to do with giraffes, animals, conservation, etc. would be considered poor practice.

So, what are the different types of links and why should you be concerned about them?

When you create a link from your website, if you have followed these five points you will have ensured that it is relevant, contextual, and above all, it adds value to your reader. But website owners I have spoken to are worried that it means that people following those links will leave their website and not come back. This is a possibility, but if you are concerned about this then best practice is to create the link and ensure it opens in a new tab. As we see in Figure 54, on WordPress this is achieved by simply ticking the top box. What it means is that your website stays live in the reader's Internet browser, which then opens another tab for them to read the resource that you have linked to. When they have finished reading that, they can simply return to your website as it's still there and live on their browser. As a matter of course, almost all the external links I create open in a new window as this not only removes the problem of people leaving your website, but I believe it makes it easier for users are well.

Having created the link, by default it will be a 'follow link'. Follow links appear in the html code like this:

<a href="https://anyoldwebsite.com">your anchor text</a>

The part that says 'your anchor text' is the words which you have chosen as your anchor, e.g. giraffe conservation.

A follow link is one which a search engine will 'follow' and they will use it as part of their algorithm to decide the relative merits of each page on the Internet.

The more 'follow' links your page gets from higher ranking websites, the more authoritative your page will become.

No Follow links on the other hand, appear in the html code like this:

<a href="https://anyoldwebsite.com" rel="nofollow">your anchor text</a>

As you can see, identical to a follow link apart from the inclusion of the 'no follow' instruction. The 'nofollow' tag tells search engines not to follow the link from your website, but in a recent 2020 update Google confirmed that when they see this tag, they still follow the link, they just don't count the value from it in any calculation of the worth of a page. So, adding a 'no follow' attribute to your link essentially says to Google (or other search engines), 'I'm including this link because it may be of value to a reader, but I don't want you to necessarily attribute value from my website to what you find at the end of this link'.

An example of a 'no follow' link could be when someone had paid for an advertisement on a high ranking website (such as a local newspaper) but the website does not want any of its value attributing to the receiving website (the business that has paid for the advert). Initially, 'no follow' links were used in exactly this way but today, there are other ways to let Google know about paid content.

If you place an advertisement on a website today, it is more than likely that the link they supply back to you will include another of the options, namely a 'rel="sponsored"' attribute. It should look like this:

<a href="https://anyoldwebsite.com" rel="sponsored">your anchor text</a>

Google suggests that this type of attribute is used for all paid or sponsored links to indicate that the website receiving the link has paid for that to happen. This makes sense of course, otherwise brands with the biggest budgets would simply pay more to advertise on high authority websites all the time, irrespective of whether it actually delivered clicks, as the value of the organic boost from getting lots of links from high value websites would be worth more than the cost of the advertising. It would also create a very uneven playing field and discourage the smaller companies from advertising.

The final attribute you can add to a link is 'rel=UGC', which quite simply tells search engines that this is User Generated Content. The link would look like this:

<a href="https://anyoldwebsite.com" rel="ugc">your anchor text</a>

This tells search engines that the link originates from something like a forum or a comment box on a website, and that again, the presence of the link should not confer any value to the receiving website. This helps to deal with the old link building tactic of spam comments underneath old articles, creating valuable backlinks for websites.

So, if you are creating an article that you feel your readers would benefit from seeing other information, such as where you got your research from or other articles on the subject, then don't be afraid to include links. Remember, the Internet relies on people being able to find information, so make it easy for users.

How to create internal links within your website.

I realise that at this point in the book I have mentioned internal links or internal interlinking quite a few times, yet not really covered them in any detail. I've explained that they are important and even told you why, but what is it about them that makes them so valuable?

Internal links are, quite simply, any link between two points within your website. The most obvious type of internal link is the one you will see on your top navigation that usually says 'Home'. Wherever you are in your website, you can click on this and it will always take you back to you home page. This is the most basic internal link.

Home   Biography   Blog   Resources   Contact

Figure 55 - The 'home' button is an internal link.

Internal links are there to help users navigate around your website and to direct them to other parts of your website they might find interesting. You often see this on e-commerce websites when you add something to your basket; it often shows you other items that you might like to buy. Internal links are also there to help the search engines understand and make sense of your website. By linking between pages, you can guide the bots to areas of your website that are related to the page they are on. This is important and links directly back to Rule 1: Google is just a machine. By inserting relevant internal links, you can help the machine better understand not only the content of your website but the context as well.

As an example, if we use the website hierarchy that we first encountered in Figure 30, we can see that if a Google bot arrived on the loft conversions page, it can only read that page and see one other link back up to the main Conversions page. It could, from there, find all the other pages, but what if you'd linked the Loft Conversions and Garage Conversions pages together (Figure 56)? Would that make it easier for the bot to understand the links between these two pages and the main conversions page? Would it help everyday users of your website to understand that you don't just provide one type of conversion? Would that give them greater confidence in your ability to help with their conversion, wherever it was? Internal links provide a breadcrumb trail for both bots and humans to pick up and to help them make connections between different parts of your website.

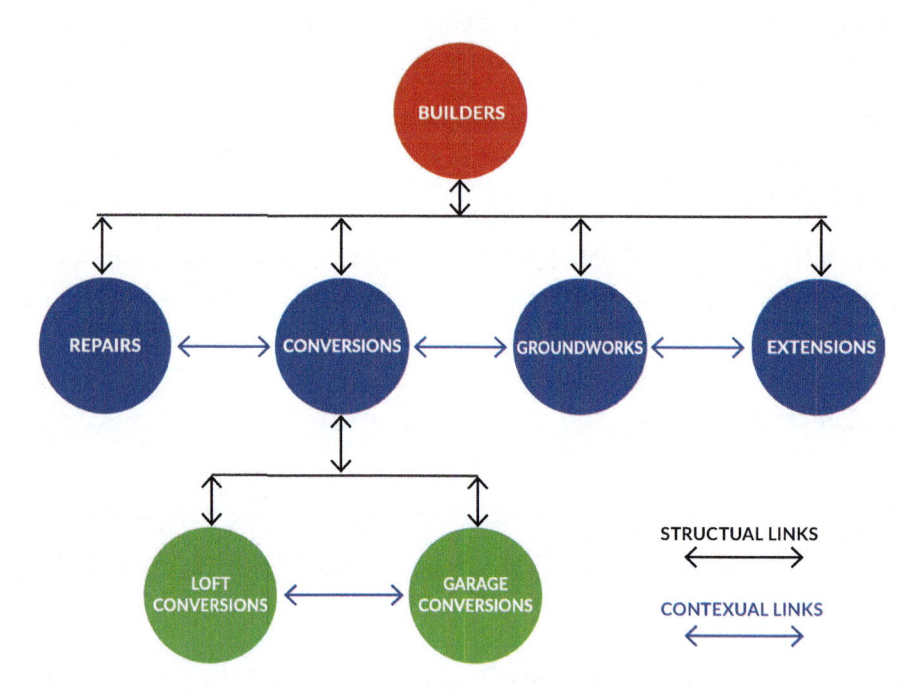

Figure 56 - Structural and Contextual internal links.

In SEO terms, the links that form the base architecture of your website are known as 'structural links', whereas the links between the pages are often referred to as 'contextual links'. Of course, some structural links can also be contextual and vice versa, but the essence here is to never forget that you are trying to make the website as accessible as you can for both users and the search engines.

As these links are all within your website, then you should aim to make the anchor text as relevant as possible to the page people will land on. Remember, every internal link should be relevant, contextual, and above all, add value to your reader. As we covered in the previous section, your internal link should be a standard 'follow' link, unless there is a specific reason for it not to be. It will look like this:

<a href="https://anyoldwebsite.com">your anchor text</a>

As I said earlier, the part that says 'your anchor text' is the words which you have chosen as your anchor, i.e. giraffe conservation in the example given.

The only times I consider making an internal link 'no follow' is where the link refers to a page that is not fundamental to the relevance of the website. Examples of this might include links in the footer to your privacy policy or terms and conditions page, neither of which will help search engines understand the context of your website. They may be basic requirements, but I'd rather not encourage bots to spend time crawling and indexing them.

There are also plenty of tools out there that can help you identify internal linking opportunities. If you run a WordPress website, there are several plug-ins out there that will help you identify pages that could link together and even, in some cases, do it automatically.

Spammy links and how to deal with them

Earlier in this chapter I talked about spammy links and how to check for them using your SEO tools, but the topic of spammy or toxic links deserves a deeper explanation.

If an SEO firm ever offers to do a free website review for you, nine times out of ten they will highlight 'spammy links' as one of the issues they find with your website. If they do, please don't panic. Pretty much every SEO tool that examines backlinks will find some that they will consider to be spammy, toxic or harmful to your website. Frankly, it's highly doubtful that any one backlink can cause direct harm to your website and SEO firms that use this as a 'fear factor' to encourage you to sign up with them should be ignored. Unless they can give you a clear reason why the links are harmful, and more importantly, show you how they are actively harming your website, this is not something to get worried about.

What is a spammy or toxic link and how do you spot them?

There are various definitions of spammy links but the essence of all of them is the same: a spammy link is a link to your website from a poor quality or low value domain. And hereby hangs the problem of spammy links, as not all low value domains are spammy.

Take as an example your own business website. Assuming you bought the domain name as new and created a brand new website on it, from day one your 'authority' is zero. You have no links coming into your website and none of your content is indexed in Google. Moreover, if (as many small business owners do) you have created a simple six-page website with minimal content on it, and the content that is there simply says what you do and why people should ring you, then there is little that will change the value of your website from 'low quality'.

If you now create a blog post and decide to link to my website at jonathanguy.co.uk, it will appear in my Google Search Console dashboard as an inbound link. But all the link tools out there will also register the link and include it in their list of inbound links to my website. Except they, unlike Google, will attribute a value to it and that value is likely to be close to zero. As such, they are also more likely to recommend that I disavow it (more of that later) as they could consider it a spammy or low quality link

The problem harks back to my 3 rules of Google, specifically Rule 1: 'Google is just a machine'. All of these SEO link tools are also just machines, and a machine seeing your link to my website may well tell me it is spammy without ever considering anything further. To fully appreciate the value of a link, you need a human to examine it for context. If I spot the link, follow it back to your website and discover that you have written something complimentary about, for example, this book, then I'm highly unlikely to be unhappy with that. But a machine may tell you otherwise.

Identifying spammy links, therefore, is a combination of understanding the mechanical aspects of a link (such as the value of a website, the type of link it is, etc.) and a human element of adding in context.

Spammy links typically are one of three main types:

Forum or comment spam – this is easy to spot and it a favourite of those looking to promote websites selling sex or drugs typically, though there has been an

The Three Key Areas of SEO

increase in forum and comment spam for both the gambling and digital currency sectors. Here's some examples from the comments capture on one of our WordPress websites, which quarantines this sort of links (and comments) rather then set them live, and some from genuine websites.

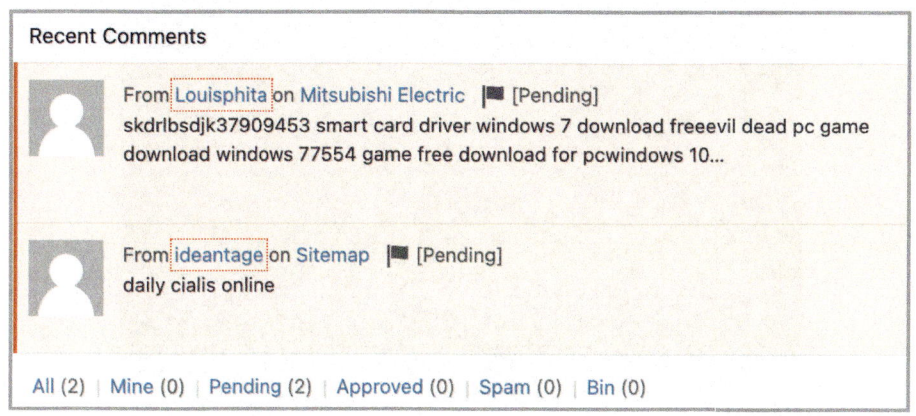

Figure 57 – Spammy forum comments.

Figure 58 – More spammy forum comments – these are clearly automated.

Search Never Sleeps

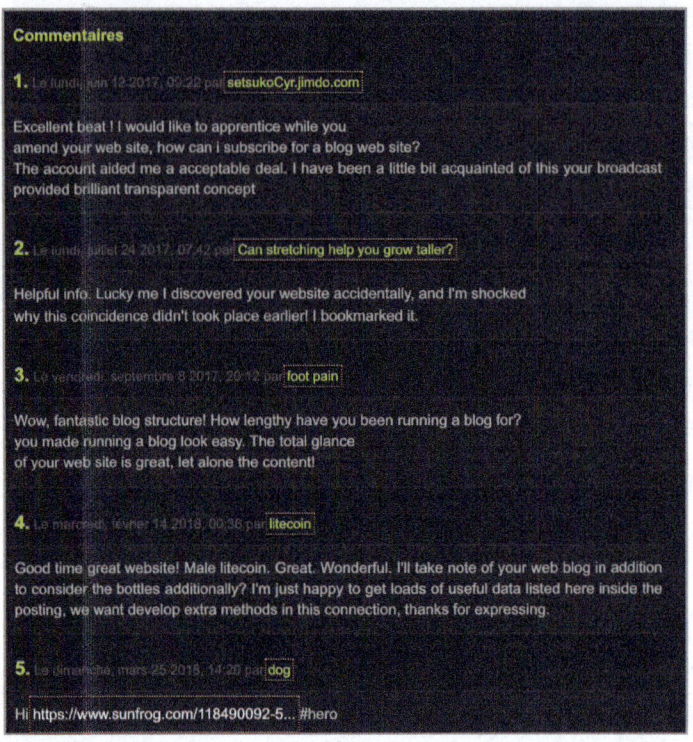

```
Commentaires

1. Le lundi, juin 12 2017, 09:22 par setsukoCyr.jimdo.com

Excellent beat ! I would like to apprentice while you
amend your web site, how can i subscribe for a blog web site?
The account aided me a acceptable deal. I have been a little bit acquainted of this your broadcast
provided brilliant transparent concept

2. Le lundi, juillet 24 2017, 07:42 par Can stretching help you grow taller?

Helpful info. Lucky me I discovered your website accidentally, and I'm shocked
why this coincidence didn't took place earlier! I bookmarked it.

3. Le vendredi, septembre 8 2017, 20:12 par foot pain

Wow, fantastic blog structure! How lengthy have you been running a blog for?
you made running a blog look easy. The total glance
of your web site is great, let alone the content!

4. Le mercredi, février 14 2018, 00:38 par litecoin

Good time great website! Male litecoin. Great. Wonderful. I'll take note of your web blog in addition
to consider the bottles additionally? I'm just happy to get loads of useful data listed here inside the
posting, we want develop extra methods in this connection, thanks for expressing.

5. Le dimanche, mars 25 2018, 14:20 par dog

Hi https://www.sunfrog.com/118490092-5... #hero
```

Figure 59 – Spam forum comments with the link in the username.

Low Quality Guest Posts – very much the flavour of the day currently, there are websites out there who will allow anyone to post any type of article and include links within the post, irrespective of whether they make sense or not. This is just

---

Local self-repair retail stores usually have a lot of regular service parts that need to be replaced. You can even buy small engine accessories such as belts, hoses and fuel pumps. Not all vendors have access to the same section. Talk to a customer and find out if you can find something in the store if you need something special. If you can't normally order, the store can show you where to find the part.

How to get old car details.

Old car parts can be hard to find. If your *pièces automobile* is more than ten years old, your first stop should be a rescue yard to replace spare parts. Check the local phone book for rescue yards in your area. Most of them focus on machine parts such as external or internal. You can save a lot of time by calling before going to the rescue yard.

Do you have a problem with your car's engine and how do you plan to replace it? Do you have a budget and do you want to be smart? Don't know the technical and financial aspects of buying a used car engine? If your answer is yes, then going to a used auto engine is the best option. The money spent on engine maintenance is not only good income. But that prevents the car from becoming unnecessary. Sometimes the used auto part exceeds the original part.

Figure 60 – Example of a low-quality Guest Post.

The Three Key Areas of SEO

one example, though I'm sure you've found many more yourself if you've visited this type of website (Figure 60).

Link Directories – directories used to be a mainstay of link building and there were companies set up to simply create directory websites and allow businesses to post on them, at scale. By clever interlinking they managed to create high authority websites that had absolutely no value at all to end users. Today, these websites still exist, though in smaller numbers than previously and you can still pay to appear on them. As a word of caution, please don't. Despite the fact that they still carry weight and can, under certain circumstances, help push a website up the organic rankings, it's just a matter of time before Google and other search engines find them and devalue them. More importantly, if firms are proven to have been using them in an effort to artificially manipulate the search rankings, then Google can – and will – apply a Manual Action (penalty).

Figure 61 – An example of a link directory.

Figure 62 – Another cheap link directory.

What damage can a toxic link cause your website?

A single spammy link is highly unlikely to cause you any harm at all. To understand this, we need to consider why the term 'spammy link' exists in the first place. It is there to help identify links from websites which might contravene Google's Webmaster Guidelines and nothing more. No other search engine currently talks about penalising websites for poor or spammy backlinks (apart from Yandex, the Russian search engine), with Bing, for example, talking about what they would prefer to see,[31] not what they will penalise.

CASE STUDY

I was approached by a limousine hire company to help them as they had just been penalised by Google for link building, and they no longer appeared in local searches for limousine hire. The previous SEO company had simply been buying thousands of links each month, each with the exact anchor text that the firm wanted. When I checked, they had over a quarter of a million backlinks, most with the same identical anchor text, all of which pointed to the home page. Most of the links were from websites in Russia and the Far East, but the firm was a small business in the northwest of England. If links are 'votes of approval' for websites, how come so many websites halfway around the world were actively approving of a small business in England?

The solution was straightforward: I created a disavow file for all the links that were not from the UK and we created some new pages, specifically aimed at the service and location they targeted. Within a few days, Google automatically reassessed the website and over the next two months, the new pages ranked top 3 for every keyword they wanted.

Takeaway:

Trying to fool Google is never a good thing. Bulk buying backlinks is a sure-fire way to damage your website.

---

31 https://www.bing.com/webmasters/help/link-building-7a3f99b7

So, individually, poor quality links will do nothing harmful to your website. Collectively, however, if there are a number of them and they all, for example, link back using the same keyword rich anchor text, it will send a signal to search engines that this could be manipulative link building. Lots of links from lots of poor quality websites, all with the anchor text 'cheap boiler repairs', is likely to be viewed dimly.

In these rare instances, Google can apply a Google Manual Action, more on which shortly.

How to 'disavow' spammy or low quality backlinks

If you've been investigating your backlinks and reading around the subject, you may well have come across something called 'disavowing' links. This is the process of telling Google about links that you don't want or don't like. The original tool for doing this was created and launched by Google in 2012, but this was in an environment completely different to the one we find today. Entire ecosystems of link farms existed, with no other purpose than to manipulate the Google search results, and as I said earlier, a great many companies were using them. One customer we acquired around this time came to us with expectations that we could do something similar to his last SEO firm. He would give them £500 every eight weeks or so and they would buy enough links to push him back to the top of Google. By the time he arrived with us, there were over a quarter of a million links pointing to his website – all, apparently, votes of confidence in his small local business. Links from all over the world, but especially from USA, Russia and the Far East. Not bad for a company that operated in a ten-mile radius of his house!

In 2012 Google was regularly penalising websites for manipulative link building through Manual Actions, whereby they deliberately either significantly reduced or removed the website from the search results. Many webmasters, faced with this fate, were struggling to do anything meaningful to clean up the mess. Google's advice was that webmasters needed to contact the websites from which they had received these poor links and ask for them to be removed. Of course, this was almost impossible as the links were largely automated and from websites which nobody monitored, so trying to remove them was futile.

On the back of this, Google introduced the 'Disavow Tool'. This allowed webmasters to upload lists of links they wanted nothing to do with, to tell

Google not to count them towards their website's position in the search results.

If you are struggling with a lot of poor quality links pointing to your website and you think that these are causing your poor rankings, then you can upload your own list. But before you do this, you need to be aware that you can cause huge problems if you do it incorrectly and ideally, this is one for an experienced SEO to review first. Google says on its support forum that:[32]

"If you have a manual action against your site for unnatural links to your site, or if you think you're about to get such a manual action (because of paid links or other link schemes that violate our quality guidelines), you should try to remove the links from the other site to your site. If you can't remove those links yourself, or get them removed, then you should disavow the URLs of the questionable pages or domains that link to your website."

It then follows that advice with a warning box that says:

"This is an advanced feature and should only be used with caution. If used incorrectly, this feature can potentially harm your site's performance in Google Search results."

Disavow links to your site

If you have a manual action against your site for unnatural links to your site, or if you think you're about to get such a manual action (because of paid links or other link schemes that violate our quality guidelines), you should try to remove the links from the other site to your site. If you can't remove those links yourself, or get them removed, then you should *disavow* the URLs of the questionable pages or domains that link to your website.

⚠ This is an advanced feature and should only be used with caution. If used incorrectly, this feature can potentially harm your site's performance in Google Search results.

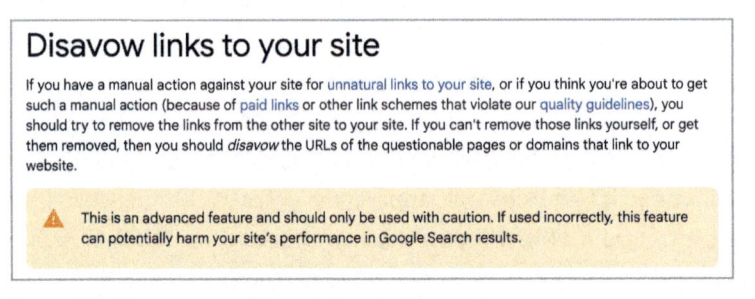

Figure 63 - Disavow Links in Google Search Console.

Today, very few websites receive manual penalties from Google and in part, this is because Google knows manipulative links building when it sees it. For the best part of a decade, Google has been accepting and receiving disavow link files from webmasters across the globe and, as you might expect, with that much data it can very easily work out which are the good and which are the bad websites. In fact, it had enough data by 2016 to be able to incorporate the Penguin update – which specifically looked for manipulative backlinks – into the overall algorithm. Since that point, rather than penalise webmasters for having

---

32 https://support.google.com/webmasters/answer/2648487?hl=en

bad backlinks, it's rewarded them for good backlinks. It's easy to spot the bad ones when millions of webmasters have sent you lists with them in.

Having said this, if you still want to upload a disavow file to Google, perhaps because there are specific websites linking to you with which you want no association, then this is how to go about it.

First, you need to create your disavow file. It needs to be in the form of a text (.txt) file and this is important – no other type of file will work. I've seen lots of people struggling with Excel or .csv files and failing to upload them, so if you know this upfront it will save a lot of time.

Next, it's worth downloading a full list of your links onto an Excel spreadsheet. To do this, I tend to use a range of different tools, such as Majestic, Google Search Console and either SEMRush or Ahrefs to download all the links they can see. Cut and paste all the lists together onto a single spreadsheet in one column and then de-duplicate the list. This means that you have taken the best available data from a range of sources and then filtered it, so you only have each link once.

The next step is to decide whether you want to disavow a single link or all links from that domain. This is important as it can save you a lot of time later. If you have found a lot of links from the same website and you want to disavow all of them because you don't want any links from that website, the simplest way is to disavow at domain level. In fact, this is the method I recommend unless you are very worried about a single link from a website. Most disavow files are made up of websites that you don't want to be associated with, rather than individual links.

As an example, if I find 100 links to my website from www.manipulativelinks. com, then rather than try to list every one, it's easier to disavow the domain (Figure 64):

Don't do this:
www.manipulativelinks.com/bad-link-1
www.manipulativelinks.com/bad-link-2
www.manipulativelinks.com/bad-link-3
www.manipulativelinks.com/really-bad-link

Do this instead:
Domain:manipulativelinks.com
domain:10seotips.com
domain:10url.com
domain:1godir.info
domain:1seodir.info
domain:1webdir.info
domain:27.londovor.com
domain:34it.com
domain:360link.info
domain:4directory.net

Figure 64 – The correct way to disavow a domain.

By using the 'domain:' instruction, Google will understand that you want nothing to do with any link from that website, rather than having to individually list all the ones you can find. Bear in mind that there may well be links that neither you nor the other tools can see coming out of that website, pointing to your website, but Google's crawlers can and will find them. Better to nuke the entire domain than try and individually pick off single links.

You can do all of these steps on an Excel spreadsheet as it makes it easier to manipulate the data, but once you have finished, copy and paste everything onto a text file before uploading it to Google. If you want to include a message to Google (on the off chance that a human might read it) then you can include comments by starting a line with a # mark. If you do this, the machine will ignore the line, but a human won't.

The final step is the actual upload, which you can do by going to https://search.google.com/search-console/disavow-links[33] and from there you can upload your file.

The process of doing this will ensure that Google is only counting those links *not* on your disavow list and in theory, if you have been penalised for unnatural or manipulative paid links, it should help to remove that penalty. Be aware though, that this process can be hit and miss so be prepared for a long wait if you are penalised with a Google manual action.

Black hat link building – what it is and how to avoid it.

Black Hat, White Hat, Grey Hat – it's enough to make anyone confused. These are terms thrown about quite happily by people who are in the know, but mean nothing to most website owners.

We should start by understanding where these terms came from, and why.

For as long as there have been search engines, there have been people trying to manipulate them to ensure their websites ranked higher than anyone else. This practice of manipulation long predates Google and ranges from what were fairly basic tactics back then to more sophisticated methods today. And yes, it still exists today, and far from being underground, a quick search on Google actually shows up firms advertising these services.

---

[33] https://search.google.com/search-console/disavow-links

The Three Key Areas of SEO

Black hat link building is anything that is specifically forbidden by Google's Webmaster Guidelines. To be clear, it needs to be specifically against the guidelines to properly qualify as black hat. Anything that does not conform to the guidelines, but isn't specifically against the guidelines, *could* be considered grey hat. This is, of course, a judgement call as Google doesn't explicitly state what it considers to be good practice for link building. All it says on the subject is:[34]

"The best way to get other sites to create high-quality, relevant links to yours is to create unique, relevant content that can naturally gain popularity in the Internet community. Creating good content pays off: Links are usually editorial votes given by choice, and the more useful content you have, the greater the chances someone else will find that content valuable to their readers and link to it."

Sounds easy, right? But of course, it's not and the fact that you are reading this shows how hard it really is to make any impact on the Google search results.

But why black hat and white hat?

I've tried to find the earliest mention of the term 'black hat' in relation to link building techniques and the first one, as far as I can see, is with a very fresh faced Danny Sullivan[35] on a website called The History of SEO,[36] where he mentions the term black hat. Today, Danny is so well known in SEO and digital marketing that he has his own Wikipedia page. The actual terms, however, relate to the old black and white Western movies, much loved in the 1940s and 50s. As these movies were monochrome, the audience needed a way of telling the difference between the good guys and the baddies. The film makers settled on one simple detail: the good guys always wore white hats and the bad guys, black hats. So naturally, in SEO terms, the 'bad guys' are known as 'Black Hat'.

The term 'grey hat' is a far more recent phenomenon, and this is generally used when people are link building but not deliberately ticking a box on Google's 'forbidden' list. As an example, one of the most popular grey hat techniques today is that of Private Blog Networks, or PBNs for short. A PBN is a group of websites that one person controls, and they are explicitly used to build backlinks to a particular website to help it rank higher in Google's search results. It's a bit like building a spider's web of links with the target website in the middle. The target website looks popular because it has lots of links coming into it from

---
34 https://developers.google.com/search/docs/advanced/guidelines/link-schemes
35 https://dannysullivan.com/
36 https://www.thehistoryofseo.com/seo-interviews/danny-sullivan/interview/

different websites. What's wrong, however, is that one person owns all the websites that link to it. And most likely, they have been paid to do this, which is definitely on Google's not allowed list. Most weeks I get emails from PBN owners asking if I'd like to buy some links for my customers. Each time, I simply ignore them as I know that sooner or later, Google will catch up with them and when they do, every website linked from it will be penalised. I simply won't do that for any of my customers.

Of course, that's not to say that there aren't links to sites I've worked on from PBNs, far from it. In some cases, I may have reached out to a website owner in a niche and asked them if they'd like to link to a great article I've written. They may have agreed and included a link to me because the content is good. There's nothing stopping them changing the following week to a paid business model and charging others for these links.

There are lots of different link building techniques that are considered black or even grey hat and rather than explain them all in detail, I'm just going to list a few and let you do your own research. If you search for any of these you will find not only what they are, but how you can do them for your own website if you choose. (NB - I do NOT recommend this!)

Keyword stuffing
Forum comments
Links in hidden text
Links in punctuation
Link farms
Directory submissions
Hijacked or hacked pages
Hidden redirects
Cloaked pages
Expired domains
Doorway pages
Spun content
Link exchange schemes

The bottom line is that from the dawn of advertising, firms have wanted to be shown above or before their competitors. Whilst the vehicle may have changed, from paper to digital, the motivations haven't. Like the old paper based media, however, the digital media has their own rules. If you want to stay on the right side of the platform that delivers most of your customers, it's worth knowing those rules and sticking to them.

Should you buy links?

I get asked this quite often and the simple answer I always give is an unequivocal NO. Google is quite clear on this, and this is exactly what Google has to say on the subject:

"Any links intended to manipulate PageRank or a site's ranking in Google search results may be considered part of a link scheme and a violation of Google's Webmaster Guidelines. This includes any behavior that manipulates links to your site or outgoing links from your site.

The following are examples of link schemes which can negatively impact a site's ranking in search results:

- Buying or selling links that pass PageRank. This includes:
  - Exchanging money for links, or posts that contain links
  - Exchanging goods or services for links
  - Sending someone a 'free product' in exchange for them writing about it and including a link.
- Excessive link exchanges ('Link to me and I'll link to you') or partner pages exclusively for the sake of cross-linking.
- Large-scale article marketing or guest posting campaigns with keyword-rich anchor text links.
- Using automated programs or services to create links to your site.
- Requiring a link as part of a Terms of Service, contract, or similar arrangement without allowing a third-party content owner the choice of qualifying the outbound link, should they wish."

In short, if you exchange money for links, this is against Google's Webmaster guidelines.

In the real world, however, it happens all the time. There are firms set up to do just this and nothing else and they can make a tremendous amount of money doing it. The problem, of course, is that Google's suggestion that you can simply create 'great content' to help your website rank is untenable. For most small businesses, the chances of anyone actually finding and linking to their website are next to zero. You can create as much great content as you like but without promoting it then no one will know about it. Which is where social media comes in, for example. Shouting about your own content on social media is good as it should drive traffic to your website. Driving traffic means people are more likely to read it and if they like it, share it as well. The more this happens the more likely you are to create genuine backlinks. But it all starts with great content and unless you are actively thinking about this and creating something new or innovative, it becomes just run of the mill to Google.

The way people get around this is to take just one of these points – 'Large-scale article marketing or guest posting campaigns with keyword-rich anchor text links' – and twist it, so the articles or guest posts don't include keyword-rich anchor text. As we saw earlier, a simple link to your home page or the article you have written can often be good enough to help it rank in search. Of course, this still breaches the earlier 'Exchanging money for links, or posts that contain links' but the reality of today's market is that this is the state of much of the link building that goes on.

The much better form of link building is solid, sustainable and generates interest from the national and regional press. There are a few firms out there already doing this by creating truly innovative content and crafting worthwhile data that adds to the sum of human knowledge. To do this, however, takes time and time is, as we know, money. The best firms I know who are doing this charge tens of thousands of pounds, putting them well out of reach for most businesses.

The bottom line on link buying, therefore, is don't. If you are tempted, you've seen the list of black hat techniques earlier in this chapter – for goodness' sake, avoid all of these like the plague!

Google penalties – what is a manual action and what can I do about it?

I should start this by covering the biggest fear people have of penalties like this, namely 'How likely am I to be hit with a Google manual action?' The short answer is that you are more likely to be hit by lightning. Knowing this, however, won't prevent some people from still being afraid of it.

The best way to avoid a Google manual action is to avoid doing anything against

The Three Key Areas of SEO

the guidelines in the first place. Given that they are pretty much common sense, if you have strayed that far off the rails then it's probably by choice, not chance. If that's the case then you should be expecting this as a consequence, much as a burglar accepts a prison sentence as an occupational hazard. In the last ten years, I have seen just three examples of manual actions from Google, and these were all in 2012 and 2013. In each case, customers came to us because they were experiencing problems ranking, and in each case, it was because Google had decided that they had been using manipulative link building techniques.

The first you will know of a manual action to your website will be when you get an email from Google telling you. They typically give you one or two examples of links they feel are manipulative, but not a definitive list. You may also notice that your website has disappeared from the search results, traffic has decreased dramatically and that customers start to tell you that they can't find you on Google. This is the point at which you need to create the disavow file we covered earlier. You will also get a notification in your Search Console. In the menu on the left-hand side, you will see the words 'Security & Manual Actions' (Figure 65) and when you click on Manual Actions, this is what you want to see (Figure 66):

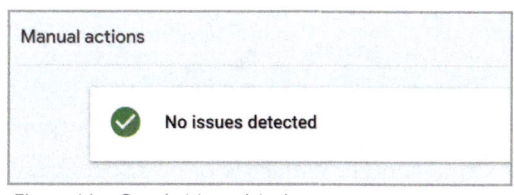

Figure 66 – Google Manual Actions.

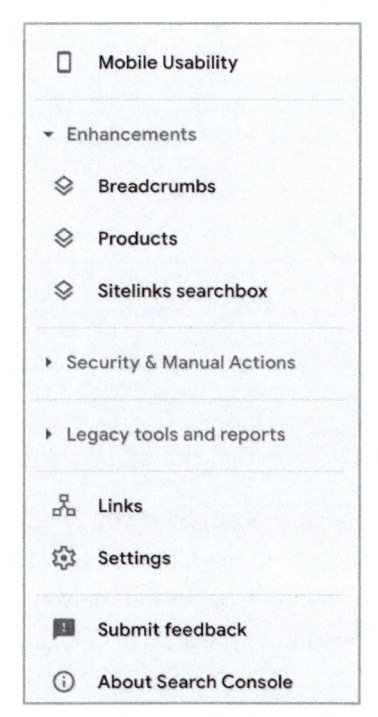

Figure 65 – Security & Manual Actions in Google Search Console.

If you have received a penalty, then you simply follow the instructions that Google gives and make sure your website is absolutely free from anything that they might consider manipulative.

What might I have done to get a manual action?

The good news is that Google covers this in some detail on their page entitled 'Manual Actions Report'.[37] The page goes into some detail about what you might have done to incur their wrath. Specifically, they say:

"Google issues a manual action against a site when a human reviewer at Google has determined that pages on the site are not compliant with Google's webmaster quality guidelines."

It's important to note that they state it is because a 'human' reviewer has flagged it up, as this means that it's not a random computer glitch causing your site to be reported. In this case, it really does mean that you've done something wrong and it's obvious to a human looking at it that you have transgressed. But remember, the chances of you getting one of these is incredibly small and to do so you will have had to trip the alarm on one of a dozen different areas. These are:

- Site abused with third-party spam
- User-generated spam
- Spammy free host
- Structured data issue
- Unnatural links to your site
- Unnatural links from your site
- Thin content with little or no added value
- Cloaking and/or sneaky redirects
- Pure spam
- Cloaked images
- Hidden text and/or keyword stuffing
- AMP content mismatch
- Sneaky mobile redirects
- News and Discover policy violations

You can read more about each of these on the Google webpage[38] if you need more detail, but they are pretty self-explanatory. In fact, apart from the last three – which relate to more recent developments in both Google and the way we search for information – these have all been around since the start of Google (and in some cases, the Internet!).

---
37 https://support.google.com/webmasters/answer/9044175?hl=en#manual-action-list
38 https://support.google.com/webmasters/answer/9044175?hl=en#manual-action-list

In summary, if you are not actively trying to cheat the system, you shouldn't ever see a Google penalty. Relax, stay calm and carry on making your website the best it can be for users.

Final thoughts

I did say right at the start that this would be a big section and I said I wouldn't apologise. But sorry anyway; it's a huge chunk of information. What I hope, however, is that you found the information useful, informative and that you can use it practically to help you build links back to the great content you are already creating.

Links and link building are amongst the hardest part of SEO, and it takes years to get your head around what you should or shouldn't be doing as well as how to go about it efficiently. This is why so many SEO firms exist, to take that strain away from you. As a business owner, your focus should be on running your business, not on being a technical wizard on the Internet. So, much like you employ an accountant to take care of the numbers, consider a professional SEO to take care of the technical side of the website.

Remember, you don't need to know how to do every job to run your business or your website, you just need to understand what you are paying people to do, and why.

Takeaways:

Links are an essential and inescapable part of the Google algorithm.

Concentrate on creating great resources for people; links will follow.

Don't try to cheat Google; you will lose.

Other SEO Fundamentals

There are certain parts of technical SEO which don't sit easily with the three key areas we've just covered. Nevertheless, they are essential parts of SEO and you will need an understanding of these to make Google love your website. I've tried to group these together here and hopefully give you a better insight into some of the lesser understood aspects of the job.

Let's start with a question I'm regularly asked when I talk about SEO, and that is which website platform is the best. There are dozens of different website frameworks and on top of these, there are even more website platforms. A framework is just an organisation of the software that is used for developing web applications and websites. To better explain this, imagine a framework as the skeleton onto which everything else is built.

There are lots of different types of frameworks and here are some of the most frequently used:

- Ruby on Rails
- Laravel
- Spring
- Angular
- Django
- ASP.net
- React
- Vue
- Ember
- Backbone

Most of these will mean nothing to you but they underpin a lot of what is currently on the web. Once you have a framework, your website platform can be built onto this; in essence, putting flesh on the bones. The final part is the 'skin', which would be your website theme or visual appearance and that goes on top of all the rest. Now you understand that, we can try to answer the question of which website platform is best...

Which website platform is best for ranking?

This is another of the 'impossible to answer' SEO questions that I get asked on a regular basis. Nobody likes hearing the 'it depends' answer, but the truth is, it depends. As a preference, I tend to use WordPress simply because it's simple to understand, easy to use and if, like me, you want to get into the code, you can do. For the majority of customers I've dealt with in the past who are also WordPress users, they like the fact that they can do what they want simply and without fuss, whether they have any technical understanding or not.

Currently, WordPress powers around a quarter of the world's websites, so you could say it's popular. But with popularity comes risks as well. As it is so well used, hackers and other bad agents will focus on code that breaks it open so they can hijack websites for their own gains. Much like makers of malware focus on Microsoft as it powers so much of the world's computing, it makes sense to them to focus on where they can do the most harm.

Is this a reason to not use WordPress? No, I don't think so. There are lots of things you can do to protect your website, which I'll cover later, but these apply equally no matter which platform you are using.

Bigger websites with more traffic generally need bigger, more scalable solutions. At the top end, there are hugely expensive website platforms and frameworks that cater to exactly that market. At the lower end, there are 'instant' platforms that allow you to sign up and go live within hours, such as Wix, Weebly, GoDaddy and so on. Whilst these platforms are generally well put together and have definitely improved over time, like all platforms, they have drawbacks. I've worked on dozens of different website platforms over the years, and whilst they all have their own quirks, none of them are perfect. But no matter which platform you use, Google and the other search engines can still crawl and make sense of them, which sort of leads us onto the question of why we need websites at all, but we'll come to that later on in this book.

Accepting for now that you still need a website and that Google is the main search engine on which you want to rank, will your choice of platform make a big difference to where you rank?

The answer is, as I write this, not really.

Sure, we've had some difficulty in the past with certain platforms because of their inflexibility when it comes to making the technical changes we need, but we've still managed to get the sites to rank. The problem comes (and will come again) when Google changes the rules by which it ranks sites. At the start of 2021, Google told Webmasters that it was introducing new rules in May 2021 which placed a higher priority on how quickly a site loaded. Specifically, it told us to work on three areas:

- LCP (Largest Contentful Paint): This tells how long it takes for the largest content element you see on the screen to load.
- FID (First Input Delay): The FID looks at how long it takes for a browser to respond to an interaction first triggered by the user. (like clicking a button, for instance)
- CLS (Cumulative Layout Shift): This is a new metric and measures the percentage of the screen affected by movement — e.g. does stuff jump around on screen?

All very techie, I'm sure you will agree, and of little interest to anyone who isn't into these sorts of things. But Google now says they are important, to the point where it will actively promote sites that have better scores in these things than those that don't. By how much, no one knows. All we know is that by getting these things right you will gain a competitive advantage.

The trouble with technical SEO is that most website owners are not interested in it and can't see how all that tinkering will make a difference. If it were a Formula 1 car and all that tinkering gave them an extra 5mph on the top speed, they'd realise at the end of the lap the difference that makes. Sadly, websites aren't like that. Each technical tweak might make only a small percentage difference to a website and cumulatively it might make 5% to 10% difference over time. But the point I always make is that the difference, no matter how small, is always a positive difference – and surely as a website owner you would want that?

Whichever platform you are on and using, the ability to affect the technical details is becoming more important. With the entry level platforms mentioned, you can't do much about Cumulative Layout Shift as this will be determined by their platform and their code. Much like you can't change how quickly your website will be shown to users, as this can be affected by the speed of the server on which it is hosted. You have to accept what you are given. Much like anyone using an iPhone must accept Apple's operating system, so you need to accept the operating system of whichever platform you use.

If you know nothing about SEO and want to remain that way, then the entry level sites might be right for you as it pushes the responsibility onto them to ensure Google can crawl and rank sites in its ecosystem. If on the other hand, you want to control what happens when Google crawls and what it reads and sees, you may need a more independent solution.

> **Takeaway:**
> Takeaway: Choose the right platform based on the size, age, and scope of your business.

Sitemaps

One of the easiest things a website owner can do to help a search engine understand their website is to add on a sitemap.

A sitemap is as simple as it sounds: a map for the search engine bots to understand what to crawl. You can tell them what you want them to crawl, how frequently you want it crawled and how important that page is to your website. You can also tell them what not to crawl and what isn't important.

Google describes sitemaps as:[39]

"A sitemap is a file where you provide information about the pages, videos, and other files on your site, and the relationships between them. Search engines like Google read this file to more intelligently crawl your site. A sitemap tells Google which pages and files you think are important in your site, and also provides valuable information about these files: for example, for pages, when the page was last updated, how often the page is changed, and any alternate language versions of a page."

Most sitemaps are appended onto the end of the domain so they read:

https://www.anyoldwebsite.com/sitemap.xml

---

[39] https://developers.google.com/search/docs/advanced/sitemaps/overview

As they are nearly always here (or a couple of other easy-to-find places, such as /sitemap_index.xml), Google and the other search engine bots know where to look.

The important bit here is hidden in the Google description, the bit where it says, "to more intelligently crawl your site." If we remember Rule 1, we know that the machine will follow every url it can find and try to make sense of it. The sitemap is a way of helping the machine make sense by both categorising and, in some cases, describing what it will find when it gets there. The subtext in that is that if a bot has a limited crawl budget and it can only spend a certain amount of time on each website each day, then surely it makes sense to point it in the direction it can do the most good for you and your website? Sitemaps are really important if you are a new website, as Google has no idea you exist. If you choose not to add on Google Analytics (and some people won't), then Google doesn't know you are there until it discovers you. It can only discover you if it finds a link to your website 'in the wild' so to speak, e.g. on a social media platform or a forum or blog. Remember, the bots follow every link, wherever they go, and if it finds your site for the first time from a third-party website, it won't know what you do or why.

XML Sitemap

Generated by YoastSEO, this is an XML Sitemap, meant for consumption by search engines.

You can find more information about XML sitemaps on sitemaps.org.

This XML Sitemap Index file contains 6 sitemaps.

Sitemap	Last Modified
https://www.aqueous-digital.co.uk/post-sitemap.xml	2021-02-19 12:51 +00:00
https://www.aqueous-digital.co.uk/page-sitemap.xml	2021-01-29 13:24 +00:00
https://www.aqueous-digital.co.uk/services-sitemap.xml	2020-01-13 11:28 +00:00
https://www.aqueous-digital.co.uk/packages-sitemap.xml	2017-09-03 15:43 +00:00
https://www.aqueous-digital.co.uk/case_study-sitemap.xml	2021-02-02 15:08 +00:00
https://www.aqueous-digital.co.uk/author-sitemap.xml	2020-09-21 09:10 +00:00

Figure 67 - A typical website sitemap.

So, unless you've told Google you exist, it won't know to crawl, index and rank your website until it finds you. A sitemap is a simple way of ensuring that when it does find you, it knows what you are about.

Now, I could leave it there on-site maps, but they contain one of my pet peeves so I'm going to get this off my chest. Above is a screenshot of the old Aqueous

The Three Key Areas of SEO

Digital sitemap, before we refreshed our website (Figure 67). Like so many others, it's powered by Yoast, which is an SEO plug-in. I'll come back to SEO plug-ins later in the chapter as they are in some cases guilty of encouraging poorly optimised websites. As you can see, the sitemap is neatly arranged so a bot reaching here can see that we want it to crawl posts, pages, services, packages, case studies and an author sitemap, which shows what I have written for the website – which in this case is pretty much all of it. Over ten years, I've written more than a book's worth of material, and by doing so, Google understands that I write about SEO quite a lot.

You will notice that it tells the bots that the last time the packages page was modified was 2017 so logically they are not going to spend any time looking there if they have a limited amount of time to spend on my site. No, they will probably focus on the posts as clearly this is something which has been active recently and there will be new stuff there for it to index. Some sitemaps, however, allow you to configure various elements, including the frequency at which you are changing the page and the priority you want a bot to place on that particular url. If you are leaving an instruction that you want search engines to visit weekly and that the page is a 60% priority on your website, but that you've changed nothing on the site since 2013, that's going to be a confusing signal for any machine. As a case in point, take a look at the data in Figure 68 from a website I was asked to optimise for a customer (I've had to redact the url details to anonymise it).

Priority	Change frequency	Last modified (GMT)
100%	Daily	2014-07-01 10:21
20%	Monthly	2014-07-01 10:21
20%	Monthly	2014-06-27 08:23
20%	Monthly	2014-04-07 09:36
20%	Monthly	2014-03-18 15:54
20%	Monthly	2013-11-27 14:01
60%	Weekly	2013-11-18 15:19
60%	Weekly	2013-11-11 14:47
60%	Weekly	2013-11-11 14:40
60%	Weekly	2013-10-23 09:57
60%	Weekly	2013-10-09 12:45
60%	Weekly	2013-09-24 15:12
20%	Monthly	2013-09-13 14:23

Figure 68 - A badly configured sitemap.

Despite the lack of url's in the image, you can clearly see that the top line (which is the home page) has 100% priority, which is correct for pretty much every website. The pages marked 60%, however, are asking Google to crawl them on a weekly basis, despite not being updated for many years. Imagine, as a machine, trying to follow a rule that says you need you to come back to a website daily, visit a home page which is 100% priority but then find the owner has not changed the site since 2014. Even the weekly frequency change pages (60%) haven't moved since 2013. It's bound to cause confusion and frankly, after some time, the bots will learn to visit your website less frequently as nothing is changing. You can, however, adjust these settings within whichever program you have used to create your sitemap, so there's no excuse for leaving these in their default 'factory' setting. If you want to play nicely with the bots, make sure you configure your sitemap correctly and don't give the search engine an instruction which just wastes its time. Remember Rule 1: Google is just a machine.

> **Takeaway:**
> Always include a sitemap on your website and make sure it is telling the search engines which parts of your website are the most important.

Schema Markup

Schema is fascinating. No, really, it is. You can get a full list of what you can do with schema, along with what it is at https://schema.org/ and as it's a simple website. I'd encourage you to take a look. But you already know, just by the way I've started this, that it's a technical bit and for many people that's a complete turn off. The good news is that there are simple tools to help you work with schema, but it's worth starting by understanding what it is and why it's important.

Schema is described on the schema.org website as:

"a collaborative, community activity with a mission to create, maintain, and promote schemas for structured data on the Internet, on webpages, in email messages, and beyond."

For those who prefer plain English, it's about a group of people who want to bring some order to the chaos of data on the Internet.

The key bit here is 'structured data'. It's a way of creating a structure to data on websites so that the bots can all read and understand them. And all over the Internet you will find helpful guides on how to add structured data to your website. Remember, the world is awash with data, the trick is turning it into usable information and from there, into intelligence.

schema.org says that schema is:

"Founded by Google, Microsoft, Yahoo and Yandex, Schema.org vocabularies are developed by an open community process."

What does this mean in practice? Well, what it means is that they have collectively agreed to standardise a way of structuring data, so that irrespective of whichever bot, from whichever search engine is crawling a website, they can understand what they are looking at.

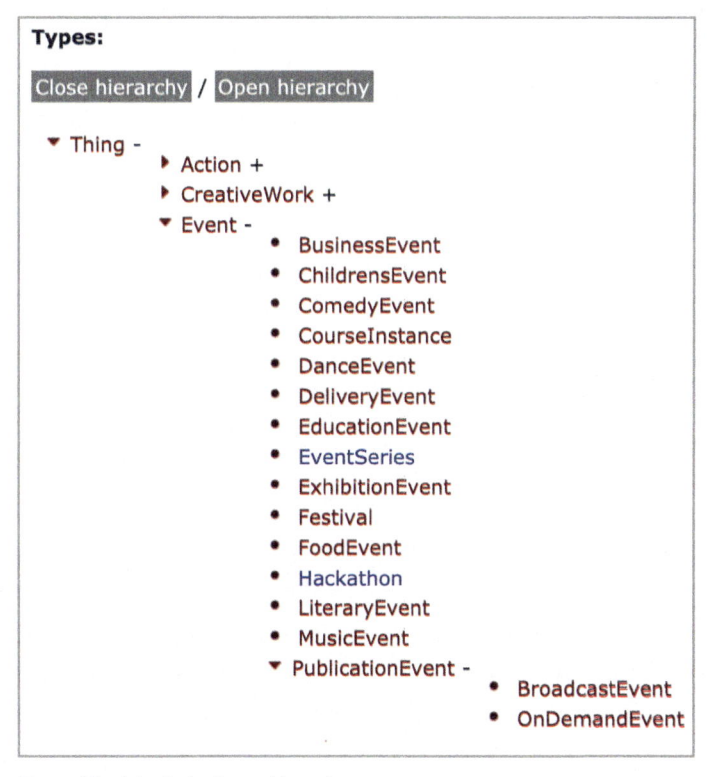

```
Types:

Close hierarchy / Open hierarchy

▼ Thing -
    ▶ Action +
    ▶ CreativeWork +
    ▼ Event -
        • BusinessEvent
        • ChildrensEvent
        • ComedyEvent
        • CourseInstance
        • DanceEvent
        • DeliveryEvent
        • EducationEvent
        • EventSeries
        • ExhibitionEvent
        • Festival
        • FoodEvent
        • Hackathon
        • LiteraryEvent
        • MusicEvent
        ▼ PublicationEvent -
            • BroadcastEvent
            • OnDemandEvent
```

Figure 69 - A typical schema hierarchy.

And there are hundreds of different schemas. No matter what your business or reason for being online, you are likely to find a schema that will fit your website.

Take, for example, if you are going to live broadcast an event; there's a schema

The Three Key Areas of SEO

Typically, there are three categories of hack, and they are:

Access control – How you log into your website or server.

Software vulnerabilities – Exploiting vulnerabilities and bugs in software.

Third-party integrations – Using a piece of software on which your website depends, to control what appears on your website.

What can you do to protect your website?

This part is relatively straightforward and as a website owner, much of this you can do without anyone's help. Here's my simple checklist to avoid a world of pain in the future.

What you can do to protect your website

- Make sure your website has an SSL installed. A simple Secure Sockets Layer certificate is the foundation of any website and whoever is building or hosting your website can help with this.

- Install anti-malware software, especially if you are using WordPress.

- Make sure there is a working firewall on your website.

- Change your log in name from 'Admin' to something less obvious.

- Use two-factor or multi-factor authentication to log in.

- Make your password more difficult. If you are using Pa55w0rd, it's simply not good enough.

- Always update the software on your website. Check weekly if you can.

- Don't click on links or attachments in emails if you don't recognise where they are from.

- Always ensure that your website is backed up securely and away from your website. As a preference, I recommend a weekly full back up and daily incremental, especially if you are regularly adding things to your website.

for that. In the hierarchy under Event>PublicationEvent>BroadcastEvent you will find all the detail you need on what you can 'mark up' to make it easier for bots to figure out what your website or page is all about.

BroadcastEvent
A Schema.org Type
Thing > Event > PublicationEvent > BroadcastEvent   [more...]
An over the air or online broadcast event.

Property	Expected Type	Description
Properties from BroadcastEvent		
broadcastOfEvent	Event	The event being broadcast such as a sporting event or awards ceremony.
isLiveBroadcast	Boolean	True is the broadcast is of a live event.
subtitleLanguage	Language or Text	Languages in which subtitles/captions are available, in IETF BCP 47 standard format.
videoFormat	Text	The type of screening or video broadcast used (e.g. IMAX, 3D, SD, HD, etc.).
Properties from PublicationEvent		
publishedBy	Organization or Person	An agent associated with the publication event.
publishedOn	BroadcastService	A broadcast service associated with the publication event.
Properties from Event		
about	Thing	The subject matter of the content. Inverse property: subjectOf
actor	Person	An actor, e.g. in tv, radio, movie, video games etc., or in an event. Actors can be associated with individual items or with a series, episode, clip. Supersedes actors.
aggregateRating	AggregateRating	The overall rating, based on a collection of reviews or ratings, of the item.
attendee	Organization or Person	A person or organization attending the event. Supersedes attendees.
audience	Audience	An intended audience, i.e. a group for whom something was created. Supersedes serviceAudience.
composer	Organization or Person	The person or organization who wrote a composition, or who is the composer of a work performed at some event.
contributor	Organization or Person	A secondary contributor to the CreativeWork or Event.

Figure 70 - Example of schema.

And as you can see, whatever you want to describe, there's probably a way of doing it using schema.

Whilst this may seem quite techie to those not overly familiar with code (and I count myself amongst them), in practice, this is quite simple to add to your website. If you are using WordPress, it's even easier as there are various plug-ins that can help by doing it all for you. If not, then just ask your SEO firm and they will be able to help.

If you want to press on and give this a go yourself, then I recommend that you start with Google's tool for doing this. It has created a Structured Data Markup Helper[40] which allows you to simply drop in any url from your website, then follow the on-page instructions. It will take you, step by step, through how to add the structured data to your website. It's worth giving this a go, if for no other reason than to familiarise yourself with the process and to understand what it does.

---
40   https://www.google.com/webmasters/markup-helper/u/0/

From an SEO point of view, using structured data is one of the quickest and easiest ways to set your website apart from the competition and for ranking higher, with more information showing than your competitors.

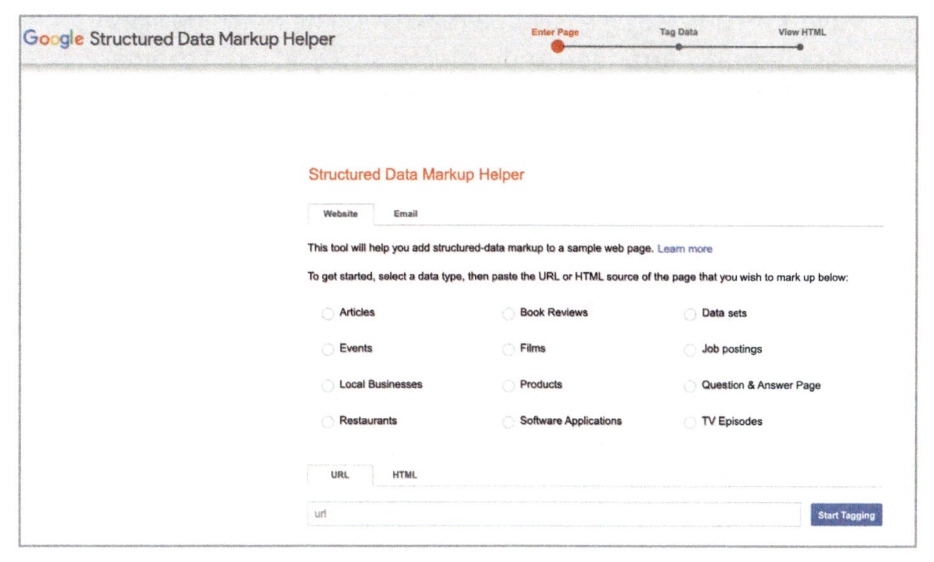

Figure 71 - Google's Structured Data Markup Helper.

If you're still a little overawed at the code bit, Google has gone one step further and included a handy little tool called the Data Highlighter[41] that will allow you to tag the data fields on your website just with your mouse. So, no technical skill needed at all with this one!

Google takes you into their Search Console[42] and as long as your website is accessible (you have Google Analytics on your website), it allows you to simply click through, highlight the text that you want to mark up, and Google will do the rest. It's that easy. No code understanding needed, just the ability to read English and to use your mouse. What could be simpler?

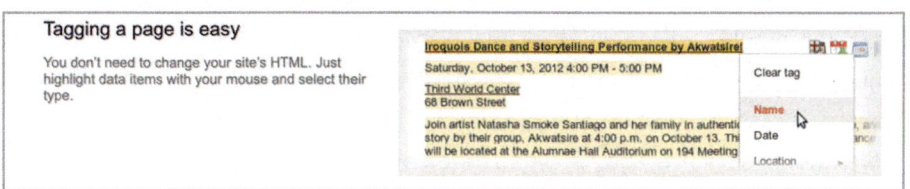

Figure 72 - Schema tagging of a page.

---

41 https://support.google.com/webmasters/answer/3069489?hl=en
42 https://www.google.com/webmasters/tools/data-highlighter

> **Takeaway:**
> Rule 1 means Google is just a machine. The machine likes things neatly arranged and ordered so if you use schema it will help the machine make sense of your website.

Mobile first indexing

At the start of 2018, Google announced that they were going to begin using mobile first indexing of search results, which meant that it would rank websites based on how well they were served to users on mobiles, rather than desktop computers. By July of that year, I'd already written a simple explainer for our website.[43] The announcement was simply building on what had gone before and continued a process Google began publicly in 2016, though it had been planned for some time before that. To fully appreciate the significance of this announcement you need to understand where Google came from with indexing and to do that, we need to go back to 1996 and the start of Google.

Back in 1996, Sergei Brin and Larry Page were both at Stanford University in California. Page was encouraged by his tutor at the time to explore an idea for his dissertation around the existing link structure of the World Wide Web. The idea became a project called 'Backrub' which looked at the interlinking that existed on pages across the Internet. That, plus the cues that existing search engines took from the number of times a word was mentioned on a webpage, eventually became Google, which was launched in 1998.

From the very start, the concept was simple: crawl as many pages as possible and from the data retrieved, create an index to answer search queries. And assume that all those queries would be made on a computer. Because at the start, the number of mobile devices which could access the Internet was tiny. Nokia had released a phone in 1996 which could get online but if, like me, you tried to use the Internet on a phone anytime in the 1990s then you'll know it was a dreadful experience. So, Google's index of webpages and search results was based completely around a desktop experience, and when you look at the graph[44] in Figure 73 you can see why.

---
43 https://www.aqueous-digital.co.uk/a-simple-guide-to-the-google-mobile-index/
44 https://gs.statcounter.com/platform-market-share/desktop-mobile-tablet/worldwide/#monthly-200901-202101

The Three Key Areas of SEO

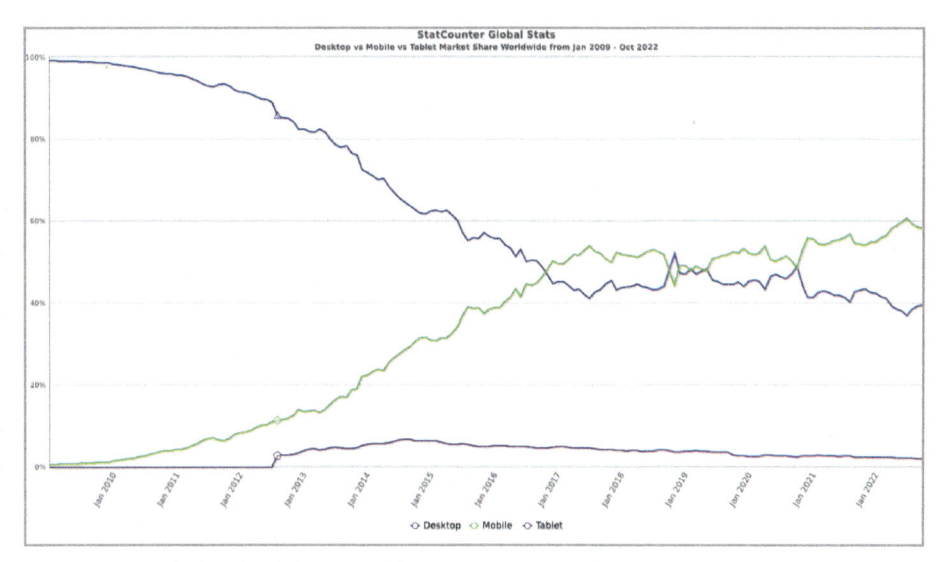

Figure 73 - Search share by desktop v mobile over time – Copyright Statcounter.

Even as far back as 2010, the share of search on a mobile device was so small that there was no reason to do anything different, but by 2013 it was evident that this was changing. More and more people were using mobile devices to access the Internet and the direction of travel was only ever going to be one way.

With the continuing growth of mobile devices and the need for Google to be able to serve search results to people on their phones, it soon became clear that the bloated code found on many webpages was simply not good enough to allow them to give a great user experience. In short, it took too long to load most websites on a mobile phone.

Google therefore did the only thing it could do in the circumstances; it started to tell webmasters that speed was important. The speed at which their website loaded on a mobile device would make a difference, not only to the way in which consumers interacted with their websites, but also, it was suggested, to the position in which your website would rank. And that was all it took for SEOs to become obsessed with site speed.

To this point, Google had simply been running a single index behind the scenes, with all the metrics based on what it was gathering from its crawl of pages designed to be served to desktop or laptop computers. But in 2016, it told us that from now on it would run two indices in parallel – one for desktop and one for mobile – but that it would continue to serve the desktop version first. This was to allow website owners time to change or update their websites to make them more user friendly on mobile devices. From there it was simply a matter of time before it moved to a mobile first index, which it did in 2018.

So, after all that preamble, what's the big issue with mobile first indexing?

Well, you can see from the graph in Figure 73 that by 2018, mobile had overtaken desktop devices as the way to access the Internet. Quite simply, more people were using their phones to get online. And that changed everything. If you were an online retailer, now you had to focus on making sure your website worked well on a mobile. In certain markets, like teen fashion, their adoption of mobile as a way of life meant that as much as 80% of all traffic to a website was from mobiles. If their customers couldn't find what they wanted quickly and buy it with a couple of clicks, they were going elsewhere. More and more, people were using mobile devices for everyday purchases and big retailers such as Amazon were making it easy for anyone to buy on their phone.

From Google's point of view, their research pointed to an impatience amongst mobile users for any webpage which didn't load quickly. Right from the start in 1998, Google had always tried to make its own home page the simplest thing on the Internet, with no adverts, no fancy buttons, just a name and a search box, precisely because it loaded quickly. Despite advances in 3G and then 4G, speed was very much an issue for mobile users.

In 2021, Google went beyond the mobile first indexing to now encouraging webmasters to look in detail at specifics, such as Largest Contentful Paint or First Input Delay, and everyone is scrambling to understand and improve these metrics. But if we step back for a moment and return to the topic of mobile first indexing, we need to answer why this is so important.

The answer, unsurprisingly, lies not in any technical issue but with us. That's right, you and me. Because we're impatient. There's not a person reading this who hasn't, at some time, abandoned a slow loading webpage, either on a desktop or a mobile. Behavioural scientists would no doubt have a theory about this, but the short version is that we need our computing to keep up with our thinking. Today, we think, react and execute those thoughts in a matter of moments, and we expect our technology to be able to do that. Google knows this and is determined to allow us to fulfil this wish by driving better speed standards across the Internet.

In short, there's no substitute for providing the right technical approach to your website and making sure that the experience desktop users and mobile users get is equivalent. And because we are all now accessing the Internet via our mobiles, then Google wants to show you websites that can help you achieve your search in the shortest possible time. Which means that the machine (Rule 1) is deciding what is fast and what is not. But we also need to remember Rule 2: when people arrive on your website, they need to find the right answer, and that is another story entirely.

> **Takeaway:**
> Website speed is essential for search engines, but most importantly, for your customers. Take the time to make sure your website is as fast as possible.

Website Security

The security of a website is rarely mentioned at any point during the planning or building stages of a website. If you have employed a competent developer, they will probably have told you that there needs to be some kind of security before the website goes live, and hopefully they will have implemented that security. The key is making sure that it's discussed before you find that you need it and, in that respect, it can sometimes be the elephant in the room for website owners. Everybody instinctively knows that if they own a website, it should be made secure, but more often than not, it is simply overlooked or ignored until it is too late.

You've probably heard of a website that got hacked and, if you've been unlucky, it may have happened to you at some time. What most people don't understand is why their website might be a target for hackers, particularly if you run a small business in a small town or village. Why on earth would your website be of interest to anyone with malicious intent? It's not as if they can do much with it, surely?

Here's comes another one of the urban myths in SEO: search Google for 'how many websites are hacked every day' and you will find one consistent answer – 30,000 websites a day. Dig a little deeper and you will see that the figure being quoted comes from a Forbes article from 2013 where the author states that this comes from his employer, Sophos Labs. Now, I'm not suggesting that this figure is made up, but it doesn't appear to have been substantiated anywhere in print, nor updated in a decade. Information on how many websites are hacked every day, week or year is thin on the ground and I suspect, being kept under wraps by the firms that sell solutions to this problem.

What is undeniable is that every day, websites across the globe are targeted by malicious actors and yours could well be next. For evidence of this you only need to look at Google's data,[45] which it thankfully makes freely available to everyone. When it spots that a website has been hacked or is potentially harmful to users, it issues a 'Safe Browsing' warning to users. You can see from the graph in Figure 74 that the volumes have dropped dramatically since mid-2019, but every day they issue thousands of these warnings as they find unsafe websites.

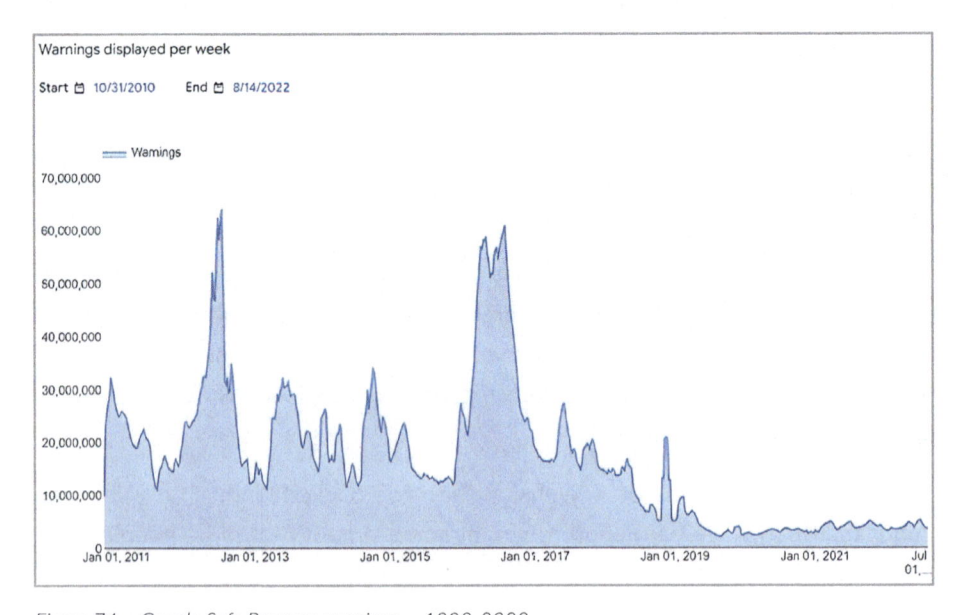

Figure 74 – Google Safe Browser warnings – 1998-2022.

---

45 https://transparencyreport.google.com/safe-browsing/overview

We can see that websites are under attack every day, but to understand why you need website security, you need to first understand why anyone would want to break into your website in the first place.

Why do websites get hacked?

Hackers across the globe want your website for a variety of reasons. First, and possibly the most common reason at the moment, is for commercial gain. Cybercriminals and gangs of hackers want your website so they can try and fool people with phishing attacks. Once they control your website, they will build hidden pages into the back of it, so you or any other casual user can't see them. They then send millions of emails telling people that, for example, their bank password has been compromised in a data leak and that they need to click on the link to change their password. When people click on this link, it takes them to a landing page they have created on your website, that has been designed to look identical to the real bank landing page. Once people enter their account number and all their password details, the criminals then log directly into the person's bank and empty their account as quickly as they can. It's a horrible and deeply personal crime.

> **Phishing**
> Phishing is where someone attempts to gain access to a person's personal information by sending an email that purports to be from a legitimate source, such as the bank.

After commercial gain, the next most popular reason is ransomware. This type of attack is normally more targeted as they are looking for a website where the owner or business will pay to recover control. The method of delivery is similar in that you are invited to click on an attachment in an email, and once you do their code literally takes over your computer and, if you are networked, anything else in the network it can reach. They then demand a ransom, usually in a cryptocurrency, to remove their software.

They can also use your website to install hidden links to another website, usually something illegal or ethically or morally questionable. These links can also act to help improve the organic positions of these illegal websites as Google, as we know, reads these as backlinks from a reputable website.

Another reason is to use your website for some other purpose, such as launching a denial of service attack on a server, distributing files, or simply stealing the data that you have, particularly if you are an online shop and your website contains customer data.

Finally, there are people across the globe who think it's funny to hack into someone else's website and they simply do it because they can. I've seen a website hacked by militants fighting a war against their government and taking over websites to broadcast their propaganda. I've also seen kids leaving messages on websites saying, 'You've been hacked by [insert name here]' and then bragging about their success on online forums.

This is not a comprehensive list, more an indication of the main types of reasons why websites get hacked. On top of this, there are ethical hackers (think back to the white hat and black hat explanation earlier in the book) who attempt to hack websites for benevolent reasons. They can be security testers, researchers or experts paid to try and hack a website to make sure that the security is good enough to repel those who would do it harm.

How do websites get hacked?

Without going into too much detail here, there are a range of methodologies that are used to take over and control websites. As I explained earlier, a large number of websites across the world are now built on WordPress and hackers spend hours looking for vulnerabilities in both the source code of WordPress (which is relatively easy to look at as it's open source) and the plug-ins that are added to extend the functionality. They love finding an old plug-in that is no longer supported by a developer but is still installed in millions of websites. One simple flaw in this code and they can easily take over millions of websites. The scale makes it worth investing time and resources, and criminal gangs will invest the time to do this.

Open Source
The name given to software where the original source code is made freely available and may be modified and reused.

In the main, hackers will use automated tools to attempt the hack as they can achieve maximum impact with minimum effort.

If your website is WordPress, much of this is available using simple plug-ins and most of this software is free, with the option to get additional layers of protection if you subscribe. Most small websites will be fine with the free versions but if your website is your livelihood, consider paying for this software. It's not expensive and it's always better to be safe than sorry. If you want more information on this, I've put a list of security software in the Resources chapter.

> ## Takeaways:
> Website security is an essential part of business.
>
> Your website is inherently vulnerable, even if you are a small local business.
>
> Even the basic security steps are better than nothing – do them today.

What are Plug-ins?

Plug-ins have been mentioned several times already without any real explanation of what they are or what they do. That's because they are everywhere in the digital world, so they need an explanation. To do this, I'm going to rely on my trusty motoring metaphor again; plug-ins are like an aftermarket accessory for your car. You can add them on to make the car look better, like wider alloy wheels, go faster stripes, etc.

> ### Plug-in
> A plug-in is a small piece of software that can be added to your website to improve or enhance its performance.

In computer terms, plug-ins are regularly used to improve the performance of websites, particularly those built on platforms such as WordPress. These platforms can be regarded as the 'entry level model' in motoring terms, in that they come with all the functionality to be a website but without the bells and whistles that people like to see. Plug-ins are typically used to add in functionality that isn't there in the standard build. Many of these are free but some of the better ones have an entry level free option with the ability to upgrade to a paid version that has considerably enhanced functionality.

What sort of things can plug-ins do?

The answer to this question is pretty much anything you want. Developers continue to write new code for plug-ins and currently, in 2022, there are over 60,000 plug-ins available in the WordPress Plugin Directory.[46] Magento has over 3,300 extensions (the same thing as a plug-in) on their website[47] and most other platforms have similar extensions or plug-ins that do the same thing.

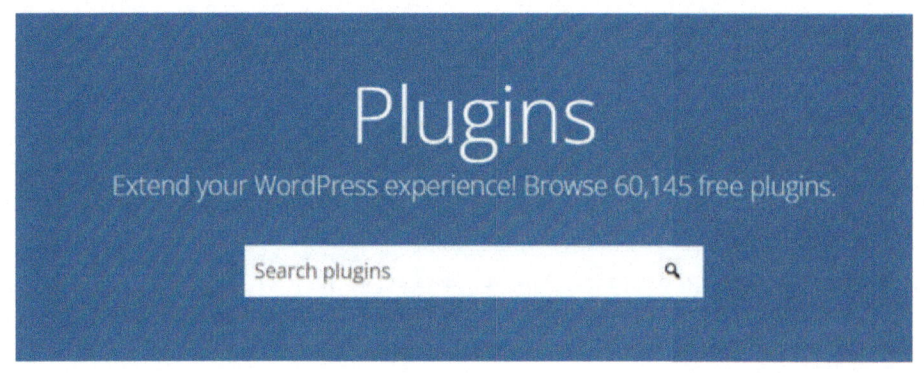

Figure 75 – WordPress Plugin Directory.

Looking in the back end of most WordPress websites and you will see a range of different plug-ins, all performing different tasks. Most frequently, they are used for things like adding in a contact form, providing security or even doing basic SEO tasks. They can, however, do so much more, including adding on functionality to turn your website into a membership site, linking to social media platforms, adding image galleries, providing automated backups and even providing a bookings platform for businesses like restaurants, or service providers like chiropractors, hairdressers or acupuncturists.

If all the traffic lights are green, my website is optimised, right?

Wrong. This is one of the biggest misnomers I have to dispel around plug-ins, especially those SEO plug-ins that have some kind of red, amber, green system of telling you when your page is optimised. I have new customers telling me

---
[46] https://en-gb.wordpress.org/plugins/
[47] https://marketplace.magento.com/extensions.html

that they have completely optimised their sites, yet they are still not ranking. When I dig a bit deeper, it turns out that they have simply made sure that all the dashboard lights are green.

The problem with this is that it misses the human element. As an example, a blog post on one of my websites is optimised with the Yoast SEO plug-in. Let me state upfront that I like Yoast and it's a great tool. It's one of several that we regularly use on WordPress websites. In this instance, the article I have written is shown as having four distinct problems (all shown as red lights) and if I'd paid for the premium version, a fifth as well (Figure 76).

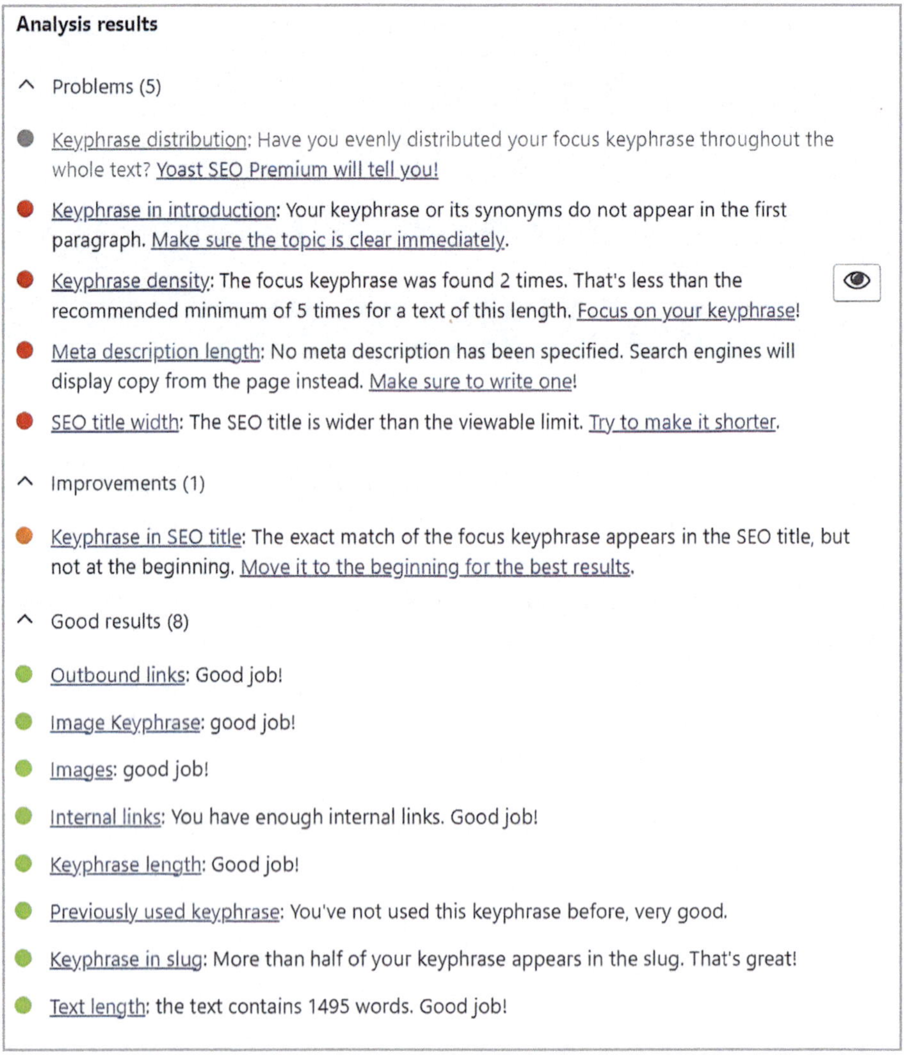

Analysis results

∧ Problems (5)

● Keyphrase distribution: Have you evenly distributed your focus keyphrase throughout the whole text? Yoast SEO Premium will tell you!

● Keyphrase in introduction: Your keyphrase or its synonyms do not appear in the first paragraph. Make sure the topic is clear immediately.

● Keyphrase density: The focus keyphrase was found 2 times. That's less than the recommended minimum of 5 times for a text of this length. Focus on your keyphrase!

● Meta description length: No meta description has been specified. Search engines will display copy from the page instead. Make sure to write one!

● SEO title width: The SEO title is wider than the viewable limit. Try to make it shorter.

∧ Improvements (1)

● Keyphrase in SEO title: The exact match of the focus keyphrase appears in the SEO title, but not at the beginning. Move it to the beginning for the best results.

∧ Good results (8)

● Outbound links: Good job!

● Image Keyphrase: good job!

● Images: good job!

● Internal links: You have enough internal links. Good job!

● Keyphrase length: Good job!

● Previously used keyphrase: You've not used this keyphrase before, very good.

● Keyphrase in slug: More than half of your keyphrase appears in the slug. That's great!

● Text length: the text contains 1495 words. Good job!

Figure 76 – An example traffic light system from an SEO plug-in.

Some customers I work with would immediately set about changing all of these to turn the lights green, but in doing so, miss out the human element. As an example, it tells me that the SEO title width is too long, but as we established earlier in this chapter, that depends on the size of the letters I've used in my title. In this case, to get the light to turn green would mean compromising on the message, hence the reason it's still red. Similarly, I could shoehorn the key phrase I've chosen into the first paragraph, but from a human point of view it would make no sense. It would seem clunky and could even be wrong.

To prove the point, if I change the opening sentence to say "Yesterday, *2nd class stamps* Royal Mail announced that they are *2nd class stamps* changing forever the world of Machin *2nd class stamps*", the entire sentence is gibberish, but the red light disappears. By following the guidance, I've inadvertently made my blog post spammy by cramming the keyword in too many times.

It's crucial to remember that plug-ins are just tools and like any tool, it can be used badly or well. For beginners looking to develop a better understanding of SEO then tools like Yoast are fabulous. Use them to build your understanding of what good SEO looks like but don't be a slave to their scoring systems.

Can you have too many plug-ins?

The straight answer is yes. Some business owners, new to owning and running a website, see the vast range of possibilities that plug-ins open up to them and add lots of them into their website. This can cause problems. Generally, I work to a rule that the fewer of them that you have to add in to your website, the better it will be. The reason for this is that whilst each plug-in will have been built to work with WordPress, they won't necessarily have been checked to see if they work with other plug-ins. Some of the most popular are well written and 'play nicely' with other plug-ins and they coexist quite happily within a website. Some though, are a problem. They may work initially but if there is a core update to WordPress, for example, some owners can find their websites breaking with no clear explanation. In these cases, when we have to try and diagnose the problem, it's usually down to having too many plug-ins active at one time and one or more are conflicting with the other. Don't be tempted to just add them in because you think they might be useful, only add those that you really need. If in doubt, ask your website developer if they would recommend it. Finally, if you are not using a plug-in, then it should be deleted from your website.

> **Takeaway:**
> Plug-ins are extraordinarily useful but use them in moderation.

CHAPTER 4

Local SEO

What is local search and why is it important?

To understand the importance of local search today we probably need to look back, as history gives us a few clues. As commerce developed alongside the Industrial Revolution over the eighteenth and nineteenth centuries, most trade was invariably local. Transport options were limited and modern conveniences such as secure packaging, storage solutions and refrigeration were some way off, so people shopped and bought locally. This wasn't a conscious decision to 'shop local', more a fact of life. The only shops that people had access to were local so that's where people spent their money. Shops and businesses grew to serve the needs of their local community and few looked beyond very local horizons. If you were a butcher, for example, your meat was sourced locally and your customers came from the local area to buy your produce. Similarly, with bakers, the grain was local and your customers lived close by. This isn't to dismiss the importance of firms that were importing and distributing their products across the country and indeed, across the globe, more to highlight that most buying and selling happened locally.

Fast forward to the twenty-first century and with the rise of digital platforms, we can now buy pretty much whatever we want from wherever we want. I can buy a camera direct from Japan, a mobile phone from China and shoes from Vietnam. When it comes to music, I can rent it from Apple in USA or Spotify in Sweden, or order vinyl and CDs from anywhere across the globe. In each of these instances I am spending money away from my local economy. Why should this matter? Why is local important?

At the start of 2021 there were 5.5 million small businesses (SMEs) in the UK, and they make up over 99% of the total business population. These businesses employ 16.3 million people and exist to predominantly serve a local market.[1] My local bakery, for example, will serve customers in a 20-mile radius, but if you ask them, they will tell you that most of their business comes from a five-mile radius, and if really pushed, they will probably agree that most customers live within two miles of their shop. Unsurprisingly, this is down to availability and competition. We can buy bread today from a wide range of stores other than the local baker. Supermarkets sell bread (and there are six in our local town), there are fast food stores that sell bread as do general stores and petrol stations. In fact, there are so many places one can buy bread it's a wonder that small craft bakers still exist. But exist they do, and they understand that being found locally is of critical importance to their business. For many of these businesses, the lockdowns which were characteristic of Government response to the Pandemic in 2020/2 made people realise just how important these local suppliers were, as people were forced to stay local and consequently, shop local.

Historically, everyone would know where their local suppliers were because towns and villages were small, there were few suppliers and most people walked to the shops. Today, if you move into a new area and don't know where your local butcher or baker is, you simply search (probably on your phone) for these services 'near me'. In fact, the 'near me' search is one of the biggest areas of increase in Google search, with US data showing that in the period between 2015-2017, 'near me' searches rose 150% more than comparable searches that did not include the term 'near me',[2] and that trend has continued to this day.

When we can buy pretty much anything we need from anywhere on the planet without leaving our homes, why is there such an importance on looking for products and services nearby?

---

1 https://www.fsb.org.uk/uk-small-business-statistics.html
2 https://www.thinkwithgoogle.com/consumer-insights/consumer-trends/local-search-statistics/

Local SEO

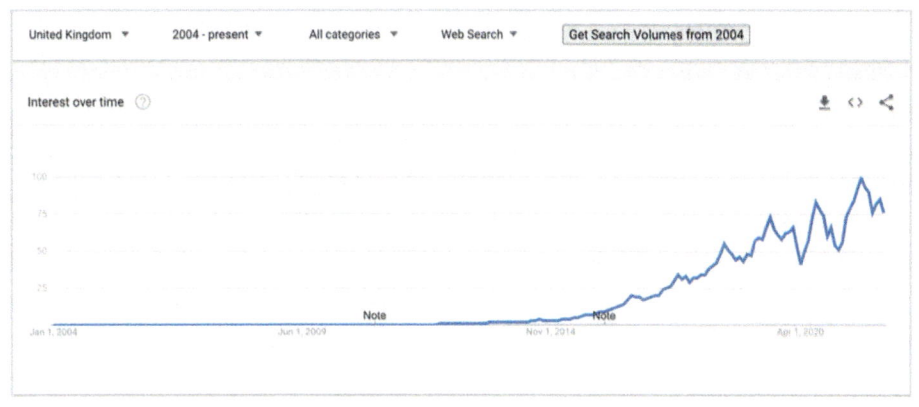

Figure 77 - The history of 'near me' searches on Google.

The answer isn't simple, as it very much depends on what we are looking for and why. Some people now search for local food suppliers in an attempt to reduce the 'food miles' and to buy more sustainably. And if you are looking for a 'dentist near me', you definitely won't be satisfied with anything other than a local provider. Personal services like this, where you physically have to attend a premises to receive the product or service, will always need to be local. Similarly, if you are looking for a 'builder near me', it's not because their proximity makes a difference to the quality of their work, nor that they need to be geographically close to do the job; it's more a question of trust. People trust local tradesmen, especially if they have seen their vehicles on the road, heard of them, seen them working on another job or they have been recommended by a friend or neighbour. There's an innate trust of 'local' and corresponding fear of outsiders and it translates into a local search.

Inherent within every 'near me' search is also a time element. Many of these searches are time dependent and rely on search engines being able to provide the correct information immediately. As an example, from a search engine's point of view, someone searching for 'concerts tonight near me' is not only looking for a product or service but has specified a timeframe in which they need it to be delivered. Historically, we would have searched the local or national papers or specialist gig listings in music publications for this type of information, but today, we expect to have the answer in the palm of our hand in under a second.

Before we had the ability to search digitally, in the paper era we typically looked for products, services or suppliers in our local newspaper or classified phone book such as Yellow Pages. Each of these listed local tradespeople and classified them under headings, so they were easy to find. We searched locally because historically, we could find pretty much everything we needed from a local supplier. These paper-based lists were a great way of finding local suppliers. Yellow Pages was always perceived as a local directory, and in the UK, Thomson Local directory even more so. Why this focus on local? The answer is because they knew that people wanted to deal locally and that historically, the further you had to travel to deliver that product or service, the more expensive it became. As we moved to digital search, the ability to search outside our local area meant that we could find a wider range of suppliers than ever before, but still, we search for suppliers 'near me' because whilst the vehicle for search has changed, the motivations behind search have not.

However, not all local businesses realise or recognise this fact and far too many have ill-defined marketing strategies which ignore the value of customers on their doorstep. There are local businesses in every major market who simply assume that 'everybody knows me' and that marketing themselves to their local community isn't necessary. These businesses are missing a trick.

If we know that consumers are looking for products, services, and suppliers near to their location, what should we be doing to optimise our websites so that we appear in those searches?

Local SEO

A quick search of Google today for the words 'Local SEO' brings me a jumbled page of paid search results, organic listings and a 'local pack' (Google's map listing which shows you which suppliers are geographically near to you), which is useful as this is a large part of what 'local SEO' is all about. The paid advertisements are all for firms trying to sell me 'local SEO' (which hopefully you will realise by now that you don't need to pay for) and the organic listings are all articles telling me how to do it. Currently, this is what I can see:

Local SEO: The Definitive Guide (2022)
Local SEO [Free Local SEO Cheat Sheet]
What is Local SEO, and How Does It Work?
Local SEO: The Definitive Guide to Improve Your Local Search

Local SEO: A Simple (But Complete) Guide
What Is Local SEO?
A Comprehensive Guide to Local SEO in 2021
Local SEO Checklist (2022) — 10 Simple Steps
Local SEO for WordPress
Top 10 Ways to Improve Your Local SEO Right Now

As you can tell, there's a lot of time and effort going into creating all of these and honestly, if you want to know how to *do* your Local SEO then there's plenty of material for you to read. I don't intend to recreate these, nor to give you a definitive list of what you should do, as these online resources are better and probably more up to date than whatever appears in print in this book. What I will do, however, is tell you *why* this is important and where best to focus your energies to get the maximum return for the minimum effort. Top of this list is Google My Business.

Google My Business

Currently, the top ranking article in the list of articles is from a website called Backlinko, created by a gentleman called Brian Dean. It's an excellent website and I refer to it on a regular basis as Brian is a font of knowledge in all matters SEO. Near the top of his article on Local SEO he uses the words:

"What makes Local SEO unique is that Google uses a different set of ranking factors to rank the local search results."

He then goes onto list those factors as:

- The location that the person is searching from
- NAP citations
- Presence of Google My Business listing
- Keywords used in Google My Business profile
- Sentiment of online reviews
- Keywords used in online reviews
- Number of "check-ins" at that location
- Shares on social media
- Google Maps star rating for that business

This is incredibly useful information apart from one small omission. Nowhere is there any reference to any article, study or resource that substantiates the statement that "Google uses a different set of ranking factors to rank the local search results." I'm not saying he's wrong necessarily, more that it's another of those areas of SEO where people accept something at face value without questioning the research behind it. As we saw earlier in the example about the number of words on a page, if you publish something and do it with enough confidence it becomes accepted fact.

As I say, the list isn't necessarily wrong, it's just that I'd like to see more evidence, for example, that NAP citations (Name, Address and Phone Number) are a key part of these 'different' ranking factors. What we can say though is that the inclusion of Google My Business in that list is correct and a critical part of local SEO.

Google My Business[3] (GMB) is a free tool from Google that allows business owners to claim a knowledge panel about their business and fill in relevant details that would help someone looking for the products or services the business owner provides. In many respects, this is akin to the free listing businesses used to get in the Phone Book, where their NAP was made freely available for anyone looking in an alphabetical list. The printed books were naturally constrained in what they could contain, because with so many names and numbers to list, providing lots of basic information would have been difficult to paginate, and more importantly, expensive to print. Firms that wanted to display more information were encouraged to pay for an advertisement and everyone else was left with a Free Line Entry containing just their NAP details. When the list became digital, the biggest constraint, that of cost, was removed. Google, as we have already established, needs content to help it decide what to rank where (remember Rule 2?), so when they created Google My Business in 2014, they actively encouraged business owners to include more than just their NAP details.

What some business owners sometimes fail to grasp is that the details they input into their GMB listing are the same details that Google use when presenting users with Google Maps. Here's an example of how this works.

If I search for 'plumber near me', Google returns a results page, at the top of which are four advertisements but underneath which is a local 'map pack'. The local map pack is Google's attempt to provide better utility to its users by geo locating their

---

3   https://business.google.com/

CASE STUDY

A small local health practitioner wanted to rank for six different treatments they offered, but only in their immediate locality. They had a simple website and as it stood, all these treatments were mentioned on the home page but not in any detail. Unsurprisingly, Google ranked them for the main treatment they provided, but not for anything else.

We identified a clear strategy for them that concentrated on creating pages built around [treatment + location] and made sure that these pages explained in detail not only what they offered, but what the patients could expect from each visit, such as how long the treatment took, what they could expect before, during and after, and even how much each treatment would cost. This additional information was significantly more than any of the local competitors had offered and within a couple of weeks these new pages ranked well in the local market. Within two months, they were number one for everything they did and getting a lot of enquiries. We followed this up with making sure all the treatments were also mentioned in their Google My Business listing, and so in any search for that health treatment in that location, they always appeared twice, once in the organic listing and once in the local pack.

Takeaway:
Rule 2 applies – if you are a small local business, create great content but localise it to where you want to appear.

---

search and offering them a local service. Underneath the map pack comes the organic listings, and whilst Google will attempt to make them as accurate and relevant as possible, the further down the list you go the less relevant some of the results become. As an example, on this search for a 'plumber near me', at #83 is a YouTube video for a plumber in Gaithersburg, Maryland and at #99 is the website for Poundland. The first of these is because it contains the word 'plumber' and the second, because on the page Google can read "...to discover this land's awesome offers as well as its awesome stores. I agree that my data will only be used as stated in the Privacy Policy. Sign **me** up!"

Google has taken the words I have searched for and separated them into 'plumber', 'near' and 'me' and when all three conditions are met, the results are near the top of the list. As time goes by, however, then the link to the initial search query becomes more tenuous.

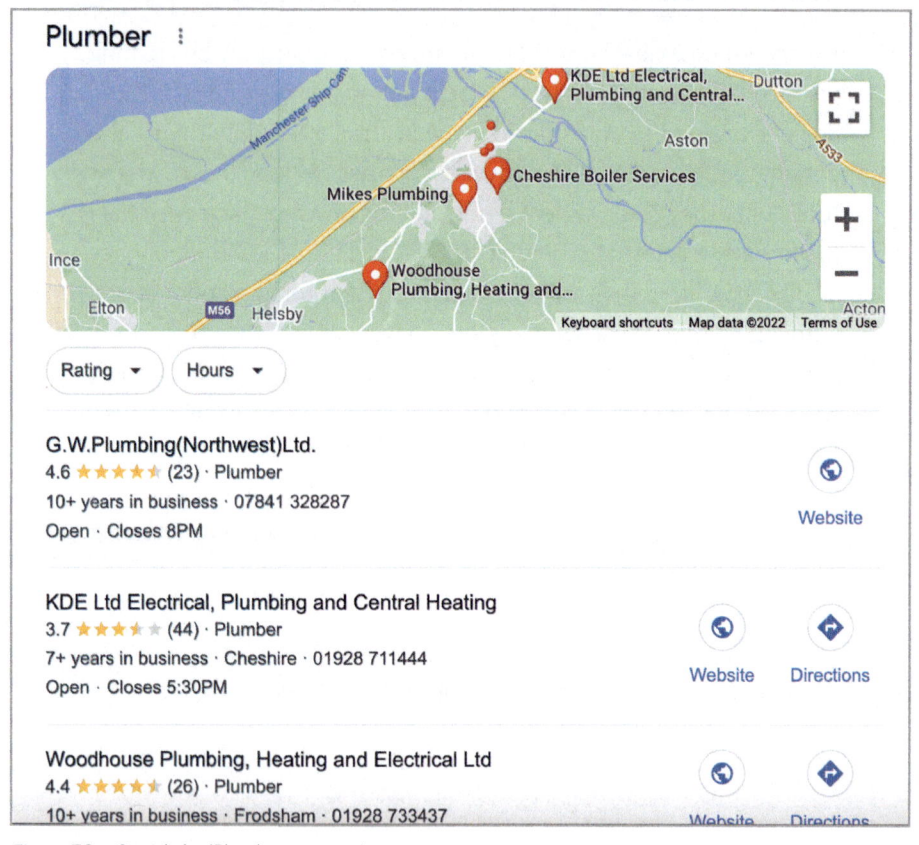

Figure 78 – Search for 'Plumber near me'.

The local map pack, however, has fulfilled the initial search exactly and has geo located me to somewhere near Runcorn, Cheshire (UK) from the IP address of my computer. It has therefore presented me with three plumbing firms near me that could possibly help in my search for a plumber near me.

Local SEO

> **IP Address**
> IP address is a unique address, made up of characters (letters and numbers) that identifies a device on the Internet or a local network.

If I click the icon in the top right hand corner of the map (a square with breaks in each side), Google transforms into a much bigger map and now includes a much wider range of businesses, located using red 'drops', all of whom it thinks might be able to help me. Remember, at this stage, all it knows is that I'm looking for a plumber near me. It has no idea why I want a plumber, nor what I need them to do.

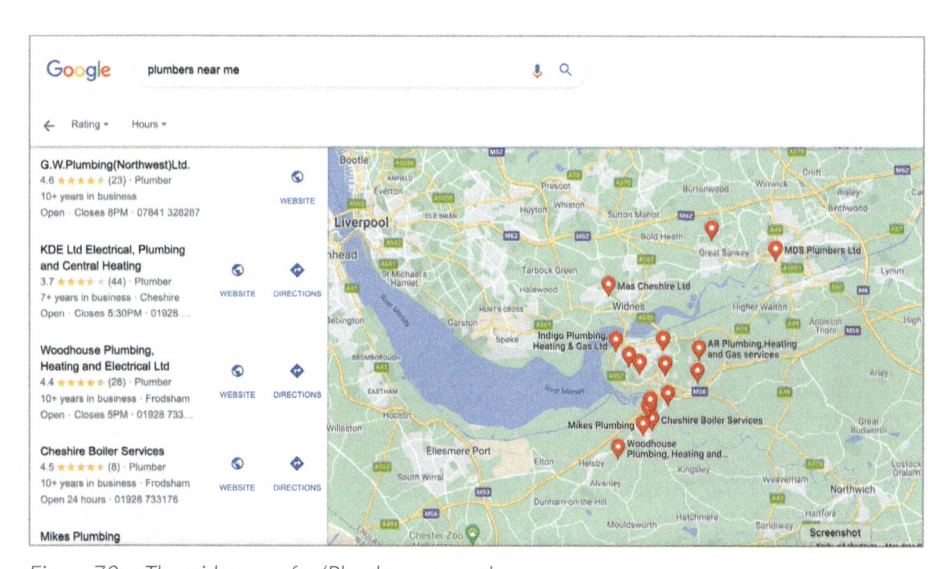

Figure 79 – The wider map for 'Plumber near me'.

How has Google decided who to include in this map and list, and why?

The answer lies, unsurprisingly perhaps, in Rule 2: nothing, but nothing, beats great content. Google uses content and other technical data it can collect to try and deliver what it thinks is the right answer to my search query. And if we

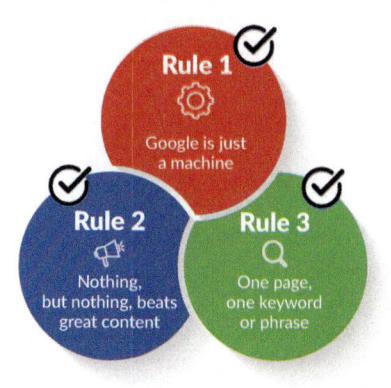

207

know this is the process Google uses, doesn't it make sense to include as much information as you can in your GMB listing?

Google will pull in information it has on each business that appears in their Google My Business listing, plus data from each company's website, which should be linked via GMB. It also follows links from websites to social media platforms and can often use reviews from Facebook or Google Reviews to add to the listings if it thinks it might help a user. If I refine my search and tell Google where I really am, it shifts the map and introduces other local firms who might help me, and in the case of A.R. Plumbing & Gas Heating, it also includes what it considers to be a useful review from a user. The review is, however, buried halfway down the Google reviews and is over two years old.

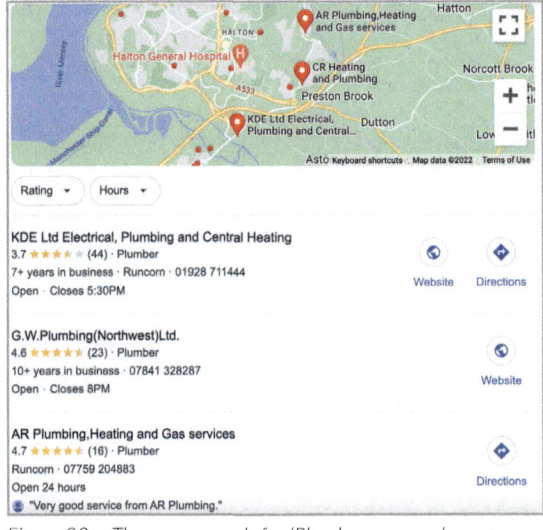

Figure 80 – The same search for 'Plumber near me' when I tell Google where I am.

What this demonstrates is that Google is simply looking for information, as much of it as it can get, to try and help it establish how my query for a 'local plumber' might be best served.

If I find I'm not entirely happy with the first search result and the firms don't quite fit my needs precisely, I might refine it and specify that I'm looking for a plumber who can service a boiler in a commercial office ('near me' of course). If I do this, then Google can refine its answer. In this case, it tells me that the nearest and most relevant 'Commercial Plumber' offering 'Boiler Servicing' is KDE, who

Figure 81 – The review that appears on their profile is two years old.

Local SEO

appeared on the first map. It's even pulled out the fact that they provide an 'Annual Boiler Service' from data it has found on their website. It's also telling me that G.W. Plumbing do 'Boiler fitting and repairs' and that Cheshire Boiler Services offer 'Commercial Oil Boiler Installation'. All this data is from their respective websites and is being used to help me pinpoint the best firm to help with my particular problem.

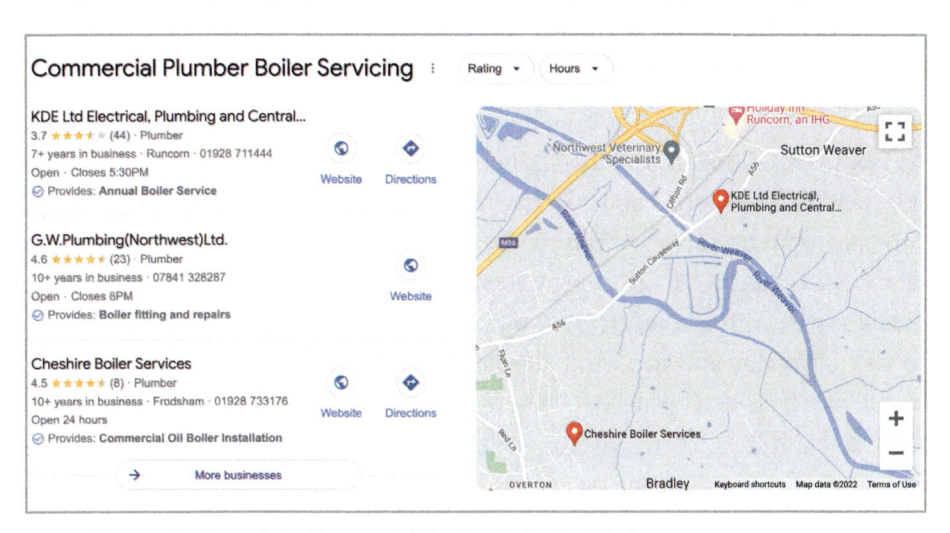

Figure 82 – A refined search for 'Commercial Plumber Boiler Servicing'.

The more specific users make their search, the more relevant the results become, but as most users aren't specific, Google has to be good at guessing what we want.

Something that people often wonder about is how Google knows where they are. The answer is simple; it knows from your digital activity. Google has access to billions of data points from an enormous range of sources, so geo data from your mobile phone, any wearable tech, or the IP address of your computer can help it pinpoint where you are. This kind of tracking looks either very clever or very sinister, depending on where you stand with privacy and tracking, but the simple fact is that it is a part of modern life. Google also looks at – and reads – every business's website and their social media feeds and makes clever interpretations of what it finds. Keeping your website and social media channels focused, clear and up to date is therefore of great importance. Underpinning all this though, is all the data you will have already given it on your Google My Business page, and this is where you can get ahead of your competition.

How to appear higher in Google My Business

This is something I'm often asked and it's not an easy one to answer. I can give business owners all sorts of tips for appearing higher in the Google My Business listings but even if you do all of them, it won't necessarily have an immediate impact. What I can say though, after years of studying how Google ranks businesses, is that if you complete (to the best of your ability) all the available fields in your GMB listing, it will help Google place you higher when customers look for you.

As I write this, Google currently has ten options in their GMB dashboard (Figure 83), five of which are opportunities for you to add more details about your company. As you can see from the examples of plumbers, Google is simply trying to best match a user's search with a company that might be able to help. It needs you to give it the information about your business, because frankly, if you don't, no one else will.

In the dashboard, you can add details about your location, opening hours, the area you service, special hours (one-offs or extended hours every other Tuesday, for example), your phone number (or numbers), your website, your products and services, and even provide a link for people to make an appointment with you. It wants to know if your premises are accessible to wheelchair users, what amenities you have on site and even what makes your business special, and that can be anything you like. That's a lot of data that will help Google make sense of who and what you are. You can also add your logo, pictures of the business and write small blog posts or offers that can appear under your listing. As Google want to own the whole process, it also gives you the option of allowing people to contact you by direct message, and if you don't have your own website, you can even create one here for free.

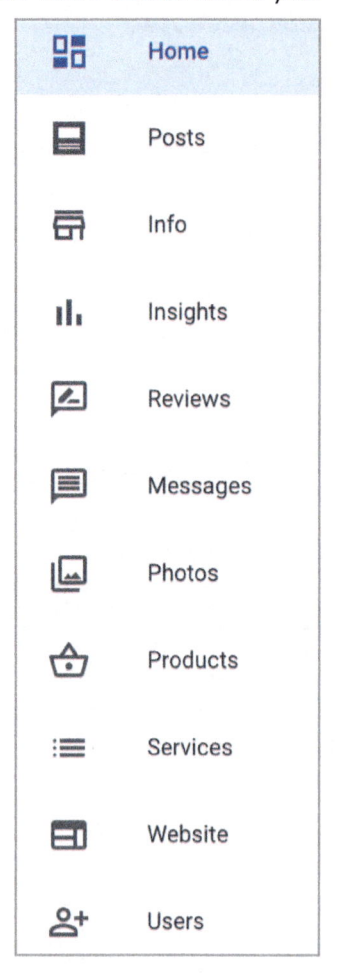

Figure 83 – Options in the Google My Business dashboard.

Most importantly though, Google likes to make it easy for people to leave reviews and these reviews always appear underneath a company's GMB listing. Whilst you can't simply say that the more Google reviews you get, the higher you will appear (because that's not true), it is true to say that more often than not, those businesses with more reviews DO appear at or near the top of the listings. Google relies heavily on 'the voice of the crowd' to help it understand which businesses are better than others and there's no better signal for Google than a genuine review left by a customer.

But these signals alone are not enough to guarantee a top listing every time and the reality is that there is no way you can guarantee that position anyway. The reason is that, as I've already explained, Google is trying to match a search query with the results it has on its database, and as everyone searches for different things at different times, then it will often throw up different results for what might seem, at first glance, the same search query.

As an example, if you search for a local solicitor, unless you know and search for them by name, it will essentially be a 'solicitor near me' search. Google starts by identifying where you are at that moment in time and then shows you those solicitors who are in the immediate proximity. Of those solicitors it will show you, the decision on the order to rank them might be done on a range of factors, such as the number of Google (or other) reviews they have, their opening hours or the type of work they do, to name a few. If you've just been searching for information about divorce, Google knows this and is more likely to show you solicitors who handle divorce matters than those who focus, for example, on aspects of commercial law. In other words, the decisions on who to rank in which position is a complex one with a great many variables. To get the best competitive advantage, you need to ensure that you have covered as many of those variables as you possibly can.

Takeaways:

Remember Rule 2 - nothing but nothing beats great content.

Complete every part of your GMB listing.

Get as many Google reviews as you can.

Google Reviews – how to get them and how to manage them

I must confess, I have something of a love hate relationship with Google reviews. On the one hand, they are a great tool for buyers in that you can see what other people think of a business before you part with any money. On the other hand, from a business point of view they are an unregulated, open access system where anyone can say anything about you, with impunity.

The problem is that the current fixation platforms such as Google, Amazon, and Facebook have with reviews is potentially quite damaging for all parties. They argue, quite compellingly, that you can't disagree with the 'voice of the crowd'. If a lot of people are leaving bad reviews for you, your service or products must be poor. QED. Logically, this makes sense. If you're getting lots of poor reviews, you probably need to do something about your product or service levels. But their confidence in this system and their belief that this process is fair is predicated on two assumptions.

First, they assume that all reviews are genuine. Second, they assume that all reviews are equal.

And they are wrong in both cases.

My issue is with the fact that these reviews are – despite the assurances from Google, Amazon, and Facebook – largely unregulated and the system is wide open to abuse. Moreover, the impact a bad review can have on a small local business is disproportionate relative to the advantage conferred by a good review.

Let's start by looking at the impact and value of reviews. From Google's point of view, any feedback a business gets must be good, and the 'voice of the crowd' is something to be welcomed. But ask any statistician how many reviews you need to make a meaningful sample and you will get a range of answers. But I bet you none of them say less than ten, and many, I'm sure, will opt for 100 or more. Now look at local business reviews wherever you are based and tell me how many small local firms can you find with more than 100 Google or Facebook reviews. They are rarer than hens' teeth. Therefore, negative reviews are disproportionately effective in this online space. A disgruntled ex-employee or a competitor can leave a damning review for your business which is enough to put off potential customers. We know that people research online before committing to spend money, so this type of review is extremely damaging. The problem here is that the onus is on the business owner to prove to Google, Facebook or whoever that the review is fake, false, or malicious, and frankly that's a pretty high hurdle to leap. I know, as I have been faced with this for some of our customers, and Google in particular has refused to remove a fake review, even when we can prove it is fake. Business owners have too often been left high and dry by this system, and with no control over who can leave a review, or where, it is open to extensive abuse.

Part of the reason why this is such a divisive issue is that reviews are easily manipulated. If I dislike a competitor, I could easily create a fake profile and leave a damning review. The business for whom I left the review would not easily be able to remove it. Sure, they could report my review to Google but it's rare it removes any reviews. To this day, some of my customers still have fake or false reviews sitting on their GMB profile and there's nothing that they can do about it. In one instance, the review was left by a genuine person with a grievance, but they had never actually visited my customer's premises nor dealt with them. They simply seemed to take a dislike to them for some reason and left a bad review. Even worse, when asked to change it, after initially refusing, they eventually did, but moved it from 1 star to 3 star and left a comment that still implied the business had done something wrong. Despite this, Google still refuses to remove it.

Add to this the fact that by undertaking a quick search (not using Google, obviously) most of you will be able to find people offering to leave fake reviews on pretty much any platform you want. Whilst all platforms like Google, Amazon and Facebook claim they are on top of this situation, the reality is that they are playing 'whack a mole', with providers often springing up faster than they can deal with them.

Despite these misgivings, customers still like to read reviews, and with sufficient reviews against your business, their value increases. The business I mentioned earlier who suffered from a fake review, after exhausting the avenues for getting it removed did the next best thing and tried to drown it out. They went from having six reviews against their name (five 5* and one 1*) to having over forty 4* and 5* reviews which more than drowned out the single bad review. More importantly, it showed anyone planning on using them that the odd bad review was just a one off and therefore something they could disregard. And it worked. Today they regularly pull in new business from people who have seen their reviews and often comment that the reason they chose them was because so many people had left good reviews.

So, how did they do it? How did they get so many good reviews?

The process was relatively straightforward, and it involved making it easy for people to do it. When they sent out invoices to customers, they included a short link and a simple instruction asking if customers wouldn't mind spending just two minutes writing something about the service they had received. Many of them were happy to do this, and as they had made it easy for them, the reviews poured in. The short link[4] is easily found and Google has worked hard to ensure this is accessible for all.

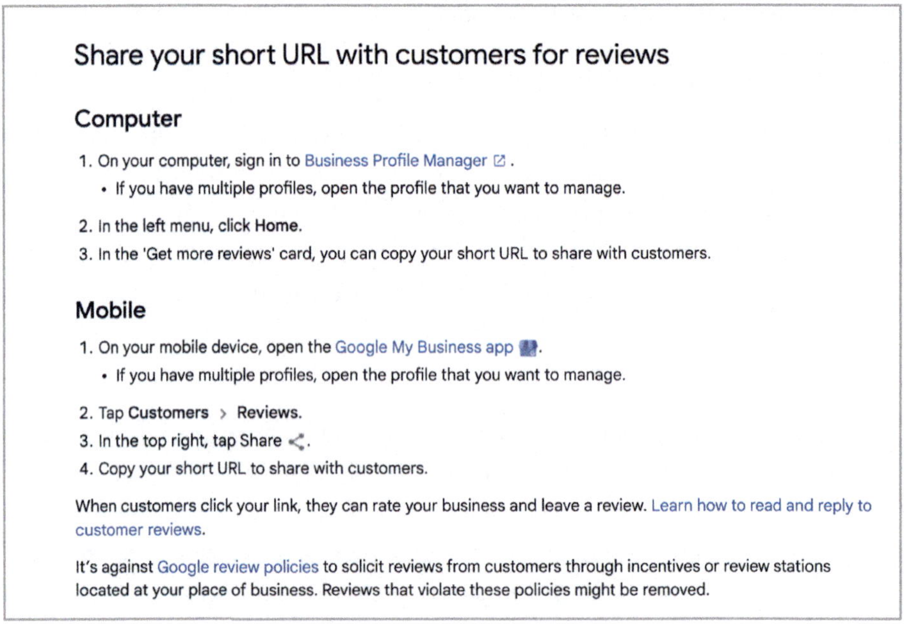

> **Share your short URL with customers for reviews**
>
> **Computer**
>
> 1. On your computer, sign in to Business Profile Manager ⧉ .
>   - If you have multiple profiles, open the profile that you want to manage.
> 2. In the left menu, click **Home**.
> 3. In the 'Get more reviews' card, you can copy your short URL to share with customers.
>
> **Mobile**
>
> 1. On your mobile device, open the Google My Business app.
>   - If you have multiple profiles, open the profile that you want to manage.
> 2. Tap **Customers** > **Reviews**.
> 3. In the top right, tap Share.
> 4. Copy your short URL to share with customers.
>
> When customers click your link, they can rate your business and leave a review. Learn how to read and reply to customer reviews.
>
> It's against Google review policies to solicit reviews from customers through incentives or review stations located at your place of business. Reviews that violate these policies might be removed.

Figure 84 – How to ask people for reviews.

The instructions are:

Computer
- On your computer, sign in to Business Profile Manager. If you have multiple profiles, open the profile that you want to manage.
- In the left menu, click Home.
- In the 'Get more reviews' card, you can copy your short URL to share with customers.

---

4 https://support.google.com/business/answer/7035772

Mobile
- On your mobile device, open the Google My Business app.
- If you have multiple profiles, open the profile that you want to manage.
- Tap Customers Reviews.
- In the top right, tap Share.
- Copy your short URL to share with customers.

Try it yourself and you will see how easy it is.

Managing Google (and other) reviews

As with any kind of communications, there's usually a good way and a bad way of doing things. Sadly, when faced with a bad review, many small businesses lose all kind of perspective and dive into the deep end, creating more problems than it is worth. Examples abound across the Internet where replies to reviews have gone horribly wrong and it's all too easy to get caught up with emotion and say the wrong thing. Probably the easiest way to deal with this is to understand what not to do and to have a pre-agreed plan in place for how you will deal with all types of reviews, not just negative ones.

As a starting point, you need to understand that you should reply to all reviews – good, bad, or indifferent. Responding to reviews makes the people who left them feel valued and listened to, and if your business relies on repeat customers then this is an absolute must. When you respond, make it genuine. No one likes to read a templated, 'Thanks, we value your feedback' after every review as it comes across as soulless and, more importantly, thoughtless.

Positive reviews are probably the easiest to deal with, as your response simply needs to be genuine and heartfelt. Thanking them is obvious but if you can, make it personal. For example, if the review says something positive about someone or something to do with your business, mention it in the reply. If they write, 'Sally is brilliant; she really made us feel welcome', you can respond with, 'Thanks for the positive feedback and we'll be sure to let Sally know that her hard work was appreciated in our weekly team meeting.' It doesn't take much but in that one response you have acknowledged them, recognised that they appreciated someone in your business and that their feedback will not only reach that person, but may help that person with recognition in a public forum.

Everyone's a winner in this scenario.

Middle of the road reviews are trickier in that they are often neither praise nor complaint. A review along the lines of 'the food was acceptable and the prices about right' is a tricky one to deal with. The temptation is to respond with, 'What do you mean, "acceptable"?' But please resist this temptation. What you need to do is to rise to the challenge in a positive way. Replying to that kind of review with, 'Thanks so much for your feedback. We try our best to make every meal an experience and every visit an occasion, and we're working hard to do even better every day. Do come back and try us again and let us know if we've achieved it.' The aim with this type of review is to acknowledge their view and their experience and to see if they might be persuaded to come back. Whether this works or not is largely irrelevant; it's more about prospective customers who might be reading this. If you'd never visited a restaurant before and read that response, how would you feel about them? Would it be a better or worse feeling than if they'd gone with the first response of questioning the reviewer? It's all about perspective and your overall aim here to is come across as positive, friendly and welcoming.

The biggest banana skin, however, is with negative reviews. These are the ones where people clearly have an issue with your business and have decided to air it publicly. From a business owners' perspective, particularly smaller businesses, the problem is that it feels personal. If people don't like your business or service, it's as if they've said they don't like you. As we all know, personal attacks generally provoke one response and that's **FIGHT!** Despite the good feeling that is often engendered by being a keyboard warrior, it will never get you the response you want, which is the retraction of the negative review if it is unfair, or the ability to publicly put it right if it is your fault. Admitting responsibility is a very hard thing for most business owners to do but often it's the first thing you should do in these circumstances. Admitting that you didn't quite get it right is difficult, but it's crucial, if you are in the wrong, to do so publicly. The best response is one that recognises it might not have been right for the customer, reaffirms your commitment to doing something about it and makes it easy for them to contact you, preferably not in the public view. In short, respond in public so everyone can see you are responsive, but ask them to send you a direct message with more detail so you can pick it up. You don't want to engage in this process in the public forum as some of the correspondence may not be right to air publicly. As my parents used to say, 'You don't air your dirty washing in public.' A good response to a negative review would be along the lines of: 'Thanks for your comments and I'm very sorry to read about your experience. This is definitely not the standard of service we strive for, and I'd like to see what I can do to help. If you'd like to contact me directly by Private Message (Direct Message) then I'd be happy to investigate this further for you.' Don't forget to add your name after this so people know it's not just a chat bot but someone they can actually talk to who might care about their problem.

The final word on responding to reviews is about tone of voice. We've already covered anger (definitely a no-no) but often, the next weapon chosen by angry people is sarcasm or humour. Whilst you may find it funny, it's a pretty certain bet that the person receiving that response won't. Trying to be funny or dismissive generally leads to a poor outcome, and if you think one bad review is a challenge, try dealing with one very disgruntled customer leaving multiple reviews across multiple channels. Before you know it, you will be spending all your time just dealing with social media reviews and no time at all on fixing the problem of what went wrong in the first place.

The bottom line here is, like it or not, the customer is always right.

Takeaways:

Make it easy for people to leave reviews by supplying a short link.

Don't take customers for granted.

Don't try to be clever with your replies to reviews.

The value of geo pages and local content

Having already established that people often buy local, the question that many business owners are faced with is how to appear in local searches when their business is not actually based in that location? Historically, businesses wanting to serve a local community would open a local shop or office so they became part of the local market. Solicitors are a good example of a type of business that would open a local branch if they wanted to do business in that area. For other businesses, like emergency plumbers for example, being local or being seen to be local is essential to their prospective customers, but not to them. Someone looking for a plumber because they have an emergency normally needs them immediately and being local is a huge advantage. For the plumber, however, there is absolutely no advantage in having an office in every town or village throughout their area and every advantage in having a single, central office, from which they can dispatch their plumbers. The problem is how can they appear local to everyone whilst retaining just the one central office?

In the days of printed media, you would often see advertisements with lots of 'local' phone numbers and the names of those locations next to the telephone numbers. In big cities, firms would list a range of phone numbers and name locations across the city that they wanted to cover. With the arrival of Google, however, that changed as Google paid little attention to these distractions and would typically only list firms for the location in which they were based. The solution to this was to create local 'geo' pages – pages that were built for a specific geographical location.

The principle was based on the way businesses found Google ranked existing businesses. Firms like solicitors who had multiple branches, but one website, found that to get a local listing for each location, they had to create a separate page for each of their branches. Each of these pages would then rank (in their own right) just for the location in which that branch was based. This trick was soon discovered by other firms, and non-geo-specific businesses, like the emergency plumber, found that by creating lots of smaller local pages, they could rank in search for that location.

Of course, as with anything that works on Google, it wasn't long before it was being abused. Digital firms sprang up offering to add local pages onto your website (at a charge, of course) and they would use a simple script to clone an existing page but then change it for the next local area. So plumbers who had a page for Manchester, for example, would be offered over 100 more 'local' pages, each of them tailored towards the smaller towns, districts and areas across the Greater Manchester area. For a short time (actually, a very short time), this worked. Then, the algorithm caught up with those websites as Google established that not only were each of these pages simply duplicates of another page on the same website, but they offered a really poor user experience. From there on, the only way was down.

Today, we still see examples of this page building (though not as frequently as before, thankfully), with business owners still believing that this is the best way to get their websites to rank in an area. Whilst this can still work, it's unlikely to do so. The basic principle, however, is still correct, and by creating a local page for a local area you can rank successfully for that location. The trick is in how you do it.

If you were to search now for 'florists near me' I'll wager that some of the results on the first page of Google will be from firms that are not actually based near you. Some of them will be national companies who cover that area, and some will be purely online players looking to capture some of the 'local' markets. Finally, there will be florists who are situated nearby. The virtual firms who have no high street presence should not, theoretically, appear unless you happen to be standing next to their head office, but they do appear. How do they do it?

The answer is that they tailor a specific landing page entirely around a single location but importantly, they ensure that the content on it is unique. Whilst they may use the same style of page for each location, the content is entirely different. In some cases, they have spent huge sums of money on copywriters to ensure that every page is completely different and appeals to the local customer in that location. One company who did this a number of years ago (and it still works today) is Serenata Flowers. I had cause to write about them on my blog[5] back in 2015 when Google hit them with a penalty for artificial link building and I have followed their progress ever since. Their approach to appearing local is simple; make every page appear as if it's been built purely for that location.

The start point is the url string. Here's their standard url string for the geo pages, using Runcorn as an example:

https://www.serenataflowers.com/en/uk/flowers/next-day-delivery/florists/online/england/cheshire/runcorn

You can see that they have inserted 'flowers', 'next day delivery', and 'florists' as core words they want to rank for, along with three geo location cues in 'England', 'Cheshire' and 'Runcorn'. That exact same url string also works if you change the location to another Cheshire town, in this case, Northwich:

https://www.serenataflowers.com/en/uk/flowers/next-day-delivery/florists/online/england/cheshire/northwich

---

5   https://www.aqueous-digital.co.uk/articles/have-serenata-flowers-been-hit-by-a-google-penalty/

Both pages look very similar when you land on them, but they are subtly different. In Figures 85 and 86, above the fold, you can see that the only change is that the town name is different over the top of the picture of the lady, and to the right, the 'Free Flower Delivery' box has a different town name. On its own, this wouldn't be enough for Google to separate these two pages as otherwise, they are identical.

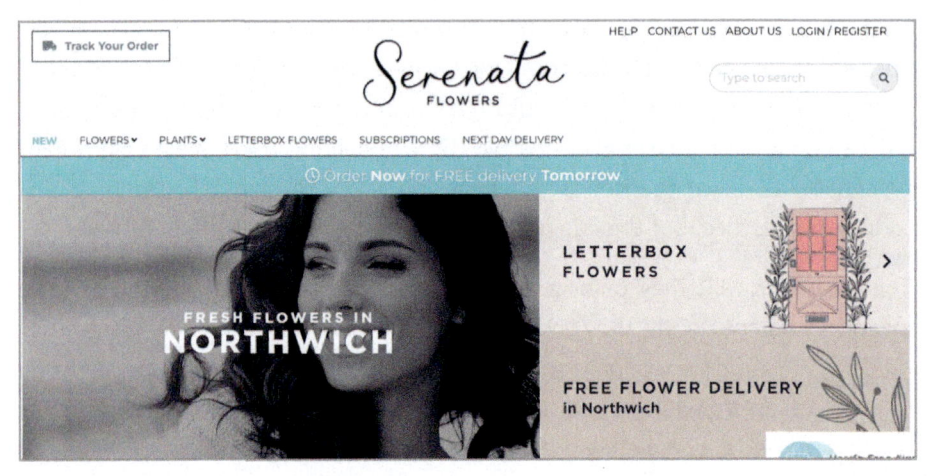

Figure 85 – Serenata Flowers Northwich landing page.

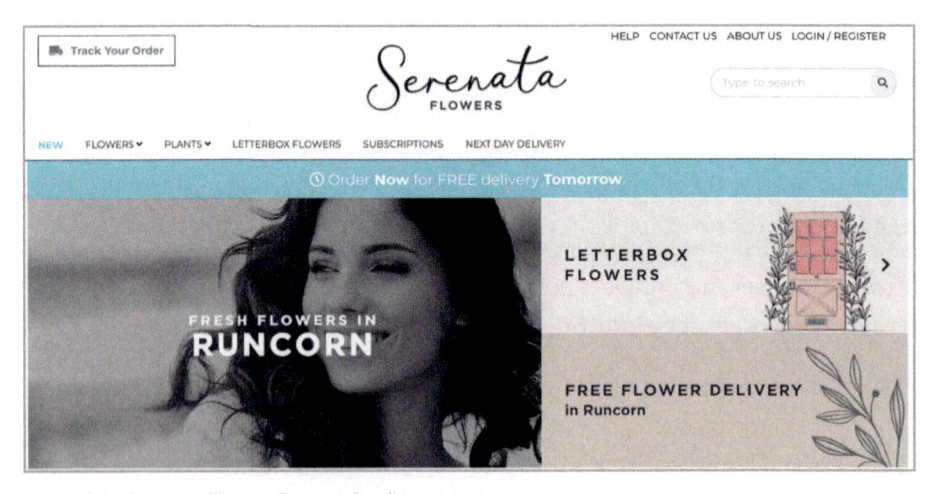

Figure 86 - Serenata Flowers Runcorn landing page.

The key changes, however, are below the fold. As you scroll down you can see that they have personalised the information so that they reflect the local area: Northwich information on the Northwich page (Figure 87) and Runcorn information on the Runcorn page (Figure 88). You might also notice further optimisation on these as they have underlined and made bold anything that relates directly to having flowers delivered; they've not missed the SEO opportunity afforded by that.

ORDER FLOWERS ONLINE FOR NORTHWICH DELIVERY

Want to send a beautiful bouquet of flowers but can't get to the high street? At SerenataFlowers.com, we've made it simple to order flowers online at any time, day or night, and have them delivered the next day to any address in Northwich. Our safe and secure online site lets you browse a selection of stunning bouquets at affordable prices. Simply pick and click, and your order will be looked after by florists in Northwich who will turn your online flower order into beautiful reality. And you can do this all from the comfort of your own home.

FLOWERS SENT BY FLORIST IN NORTHWICH

Booking a bouquet through a florist online is a great way to send someone a very special gift. Our florists in Northwich are skilled artisans with years of experience in working with the freshest and most beautiful blooms to create wonderful memories in flowers. Delivery is guaranteed the next day, so with SerenataFlowers.com you can be sure that when you send flowers in Northwich they'll be as fresh as the moment they were picked. Our delivery service makes sure they arrive on time and in perfect condition too. Simply pick and click, and our team of experts will do the rest for you.

ENGLAND CHESHIRE NORTHWICH

FLOWERS DELIVERED NEAR NORTHWICH

Barnton	Cuddington	Davenham	Hartford
Lostock Gralam	Rudheath	Weaverham	Wincham

Figure 87 – Northwich data on the Northwich page.

FLOWERS SENT ONLINE NEXT DAY TO RUNCORN

Once you've picked your blooms, it's time to get them delivered. SerenataFlowers.com can ship flowers to any address in Runcorn thanks to our easy and fast service. Simply pick and click from our fabulous selection, pay using our secure online payment method and we'll take care of everything for you. Our skilled florists will create a beautiful bouquet for you and send it to the destination of your choice in Runcorn with our next-day flower delivery service. Our florist service offers a seven-days-a-week service, delivering fresh, fabulous flowers and gifts with your own special message.

FLOWERS SENT BY FLORIST IN RUNCORN

Did you know that maidenhair ferns, often used in bridal bouquets, symbolise undying love? At SerenataFlowers.com, our florists in Runcorn understand the nuances and symbolism of every flower, and how picking the right one can send a clear message of love and affection to someone you care about. Our florists Runcorn will take your order and turn it into something truly special, and will ensure that your bouquet is delivered in tip top condition. The hardest bit is deciding which bouquet to send!

FLOWERS ONLINE NEAR RUNCORN

Online shopping is all the rage these days, so we've made it even easier for you to buy flowers online from the comfort of your own home. At SerenataFlowers.com, our florist online service means you can order a beautiful bouquet 24/7, and skilled florists in Runcorn will turn your order into reality. Our flowers delivery service in Runcorn also makes sure your fresh flowers reach their destination the very next day - and all this with just a few clicks! It's the easiest way to buy flowers online, and all at a price to suit any budget.

BUY STUNNING FLOWERS IN RUNCORN

It's never been easier to send a perfect posy from SerenataFlowers.com to any address in Runcorn. Our florists use all their skill and experience to ensure your chosen flowers arrive looking fresh and fabulous. Whether you're sending blooms in Runcorn or an impulsive gift, our expert florists will hand pick your blooms from only the freshest flowers available. From delicate orchids to fragrant roses, sending flowers to someone special couldn't be simpler. Choose from a wide range of our flowers online, add a special message and let us do the rest.

ENGLAND CHESHIRE RUNCORN

FLOWERS DELIVERED NEAR RUNCORN

Beechwood	Brookvale	Castlefields	Murdishaw
Palacefields	Windmill Hill		

Figure 88 - Runcorn data on the Runcorn page.

Below the fold

Below the fold refers to the part of the page you cannot see at first glance. Much like a newspaper used to be folded in half as the vendor handed it to a customer, the headline was always 'above the fold'.

Finally, underneath the testimonials they have some local content (Figure 89). This is much shorter for Northwich, perhaps because it is a smaller location than Runcorn (20,000 inhabitants compared to 60,000 inhabitants), but it still includes headings (h1, h2 and h3) which contain the location name, and the name of that location is also within the copy underneath those headings. They've worked hard to make it appear natural and haven't simply shoehorned the name of the town into a sentence, and for the most part, it works. Underneath that there are smaller, local locations that relate to that town, but click on any of these and they open up another geo page with exactly the same structure as the main page. In fact, when you start digging, there are over 1,600 of these geo pages, all personalised to a specific location and all unique. This affords them extraordinary coverage of the UK with every major city, town and local district covered by a specific geo page.

Figure 89 – Local testimonials on the Runcorn page.

Why do they do this? Because people like to buy local and by appearing local, they hope you will choose to use them to have your flowers delivered.

Behind the scenes, all the meta data on these pages is further tweaked to reflect the local nature of these pages. On the Runcorn page, as an example, this is what they have put.

Page Title: **Flower** delivery in **Runcorn**, Cheshire

Meta Description: **Flower** delivery in **Runcorn**, Cheshire. Order gorgeous fresh **flowers** with FREE next-day delivery Monday to Sunday from award winning Serenataflowers.com with a customer satisfaction of 93% in our customer reviews h1: Fresh **flowers** in **Runcorn**

h2: Free **flower** delivery in **Runcorn**

h3: Letterbox **Flowers**

h3: **Flowers** sent online next day to **Runcorn**

h3: **Flowers** sent by florist in **Runcorn**

h3: **Flowers** online near **Runcorn**

h3: Buy stunning **flowers** in **Runcorn**

h3: **Flowers** delivered near **Runcorn**

You'll notice that they have used multiple h tags across the page but each of them relates to the nature of the page and the location of that page. The bold emphasis in this instance is mine, simply to show you how many times the main keyword or location are mentioned in this critical meta data.

The result is that each of their local geo pages are tailored to a specific location and in this case, they follow Rule 3 by being specific to a single thing – that location and the word 'flowers'.

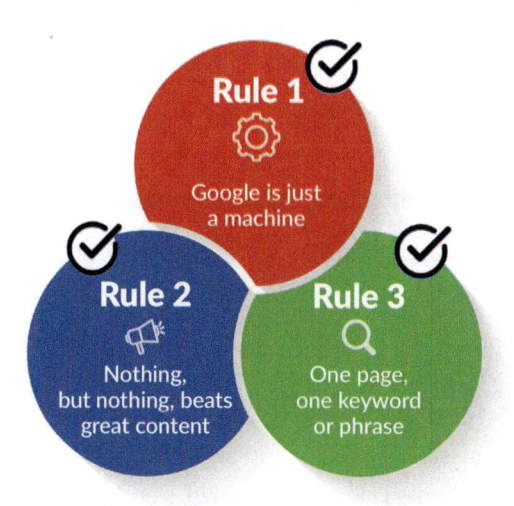

Rule 1 — Google is just a machine

Rule 2 — Nothing, but nothing, beats great content

Rule 3 — One page, one keyword or phrase

You can see from this example that local geo pages can be hugely powerful if they're done correctly. Simply throwing up a page on your website with the name of the next town won't be enough, you need to make it specific, relevant and compelling. If you want to appear relevant to people in the next town, you need to include reasons why they should deal with you. Serenata use the reason that the florists they use to fulfil these orders are based locally in that town, but you can use any reason you want. It might be that the next town is where you work every day, so you can say you are there when they need you. It might be that you employ someone who lives in that location, or that you already deal with customers in that location – the possibilities are endless. Just consider what might make you choose a firm from further away if you were searching for a local service and think about using that as a selling proposition.

Local pages, if created correctly, can be hugely powerful and help drive enquiries from a range of locations outside your local area. Spend the time to make each page relevant and unique and you have a great chance of making this a successful strategy.

Local Schema

There is one more way you can localise your pages so that Google can make sense of them, and that is by using local schema. We saw earlier that schema is a hugely powerful tool to help the machine understand your website and by adding in a 'local' element to your local pages, you are helping it make sense of what you are doing and what information may be relevant to local people.

As always, Google is keen to help you add this type of information to your website and it has a simple 'how to' page on its developer blog[6] that explains what you need to do. For the more tech savvy of you, the local business page on schema.org[7] contains every field you can possibly imagine to capture your local data.

This type of data markup is extremely useful for businesses dealing directly with the public – especially restaurants, cinemas and department stores. If, however, you are a local tradesperson, then this is also for you, as you can put things like your opening hours, specialisms, location and star ratings from online reviews. Anything you add as schema is likely to be used – and therefore appear – in your GMB listing that appears in search.

---

[6] https://developers.google.com/search/docs/advanced/structured-data/local-business
[7] https://schema.org/LocalBusiness

Remember Rule 1 states that Google is just a machine. If you can help the machine make sense of the data, it's far more likely to show you properly in its search results.

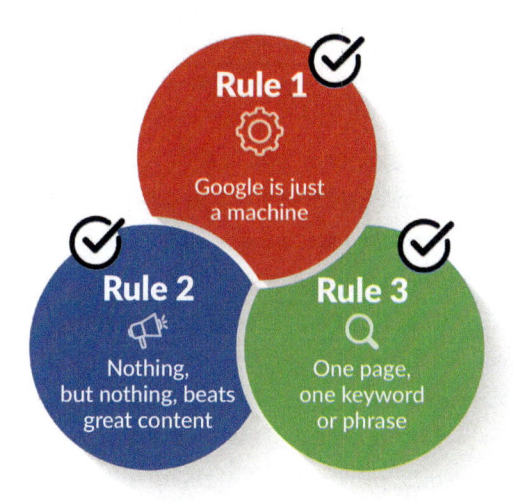

Rule 1 — Google is just a machine

Rule 2 — Nothing, but nothing, beats great content

Rule 3 — One page, one keyword or phrase

Other local signals to help customers find you

In a chapter on local SEO, it would be remiss if I didn't mention other ways you can be found locally. Sometimes, in the rush to the new, people forget the old tried and tested ways of doing things, and the stampede to digital means that some great opportunities often remain untapped.

What people often overlook is the fact that offline activity can also translate into online gains, so all your promotional efforts can add value if they are planned and executed well.

Before we get to the offline elements though, there are still online areas that are overlooked. As an example, most town and local areas across the western world now have a local website dedicated to the town, district or area. To find yours, try searching on Google for 'local [insert town name here] directory' and check the list that appears. In there you will find a range of local websites on which you can create an entry for your business. You don't need to be on all of them but a decent range of those on page one should suffice. Add to these the obvious candidates such as yell.com (or yellowpages.com in the USA), Thomson Local and BT and you will have covered the basics. Add to this local Facebook and Instagram groups and you have a ready-made local platform for your products and services.

When it comes to offline activity, there's generally someone locally who creates a small local magazine, no matter where you live. If there's one that comes through your door or is made available locally in shops, consider advertising in there. Typically, they are not expensive, but they will get your name in front of an audience, some of whom may not be tech savvy. You should also not be afraid to talk to your local newspaper about both advertising and promotional opportunities. If you and your business are a good story, they may well print it. All you need to do is read the paper each week, establish what sort of story they like to run (turnover milestone, new premises, new staff, expansion, etc.) and then create your own press release. Try to write the story in the style you can see them printing every week and above all, make sure you get a good, high quality photograph to accompany your story. Print relies on people reading the stories and superb photographs make people stop and read. Don't be afraid of paying a local photographer to take some professional shots for you, as stories that arrive in newsrooms accompanied by an original, high quality photograph are far more likely to be printed than a random snap from a mobile phone. Remember, local papers want to print local stories. Help them and they will often help you.

Takeaways:

Local geo pages can work if done correctly.

Make sure each page contains relevant local information and cues.

Don't forget the meta data.

CHAPTER 5

E-Commerce

What is e-commerce?

The simplest definition of e-commerce I could find is:

> **"Commercial transactions conducted electronically on the internet."**[1]

But this definition doesn't really capture e-commerce the way most people understand it. Perhaps a better definition is:

> **"The buying and selling of goods and services over the Internet. It is conducted over computers, tablets, smartphones, and other smart devices."**[2]

Today, there are business to business (b2b) segments of the market, business to consumer (b2c) interactions, and the increasingly popular consumer to consumer (c2c) e-commerce solutions. Whichever definition you prefer, all of them attempt to simply describe what was a seismic shift in the way people and business buy and sell goods and services.

---

1   https://languages.oup.com/google-dictionary-en/
2   https://www.investopedia.com/terms/e/ecommerce.asp

When did e-commerce start?

Astonishingly, the birth of e-commerce can be traced all the way back to 1979. I say astonishingly as I distinctly remember at that time, the height of computing was a dumb terminal linked to a large printer in the corner of the Computing Room in school, which churned out the green and white lined paper so familiar to anyone who had anything to do with computers in the 1980s. At the time, Computer Science qualifications were still being taught by asking pupils to write out code on triplicate forms (three copies of the same form with carbon paper in-between – yes, this really *was* a thing) and then they would be put in the post to a data entry bureau. It seems incredible to think that at the same time, Michael Aldrich[3] is credited with inventing online shopping.

> **Continuous Stationery**
> Did you know that the green and while lined computer paper is known as Continuous stationery in the UK, continuous form paper in the USA and Computer Printout paper across most of the world?

From small beginnings, e-commerce didn't really take off for the next fifteen years, as the technology needed was simply not a part of people's everyday lives. As computers spread and become ubiquitous and mobile phones became better, faster and more able to handle online browsing, so e-commerce grew. The year 1995 became a significant moment in its development, as Amazon was launched by Jeff Bezos as a platform to buy and sell books, but still the revenues being transacted online were relatively small. Fast forward to today and almost US$5 trillion is being traded through e-commerce and this figure is forecast to rise to US$7.5 trillion in the next few years. By 2025, it is forecast that a quarter of global retail sales will be through e-commerce platforms.

Against this backdrop, the number and type of e-commerce solutions have ballooned and the barriers to entry have dropped dramatically. This has allowed more and more people and businesses to get online with some type of shopping solution. From a casual part-time seller to multinational businesses, if they need to be online there is no longer any excuse for not doing so.

---

3   https://en.wikipedia.org/wiki/Michael_Aldrich

Should I have an e-commerce website?

Theoretically, this should be a fairly easy question to answer, but in practice, I've seen it lead to a great degree of confusion amongst some business owners. As an example, one customer I've worked with arrived with a fully-fledged e-commerce website, but they had chosen to disable the pricing and checkout options because they didn't want people to be able to buy straight from the website. Primarily, they were a wholesaler and wanted enquiries from businesses, not the general public. However, they wanted to show their product range and the developer they worked with thought an e-commerce shop with the checkout removed would be the ideal solution. You can see lots of websites like that all over the Internet and whilst it might solve their business problem, what does it feel like from a customer's point of view? And how will Google assess them?

The answer to these questions can be seen when you search for 'wholesale [anything]' on Google. Try it and see how many of the websites that are on the first page are 'dumb' websites that won't let you buy online. However, there is a general expectation – certainly amongst the savvier shoppers – that they should be able to buy online, and no matter what you are selling, they will buy if the option is there. If you are selling products (or some services), you should be asking yourself the question 'Why DON'T I have an e-commerce website?' rather than 'Why should I have one?' Wholesalers and those in the b2b space are the worst offenders in this, as often they think that they don't want to show competitors their prices, that they can sell more if they get a customer on the phone or that they just want to build a personal relationship with everyone they sell to. That's fine; however, it misses the point. Business operates 24/7 and people will be buying at different times of the day. If they can buy their supplies at 2:00am because that's the only time they have to do it, then that's what they will do. And to anyone who thinks that no one in their industry will buy what they are selling online, for whatever reason, I simply refer them to Alibaba.

Alibaba.com is probably the world's largest online retailer, with revenues of US$72bn in 2021 – and it's a wholesaler. Its business model is to wholesale in bulk so if you search on this website and find any of the products that your company sells then you can be sure that your customers will be happy to buy online.

Therefore, the question of whether to have an e-commerce website comes down to whether you are selling something that can be bought as a product. There are millions of different products that lend themselves to this. With some creativity, some services can also be packaged this way. Your starting point is to decide whether what you have can (and should) be bought as a product. If you are selling jewellery or cosmetics, books or CDs, the answer is fairly simple. If you are a tradesperson, however, it's unlikely that you will need an e-commerce website as no two jobs will ever be identical. That's not to say that there's nothing you could sell on an e-commerce website, as if you wanted to create a package price for something you do regularly, then you could sell it online.

Most retailers now have a website of some description and millions of small home-based or small business entrepreneurs have also joined in, meaning there are now estimated to be over 25 million e-commerce websites amongst the 1.2 billion websites globally.

What is the best e-commerce platform?

Decisions on which e-commerce platforms to use can be made for a range of reasons, such as convenience, price, or accessibility. Often, businesses who have e-commerce websites have ended up with what they have because that's the platform that their preferred developer likes to work with. Little consideration is given to whether the platform is suitable for the type of e-commerce, or even

Top In eCommerce Usage Distribution in the Top 1 Million Sites

Technology	Websites	%
WooCommerce Checkout	37,341	3.73
Shopify	27,054	2.71
Magento	10,482	1.05
Shopify Plus	3,839	0.38
Squarespace Add to Cart	3,052	0.31
PrestaShop	2,802	0.28
OpenCart	2,769	0.28
BigCommerce	2,350	0.24
Salesforce Commerce Cloud	1,816	0.18

Figure 90 – E-commerce platforms used for the top one million websites, courtesy of BuiltWith.

whether it is scalable or sustainable. Looking at the most popular e-commerce platforms of the top one million websites globally will give you an insight into which are being used the most by the successful e-commerce companies, but this information won't tell you what is right for you. To make that decision, you need to start with an understanding of what you are trying to achieve and why.

The list in Figure 90 is a summary of the different e-commerce platforms used by the top one million e-commerce sites in the world. It shows the name of the platform, the number of websites in the top one million that run using this system, and what percentage that is of the whole. What becomes immediately apparent is that the most popular platform (WooCommerce, which runs on WordPress) is less than 4% of the global total. What this means is that outside of this top ten, there are so many other different e-commerce platforms available that if I were to list them here, we'd probably fill an entire chapter! This highlights that there is no 'one size fits all' solution and that different platforms can work equally well for business – as long as they are well built and follow the 3 Rules.

The list contains some platforms which may sound familiar, and over the last decade I've worked with businesses on all of these. The biggest decision that most of the businesses have had to make is which type of platform to build on, and in many instances they will have started on one platform before moving to another as they grow. Whilst WooCommerce is the biggest in this list, it's not automatically right for everyone, so the start point needs to be an understanding of the differences between these platforms.

> E-commerce platforms can be categorised into three distinct types:
> **Enterprise solutions**
> **Hosted solutions**
> **Independent solutions**

Let's look a little closer at each of these to understand what they do and what they are good for.

Enterprise Solutions

There's a pretty good chance that the majority of you reading this book will not need an enterprise system. Typically, these are full software systems, often referred to as Enterprise Application Software (EAS), which are used by large global businesses, governments, and major retailers to integrate not only the e-commerce elements of a website but also to provide a portal with a variety of other tools included. Often, these systems will include various databases, including a Customer Relationship Management system (CRM) and other useful additions such as a stock management and inventory system, a pricing and discounting system and integration into a vast array of other systems.

In short, these are massive digital hubs that provide an e-commerce platform as part of a suite of other tools, and unless you are turning over a few million pounds (or dollars), then you probably have no need of this type of system.

Hosted Solutions

A hosted e-commerce solution is one where you do not need to set up your own server. The e-commerce platform chosen will be storing your files and data in the cloud. The e-commerce platform is responsible for ensuring that the platform is online, available, and updated on a regular basis. There are lots of different solutions available in this space and generally, they are known as SaaS solutions (Software as a Service).

Examples of this include Go Daddy, Wix and Ionos, all of whom will allow you to set up an account with them, create your own website using templated designs and get a shop live in as little as a day. They take care of everything you might need including hosting, maintenance, and the provision of a secure payment system included. For many small businesses, this is an affordable and low maintenance option that suits their business.

Independent Solutions

A fully independent solution is one where you are responsible for the hosting environment. Once you have a suitable hosting platform (server), you can build your website using a framework of your choice.

Examples of this include WooCommerce and Magento. Once you have chosen your platform, you typically need to work with a developer to create your own online shop. As well as hosting and backups, you will also be responsible for all ongoing maintenance, the design, look and style of your shop and any

E-Commerce

integration, such as payment systems, a CRM or other software products such as those for inventory management (often referred to as 'middleware').

Each of these solutions have their pros and cons and Figure 91 lists some of them:

	Hosted Solution	**Independent Solution**
Hosting	Included.	You will need to arrange this.
Maintenance & Updates	Included.	You will need to arrange this.
Security	Included.	You will need to arrange this.
Design	Generally provided for you as a template. (customisation and design now often allowed)	You will need to design and build the website. (usually with a developer)
Features	Some are provided by the platform. (usually at extra cost but they are often limited)	Vast numbers of third party solutions means there's usually a solution for whatever you are looking for.
Non-standard features	Generally, you are unable to customise something that doesn't already exist on the platform.	You can usually get someone to build a custom solution that will work.
Pricing	A single monthly payment to keep the shop open.	You only need to pay hosting and maintenance costs.
Ownership	Not owned by you. Copyright for everything you build may remain with the platform.	You own the website and the copyright for everything on it.
Technical SEO	Limited to the features of the platform.	Unlimited.
Transaction fees	Fees typically a percentage of sale – often higher than Independent solutions.	Fees determined by payment system provider – typically lower than hosted systems.
Website speed	Fixed by the platform.	Only dependent on your website and hosting.
Bespoke solutions	If you want something bespoke, a hosted solution is probably not for you.	Fully customisable.
After sales	Dependent on Customer Support.	You are in control.
Limitations	The platform and the tools they provide.	None other than cost – the more you want the more it costs.

Figure 91 – Pros and cons of hosted versus independent e-commerce solutions.

The key difference between these two solutions is the flexibility and ownership. Hosted platforms mean you are locked into their environment and you have to continue to pay them monthly, whether you sell anything or not. I've worked with customers who have found themselves paying monthly subscriptions to a hosted platform, unable to move off the platform as they subsequently find that they don't own anything other than the data. If you've used one of their templates and then wish to move to an independent solution, you will literally have to start from scratch again, as most hosted solutions own the copyright on their designs.

This might sound as if I have a problem with hosted solutions, but nothing could be further from the truth. This type of website is ideal for a small business or home-based start-ups who need a simple way of getting an online shop up and running. It can work extremely well for testing a market to see whether you can generate sales for a new or different product. These platforms have also extended their offerings over the past few years, and some will now allow website development companies to develop websites for customers on their platform, rather than just using the available templates. As a quick and easy way of getting an online shop up and running, they're hard to beat.

Looking again at the chart in Figure 90 we can see that of the top one million websites using an e-commerce solution there are enterprise, hosted and independent solutions. Remember, these are the top one million websites globally, so the amount of money transacted through these will be enormous.

Figure 92 shows the top one million e-commerce websites divided by platform choice.[4] As each of these are in the list of top one million e-commerce websites, this should highlight that no matter which solution you choose, the ability to scale should not be something that holds you back.

Enterprise	Hosted	Independent
Salesforce	Shopify Prestashop Big Commerce Squarespace	WooCommerce Magento OpenCart

Figure 92 – Breakdown of the platform types of the top one million websites.

---

4   statista.com/topics/871/online-shopping/

How do I optimise my e-commerce website?

Once you've decided which platform is best for your business, you then get to do the exciting bit and build your own shop. Whichever solution you opt for, there's nothing as exciting as seeing your dreams come to life in an online shop. I say this from experience, as I run my own small online shop in a tiny niche. Typically, I will turn over no more than a few hundred pounds a year, and I'm fine with that. It covers the hosting costs, I can do my own maintenance, and more importantly, it allows me to experiment with SEO in a shopping environment, which brings me to how you can optimise your e-commerce website for SEO.

A quick look on Google turns up innumerable guides on how to optimise an e-commerce website for search. Worthy though they all are (and do have a look if you want step-by-step guides), they all tend to repeat each other. My views (as you probably gather by now) diverge from the everyday in this respect as I have my own solutions for optimisation.

Having built, worked on, consulted on and optimised many e-commerce websites over the past decade, I can sum up the things that make a difference in simple terms. Unsurprisingly, the biggest hurdle you will have to overcome and the one thing that makes the biggest difference is Rule 1.

It's just a machine

Pretty much all the online guides will tell you that to be successful you need to:
- Perform keyword research
- Create your website architecture based on the research
- Optimise your pages for content and meta data
- Tidy up your technical SEO
- Undertake local SEO if you want visitors
- Create lots of backlinks

Rule 1 — Google is just a machine
Rule 2 — Nothing, but nothing, beats great content
Rule 3 — One page, one keyword or phrase

If you can do all of these, the tills should be ringing and people queuing around the block. Except they aren't and they probably won't. So, what are you missing?

What everyone misses is the fact that Google is just a machine and will never be buying what you are selling. That part is reserved for human beings who need something more than the information required by the machine. Whilst you need to optimise for the machine and help it understand what your website is all about, the prime focus needs to be on the user.

> **CASE STUDY**
>
> Working with a startup e-commerce website in the health sector, we quickly developed a strategy for them that ensured they would appear high in Google searches. They were early to market with a particular treatment, and we needed to ensure that when anyone was searching for this treatment, they found their website.
>
> We started by exploring the questions that a potential patient would research online and then we ensured that the page answered as many of these questions as possible. We helped them scope out the page design to include as much content as any prospective purchaser would need and that Google would need to ensure the page was authoritative.
>
> The results were that the page went from no traffic at all to over 2,000 users a day in under six months. Within a year, organic search was delivering over 80% of their traffic and generating over £500,000 in sales revenue. More importantly, once users were signed up, the company were able to email them about repeat prescriptions and this generated another £1m in sales.
>
> **Takeaway:**
> With e-commerce websites, make sure the landing page has all the content that a customer will need to make their purchase decision. Once you have the customer, remember to keep in touch with them!

As another practical example of focus on the user, consider the Samsung WW10T684DLN washing machine. If you were looking online to research this machine, what would you type in? Would it just be the code 'WW10T684DLN' or would you include the name Samsung? Would you even bother typing 'washing machine'? Google (or any search engine) only needs the code to completely understand what you are looking for (try it and see), but when you get the search result back, what do you expect to see and what do you want to see? The answers depend on your search intent. If you are researching before buying this washing machine, then you might want to see product details, specifications and reviews. If you have already decided that this is the washing machine for you and are looking to buy it, you may be looking for price, availability and delivery. Given these different searches for the same thing, how can you best configure your website to cover all eventualities?

Key to this is to start with the product code. We know Google needs the code to understand your search and we also know that potential buyers, whether researching or price shopping, will also use the code. The code should be in the page title, description, h1 tag and the meta description as a minimum. The other details (such as the brand name and features of this particular model) will be essential for anyone researching, so need to be included prominently in the h1 tag and the description, as well as the meta description if you can. The reason for including them in these areas is because those are the most obvious ones that people will see. Whilst Google doesn't need to know it's a Samsung in order to list it and rank it, people like to see the name as the brand carries weight. Think of all the advertising that Samsung do; it's for moments precisely like this where an unsure buyer is looking for a product and Samsung hope that all the positive brand affirmation they have worked on over the years will sway a buyer towards their product.

Similarly, Google doesn't need to see how many people have reviewed or liked this product in order to rank it, as from a machine point of view, all it knows from a product code search is that you are looking for it. As a buyer, however, you might well be interested in seeing how many people have bought and liked the machine, and you may want to read any reviews they have left – especially bad ones.

Given that different searches will yield different result and different people are looking for different things, how can you create your product pages in such a way as to cover all the bases? Here's my handy six step guide for doing this.

Let's look a little closer at each of these.

> Six Steps to great Product Pages
> 1. Make your products easily found
> 2. Don't just use manufacturers' descriptions
> 3. Create great content on your product pages
> 4. Use product schema
> 5. Tell a story about the product if you can
> 6. Demonstrate expertise where possible

1. Make your products easy to find

As I said earlier, the simplest way to do this is to use the product codes. Machines understand these, people understand that they are a way of differentiating between products, and it's the quickest way of connecting the dots. Whatever you are selling, unless it's a unique item, there should be a product code, a SKU (Stock Keeping Unit) or UPC (Universal Product Code). If you're unsure, try searching online for the thing you are listing on your shop and see what comes up in search. Include the product code in the page title, h1 and meta description as a minimum and make sure it's obvious when placed on the page. You can also include it in product descriptions as well.

2. Improve on manufacturers' descriptions

If you're selling products that you buy in from manufacturers, they will often supply product descriptions to help you. The best examples of this are typically in the white goods and electronics categories, where they supply large amounts of data on every product that they manufacture. Along with the basics such as size, weight, colour and as many features as they can think of, there's usually a narrative description along the lines of 'Product XYZ is the latest in the range from [insert manufacturer here] and is ideal for people with busy lives.' Mostly, it's marketing content, but what most people do is simply copy and paste this into their product description on their website. Whilst this might 'tick a box' in that you have put something in as a product description, it does nothing towards helping you rank in search. What people forget is that this product description is already on the Internet, usually on the product page of the manufacturer's website. Which means that you adding it to your website is, as far as Google is concerned, a copy. As it already knows where the original content is, why would it rank your website above that in a search result? If a dozen retailers all do the same thing, how can any search engine possibly differentiate between the websites and decide who to rank in which order? If you want to differentiate your website from your competitors, by all means use the manufacturer's descriptions, but change them. Add to them, find another angle, and develop something that makes the product more interesting than just the standard narrative. After all, if you were buying that product, would you fall for the allure of the manufacturer's description alone?

3. Create great on-page content

Moving on from the manufacturer's description, if you are changing that then why not consider what else you could add? In reality, the only limit is your imagination. You can add your own description, buyers' reviews, a user test result, an unboxing video, a video showing how to use the product or what it looks like out of the packaging – the list is endless. Today, more and more buyers expect rich content to help in their buying process and this is evidenced by the proliferation of short product videos you see daily on social media. These all try to convince you to buy a product in the first ten or fifteen seconds, and in many cases, they are hugely successful. But these short videos are only part of the story. Some of the more developed online retailers now create their own videos about each product that can be up to ten minutes long. The key thing is that if people have been lured to your page because they are interested in the product, showing them an extended video is perfectly fine. Don't think that they will be put off by longer videos. Google's own research on YouTube shows that people are more than happy to consume longer videos if they already have an interest in the subject.

The other benefit of this is that it ticks every box in my 3 Rules. It gives more data for the machine to help rank your website, it develops great content which users like, and as it's only about a single product, it's focused.

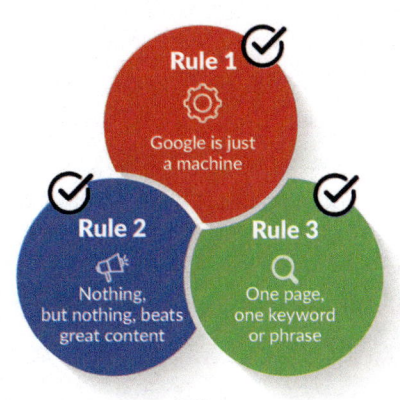

Rule 1
Google is just a machine

Rule 2
Nothing, but nothing, beats great content

Rule 3
One page, one keyword or phrase

4. Use product schema for every product

We've covered schema earlier in the book – if you recall, schema, in the context of SEO, is simply a way of organising information so that a machine (in this case, Google) can make sense of it. If you need a refresher, take a look back to Chapter 3. In e-commerce, it's essential, and there are lots of different schemas you can use, depending on the products or services you sell. Google lists a range of different schemas it feels are relevant to e-commerce, though this list is not comprehensive.[5]

On its developer's website, it features:

- Local Business
- Product
- Review
- How To
- FAQ Page
- Breadcrumbs
- Website
- Video Object

On top of this you can also use:

- Item list
- Person
- Organisation
- Sitelinks
- Q&A

Remember, this isn't a comprehensive list – for that, you should visit schema.org, where you will find every type of schema for every type of business.

I'm often asked which is better and I'm afraid there is no straight answer to that question. It depends on the type of website you are running and what you are selling. You can try experimenting with different types of schemas, but if you find you are still confused, as always, consult a professional SEO firm who will be able to point you in the right direction.

5. Product stories sell

Have you ever wondered why TV shopping channels are so successful? Why the products they sell appear to go for prices in excess of those at which you might consider paying for the product? It's because people love buying into stories. The presenters are well versed in understanding how to tell a story and how to convince people that they simply cannot live without this product in their lives.

This also works in print, as demonstrated by a friend of mine who runs a very small e-commerce website for men's clothing. One of the products he sells is

---

5   https://developers.google.com/search/docs/advanced/ecommerce/include-structured-data-relevant-to-ecommerce

something he buys from a niche manufacturer, and he only sells it because it's something he uses. It's a particular piece of clothing that has been adapted beyond its everyday use and is ideal for people who are outdoors a lot. The problem he has is that he cannot keep up with demand; he sells out almost as soon as he gets stock in. Moreover, when you search on Google for this item, he's usually top. Why? Because on the product page, along with not using the standard manufacturer's description (pretty dull, when all it says is what it's made of, how many buttons it has and how to wash it), he tells a story. The story he tells is how he found this product, how he uses it and how it changed his entire outdoor experience. Unsurprisingly, this works, as not only does the machine find it interesting and is therefore a great reason to rank him highly, but it also ticks the boxes for customers who can relate to his story and can visualise this product helping them in a similar way. I'd love to be able to tell you more about the product, but I had to promise I wouldn't. He's still number one today and it's his best-selling and most profitable line. Product stories sell and if you make your stories compelling and relatable, yours will too.

6. The importance of EAT

Finally, we covered EAT in Chapter 3 and explained how Expertise, Authoritativeness and Trustworthiness are critical ranking factors for any website in the YMYL (Your Money Your Life) space. Nowhere is this more evident than on e-commerce websites. I've worked with a number of these websites, including some that have been hit by Google algorithm changes, and I can tell you that proving your expertise is vital in e-commerce.

Initially, the machine will want to see these cues in your content, but ultimately, it's for your users. Users want to know why they should trust you, why you are an expert in this field and what credentials give you your authority. As an example, if you were looking to buy medicines online, what sort of website would you trust? Would you trust one that shouts loudly about the product, makes wonderful claims about its efficacy, and pushes you to 'buy now', or would you prefer one that lists the product, its benefits, describes what it will do, lists any side effects and even tells you when you shouldn't be buying and taking it? Would you be further assured if you could see the name and photograph of a registered and licensed dispensing chemist alongside the information, and clear and easy ways to contact the company if you have any queries? Oddly, these same qualities of reassurance that we prefer as humans are exactly what Google builds into the algorithm, so websites tend to rank better if they have all these boxes ticked.

We've all heard stories of people getting scammed online; it seems to happen on a daily basis. Google and all the other search engines know this, and they work hard to make sure that 'dodgy' websites are not pushed to the top of their search results. How do they spot a dodgy website? Well, most are thrown up quickly, have thin content and use black hat techniques to try and help them rank. They are purposely designed to be 'burner' websites. Search engines can see through this.

To make sure your website is seen as one that should be included in the search results, particularly one that should be ranking high up, make sure you take time to develop great content and tick the boxes that you know they are looking for.

Should I use Google Shopping?

You will have noticed that to this point, I've made very little mention of paid advertising, other than to acknowledge its existence. On Google, it's in evidence at the top and bottom of most 'transactional' search results. Once you know they are there, it's quite easy to ignore them. But understand that most people don't ignore them. In fact, a huge number of people find them useful and click on them when they appear – and this is highly lucrative for Google. In its 2021 financial year, over 80% of all Google's revenue was reported to have come from advertising revenue. That's over US$200 billion, and whichever way you look at it, that's a lot of money. Google's suite of advertising options now includes search, display, video, app, shopping and local ads, all of which deliver revenues for the company. Of these, the one most associated with e-commerce stores is Google Shopping and it's worth digging a little deeper into what this is and how it works.

Currently, the best description is one provided by HubSpot, who also provide a handy guide to Google Shopping.[6] They describe Google Shopping as:

"a Google service that allows consumers to search for, compare, and shop for physical products across different retailers who have paid to advertise their

---

[6] https://blog.hubspot.com/marketing/google-shopping

products. This is also known as a Comparison Shopping Engine (CSE). Google Shopping results show up as thumbnail images that display each product's retailer and price."

> Types of Google Advertising
>
> **Search** – the standard text advertisement that appears at the top of many searches
>
> **Display** – image advertisements that appear on websites other than Google
>
> **Video** – video advertisements designed specifically to appear on YouTube
>
> **App** – Pulls information from your app to automatically show ads (to a relevant audience) across Search, Play, YouTube, Discover and other websites and apps
>
> **Local** – help promote local traffic to shops and venues
>
> **Shopping** – product listings that appear specifically when Google thinks you are looking to buy something, and also appear on the Google shopping tab

If you've ever bought anything online, the chances are you will have seen (or perhaps used) Google Shopping, even if you didn't know what it was. To reprise my much earlier example of 'ladies red stiletto shoes'[7] (honestly, I'm not obsessed with these!) this is how shopping looks for that search term today (Figure 93).

Figure 93 – Google Shopping result for "ladies red stiletto shoes".

---

7 To be grammatically correct, this should really say ladies' with an apostrophe, but Google users typically search without using the correct apostrophe, or indeed any other punctuation!

You can see that there are five different options immediately available, though this will expand to more if you click on the arrows on the right hand side of the advertising box. Advertisers can pay to be in these boxes, and the more they bid, the higher they come in the list, with the top five shown being the highest bidders for the term 'ladies red stiletto shoes'. The good news is that even if you appear in this list, you can still also pay to advertise in the normal text only 'search advertisements' (referred to as PPC - Pay Per Click) and you could also appear in the organic listings, which is what we've been talking about in this book, so if you are lucky (and can afford it) you can have two paid and one organic entries on the same page. All of these entries will give you a much greater opportunity to get a click, and therefore a customer. However, consumer research shows that advertisements with a picture can generate up to a 30% higher conversion rate than text only advertisements.[8] You can quite clearly see why from the example in Figure 93. If you were looking for ladies red stiletto shoes, you can see at a glance not only the colour, style, and brand, but also the price. Why, with this much rich information available, would you look anywhere else? This is, of course, a rhetorical question as every day, millions of people searching online simply ignore these ads and click on text ads, videos and normal organic listings. Not everyone is swayed by a pretty picture.

What Shopping does, however, is reinforce Rule 2, which is that nothing, but nothing, beats great content (in this case, visuals, pricing information and star ratings). The better the content, the richer the content, the more likely people are to respond to it. This is why, with e-commerce, I typically recommend using Google Shopping ads, even in a limited form.

Google tries its best to make it easy to set up Shopping Ads, but even so you will need to create a campaign on Google Ads and send all your products through Google Merchant Centre, for which you need a separate log in. Despite this, the ability to list your products right next to major competitors makes it a useful tool in the marketing armoury. The best part is that if you are clever about your bidding strategies, you can get a lot of 'free' publicity, as it costs nothing to be on Google Shopping, you simply pay when someone clicks on one of your advertisements. In Figure 93, it has cost Jimmy Choo nothing to appear, but everyone who searches for 'ladies red stiletto shoes' will see their name. Free publicity and an image for their red stiletto shoes – what's not to like?

---

8   https://www.marketingcharts.com/digital/paid-search-79142

"Retail is detail."

James Gulliver

There are plenty of online resources covering how to set up and run your Google Shopping Ads campaign and more resources about how to set a 'minimum bid' (the lowest amount you are willing to pay Google if someone clicks on your advertisement for that product) on Google Shopping, so I don't intend to cover them here. What I will say though, is that if you intend to spend money on Shopping Ads, read up as much as you can before you embark on this journey.

You may be able to manage Google shopping yourself, and if you are comfortable doing so, you may also be able to set up the feeds and create the Ad Groups yourself. But be aware, you can lose huge amounts of money if you don't control your spend on paid advertising. I often hear people who specialise in paid advertising refer to 'turning the taps on' (and this includes Google staff who support PPC advertisers) but they often ignore the fact that this is someone's hard earned cash they're talking about. The principle is that if you throw enough money at the paid advertising platform, you can find out what works and what doesn't. From this, you should be able to refine your campaigns and dial down the unprofitable areas, focusing your cash on where you are getting the best return.

This sounds perfect but is fundamentally flawed. It is built on the assumption that you can make a profit in the first place, and I've worked with a number of businesses who, for whatever reason, simply couldn't make it pay. The more they spent, the more they lost, so today, I caution anyone thinking of using Google paid advertising to seek professional advice. A professional Google Ads-qualified individual should be able to help you set up and run your campaign, and if you ask them nicely, most of them will help you become self-sufficient.

The bottom line is that when your e-commerce website becomes sufficiently developed and you have enough products (and stock) available, it makes sense to advertise. Google ads are the easiest and most obvious way to align your stock lists with people's searches, and as long as you are sufficiently rigorous in checking your spend and profitability, it's a great way to make additional sales. Remember, however, that as with all paid advertising, the moment you turn it off, the sales stop. This is part of the reason I prefer organic search, as once you have optimised a page or a product, it typically ranks for a specific keyword or search phrase for some considerable time. It works 24/7 and doesn't take a holiday, and unlike paid advertising, it also doesn't cost you every time someone clicks on a product. So, paid advertising has a place but if you can, you should aim to build it on top of a well optimised store which is already getting good, strong organic traffic.

Takeaways:

e-commerce websites continue to grow as more people become familiar with online shopping.

Making it easy to buy is essential for any e-commerce website.

Rules 2 and 3 are particularly applicable to e-commerce; write great content for each page and make sure it is unique to that page or product.

CHAPTER 6

How To Build a Better Website

So far in this book, we've spent a lot of time talking about how to make changes to your website to better optimise it for Google and the other search engines, but what if you didn't need to make all those changes? What if it was fully optimised from the start? If that sounds appealing, then how about building a new website? Starting again gives you a chance to overhaul the optimisation on your website and to begin afresh, leaving behind some of the issues and errors that might be dogging your current website's performance. You could even be in the lucky position of only just starting to build your website, so you can take all these factors on board from the start.

It is estimated that a new website is created somewhere in the world every three seconds, which means over a quarter of a million new sites are launched every day.[1] Of these, the majority simply won't be properly optimised when launched, not because they can't be, but because the developers don't know how to do this. At this point, I should stress that is not a criticism of website developers, merely an observation that in my experience, many developers have little or no idea about how SEO works. Despite appearances, I have nothing but respect for

---
1 https://siteefy.com/how-many-websites-are-there

people who build websites as they are generally very good at their job. However, they have had limited exposure to the world of SEO. Like asking a car painter and sprayer to service your car, they may know a lot about cars but very little about the bit you are asking them to work on.

Google and the other search engines are faced with something of a dilemma. They know that there are over a billion websites they can crawl and index, but with so many different types of websites, frameworks and styles, how can they make sense of what is out there? Fortunately, what they have all developed is a system that enables search engines to crawl, read and understand the html code, and from that they try to decipher what might be useful to a user. But this system has its limitations. If the crawlers can't make sense of the code they encounter, if the structure is configured oddly or the writing is indecipherable, then they simply can't do anything with what they have found. This is where search engine optimisation really comes into its own. Because it is more often abbreviated to SEO, people tend to forget the true meaning of the words; search engine optimisation – optimising for search engines. It's our job to help make their job easier, because if we can make their job easier, they will be able to use what they find on our websites to help their users – and everybody wins! With this in mind, wouldn't it just make sense to optimise a brand new website as you build it, so that it's perfect out of the box and search engines can understand it?

Building a fully optimised website isn't as hard as it might seem; all you need to do is follow a few simple rules and work closely with the person building your website. To do that, however, you need a coherent framework. To make things easy for you, here's my framework for success.

Things to consider before you create your own website

There are thousands of articles online with advice on what you need to consider when building a website, but pretty much all of them focus on the same things – making it look shiny and accessible for users. If they do mention the bits that are important to search engines, then it's more often in passing rather than as a specific item on which you should focus. However, unless the search engines can understand your website, they can't show it to people. If they don't show it to people, then it doesn't matter how lovely it looks, how much you've spent on user experience items or how easy it is for them to navigate, it's a good looking white elephant.

With this in mind, you need to start with the aim of making it Google friendly as well as user friendly, and to do that, you need a developer who understands how SEO works. If you can't find one of those, then go with a really good developer and use the following as your framework for helping them understand what you want built.

Top 5 considerations for creating your own website

1. Purpose

At the heart of any website is what you want it to do. Are you simply going to publish information, such as a blog or an online resource for people to access, or are you looking for people to interact with your site? Is it a resource for a community group or a shop that is looking for customers? Whatever it is, that's the purpose and you should stick to it. A manager I used to work with once intoned: "The main thing is to keep the main thing the main thing." From this, you can determine objectives – what you expect the site to do once it's live.

2. Audience

Who will be using your website? Here's a clue – it's not 'everyone'. You cannot build a website that will appeal to 'everyone', or at least not on the budget you have. You are not at the stage where you need to build a multi-layered, multi-faceted, multi-lingual website that will be accessed by millions daily. When you are in charge of the website build for the BBC or Wikipedia, then perhaps the answer is 'everyone', but not now. Think carefully about why someone would find your website useful. If your website is solely about Ferrari cars of the 1960s, then that's a very niche audience. Consider what characteristics they are likely to have and what binds them together, then build something that fits.

3. Technical Considerations

This includes which platform you are going to use to build your website (WordPress, Wix, GoDaddy, Magento, etc.), how easy it is going to be to configure from an SEO perspective and how easy it will be to make changes once it is live. More importantly, these days the biggest considerations are that the website works well when viewed on a mobile device (mobile friendly) and that it is quick. Website speed is one of the things Google is currently trying to drive by actively pushing faster websites higher up the search rankings. Your new website should be built as if it will only ever be viewed on a mobile phone, and it needs to load in under half a second.

4. Content

If you are still in any doubt about content at this point, go back and read the earlier chapters. Your entire website is about content and getting the right content in the right structure. Then ensuring search engines can crawl and understand it is a primary purpose of building a new website. Moreover, without content, your developer is designing something when they have no ideas what the final look will be. If they design a page with a box for a paragraph of text and you then supply 5,000 words, it's going to look a mess. In fact, they will probably have to redesign the entire page again.

5. Maintenance

This is the part people forget, namely who is going to maintain it after it is built? You need to have the answer to this firmly in your mind before you start the process of building a website. As an example, if the answer is that you are responsible for maintenance, and someone is going to hard code your website in html, then unless you know how to make changes (without breaking the website) and are familiar with ftp (File Transfer Protocol – the way computers talk to each other on the Internet), then you are going to struggle. Don't make life difficult for yourself just to save a few pounds (or dollars) at the start. Spend decent money and get a good job.

How to work closely with your developer

Over the years, I've been on both sides on this equation. I've paid to have my own websites built and I've worked with developers who have built websites for our customers. In each case, I can honestly say that I've walked away at the end having learned something. Every website build is different, and whilst the process may be similar, the issues that arise can vary considerably. Out of all this experience though, and after talking to the developers I know, their view is very much that many of the issues that arise are entirely avoidable. For what it's worth, I agree. People who engage developers to build websites sometimes expect miracles and forget that any website developer is just like you – human. They are entirely fallible, as are you. They need to sleep occasionally, as do you. More importantly, unless you possess some kind of superpowers that you've never disclosed, developers, like you, are not mind readers. Which brings me to the top five things that developers need to get the job done properly, and on time.

Top 5 tips for working with a developer

1. Communication

At the very top of the list for any developer I speak to is communication. Developers are not psychic. They don't inherently understand your business, even if they have built a similar website before, nor can they second guess your business plans. On that basis, understanding what you want is not part of their mindset; you will need to specify it. Keeping communication channels open is critical to the success of any project. Many of the developers I know will want to use a communications and project management tool such as Trello or Basecamp, rather than emails, to keep everything in one place. These tools are designed to capture every comment and all communications and to record decisions and prevent things being lost on email. Developers generally use these tools, but they sometimes forget that you don't. They fail to understand that you may be unfamiliar with how these software programmes work, and though it makes their life easier, it simply gives you another job. At the start, agree how you are going to communicate with each other and stick to it. It's better to find some common ground before you start rather than halfway through, as making things fit retrospectively is never as good as getting it right from the start. It needn't be a conflict, but it's better to disagree before you start than to try and amend things as you progress. I know it might seem that I am labouring this point, but breakdown in communications is one of the top reasons that developers and customers fall out. We've picked up what we consider to be simple website build projects from customers who have spent a year arguing with a developer and getting nowhere. The reason? They didn't communicate properly at the start and set off without agreeing who was doing what, when and why.

And finally, on the subject of communication, never ghost your developer. If something is not right, tell them. Picking up the phone is generally the best way to get a solution as you can explain what you are unhappy with and give them the chance to ask questions, understand your issue and propose a solution. Email exchanges are prone to misunderstanding and often end with using lawyers to sort the problem out! Typically, if it gets to this stage, it eventually results in mediation which, oddly enough, relies on both parties talking to each other. You find yourself back at the start of the problem but several thousand pounds lighter in the process. Communication really is the key to everything.

2. Guidance on design and framework

A developer's job should be to help you design and build your new website. It's their job to inspire you, but it helps if you tell them what you like or don't like. Often, they will start this process by asking you to point to any websites that inspire or annoy you and explain what it is that you like or dislike on them. This helps to narrow down the design ideas and to start to create something that you are comfortable with. The problem you will have is that if you are not a designer or developer, you may have no idea what is good or bad, nor even where to start. A developer, however, is in a similar position, despite their skill and expertise in this area. They simply cannot read your mind or visualise things the way you do without communication. Remember, whilst the people building websites can often do everything, designing and developing are two entirely different skillsets.

To help your developer, think about websites that you regularly visit. These might be websites that you have used to buy products, read blogs, or even read online newspapers. It could be a website where you are on their mailing list, or a website that has recently changed from something you like to something new that you find difficult to navigate. Whatever you are seeing on whatever websites you visit, there will be bits you like. It might be the colour scheme, the buttons, the simple checkout, or anything else. It could be the fact that there's a nice video or that it's easy to find what you want through their search functionality. Whatever it is, let your developer know. Every piece of additional information you give them can help to narrow down the specification for your website design. Often, people say that they want something like their competitor's website. This isn't ideal. Try not to use your competitors' sites as a reference point as you may inadvertently end up copying what they have or creating something similar. If you really want to stand out and to leap above them in design terms, use other companies' websites as the benchmark. You may not be able to have the same website as Apple but that doesn't stop you admiring and aspiring to some of their design elements.

Specifying what you want on your website is critical, and to that end there is a simple checklist for you in the Appendix at the back of this book. It includes a list of the things you need to think about before you talk to a developer: like who is the target audience, what the website needs to do, and smaller but important things, such as who is supplying the images and content. Developers need clarity. They are not, as I have said, mind readers. As an example, if you are developing an e-commerce website, the developer will need to know how many products you plan to sell, both now and in the future. Selling 10 products is a fundamentally different proposition to selling 20,000 products and the solution they will propose to you will be wildly different. On that basis, don't try and buy on price, buy what you *need* for now and in the future as your developer will be recommending the correct software solution for your ambitions. Whilst it might be more expensive to buy the better product, if your business is going to grow, then it will be cheaper than trying to retro fit your website with the functionality you later need.

3. Produce the Content

When a developer builds a website, they typically include space on the page for the content. The box they include will often be filled with placeholder text or dummy copy. This copy is referred to as Lorem Ipsum, which is the standard dummy text used by the printers and typesetters since the 1500s. The standard text starts "Lorem ipsum dolor sit amet, consectetur adipiscing elit..." and a quick search of Google for an exact match of this phrase shows that there are over 27 million examples it can find. This is often because people set websites live with the dummy text still included and Google finds and indexes it. If you build in WordPress, for example, their standard blog comes complete with Lorem Ipsum included. You may wonder why on earth people would launch a website with this still included. Sometimes, it's simply a case of a random page being overlooked, but often it is because the copy needed simply hasn't been written yet.

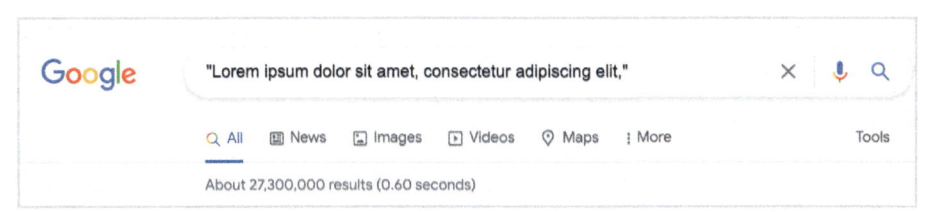

Figure 94 – Google search results for 'lorem ipsum'.

The problem with content is that your developer is highly unlikely to be able to write it for you. They won't know enough about your business, and frankly, it's not their skill set. Some, a rare few, are fully capable of doing this for you but most simply won't or can't write your copy. More importantly, it's up to you to give them the content they need to help with the design of the page. As an example, if they create a wonderful looking page but the area for the copy is just 200 words, when you supply 1,500 words of copy, they have to break apart their design to try and make everything fit. Aesthetically, this is unlikely to be pleasing, so most developers we work with prefer to have the content in advance of the design, so they can truly understand what you are trying to say and design something to better showcase your business.

4. Pay your developer

This might sound obvious, but developers are people too. They are often sole traders and rely on businesses like yours to keep their business afloat. Cashflow for them is often the difference between putting a meal on the table for their family or not, so always pay them for the work they do. Most developers will ask for some money upfront, and whilst the amount may vary, between 25% and 50% appears to be standard. If you want them to meet the deadlines, most that I know will be happy if you agree to stage payments after that, based on delivery of each aspect of the build. Even easier is to pay them a further 25% once the site is ready, but not live, and then the balance on going live.

Most developers, if they are honest with you, will tell you that they have unfinished website projects on their books. These are jobs which started well but have stalled (often through lack of content) and are awaiting the client to do something to clear the logjam. These become a burden on the developer as they have done most or all of the work they were engaged to do, but they still haven't been fully paid for the job. Unfinished jobs become a waste of everyone's time and money and, more often than not, the client is (in the developer's eyes) responsible for the project stalling. To ensure this doesn't happen, the next point is vital.

5. Stick to a schedule

Meet your deadlines and make sure developers meet theirs. Overruns are standard on website build projects, but they shouldn't be. At the start, agree a schedule with the developer and make sure you meet your part of it. Deliver your content on time. If you are supplying images, get them done sooner rather than later. Have regular catch ups with the developer (see Communication) and make sure you are both working towards the same goals.

Understand what happens once the website is live

In essence, websites are a collection of interlinked moving parts, much like a car engine. Like a car, they will need ongoing servicing and maintenance. Before you get to this point you will have needed to decide on who is going to host your website, and where. On top of this, you need to know who is going to make any updates to the website. Finally, you need to be clear on what happens if the website breaks (or is broken by, for example, a hacker), where the backups are stored and who is going to clean up or restore the website.

Most developers offer an ongoing maintenance contract, and frankly, unless you are entirely happy doing all of these things yourself, then this will be money well spent. Make sure you are clear on what you are paying for and how much it will cost. The things worth paying for are:

- Updates to any plug-ins, themes, and framework versions. (Typically needed on WordPress.)

- Ongoing server maintenance needed. (Removing redundant backups, updating php versions, etc.)

- Making changes and design tweaks.

- Repairing elements that occasionally break. (Some older websites may have been built on a software version that is no longer supported.)

- Ensuring your website is secure from hackers and spam bots.

- Making sure you have a full website backup available at any time to restore the site if the unthinkable happens.

- Stepping in to help if disaster strikes, such as a website hack. (The more important your website, the more you should pay for this – including 24-hour response.)

- Developer's time to check these things and make the changes if necessary.

In essence, you are buying insurance, except in this case you will be making a claim every month. Every month, there is something needed to keep a website up to date and a good developer will be able to help you with this.

As you can see, there's no real secret to working well with a website developer and most of what I've written should just be common sense. In practice, however, it can be hard to remember some of these seemingly simple guidelines. The essence is to remember that developers are people too. Like you, they have hopes, fears, desires and worries, but also like you, they want to deliver a good website. If they build a great website for you, on time and on budget, they know that you are likely to recommend them to other people, and from that, their work flows in. Do a bad job and they know that they are unlikely to get a future referral from you or anyone you know. The irony in the fact that website builds go wrong is that no one sets out to build a bad website or to enter into an unsuccessful project. I don't know a single developer who has ever taken on a job they want to deliberately mess up. As with so many things in life, trust and communication play a vital part in helping everyone deliver the right result.

Fifteen things people get wrong on new websites

When you build a new website it's probably worth starting with the understanding that there are things your developer will get wrong and there are things that you will get wrong. Some of these will be down to a lack of knowledge or experience and some will be down to unrealistic ambition or expectation. Whatever the reason, understand that mistakes will be made. The purpose of this part is to help guide you through the bits that, in my experience, developers get wrong more often than not. If you know this in advance, you can create your own checklist, with specifications of what you expect as a minimum delivery. If you do this at the start, developers may well price for this and charge you more, but trust me, it's cheaper to pay for this upfront than to spend hours, days or weeks afterwards trying to patch up a poorly delivered job.

I've grouped these together as a list of the top fifteen things I regularly see wrong with brand new websites. It's not a definitive list; these are just the most common mistakes I've observed over the past decade. These are also not in order or importance nor frequency, but simply a logical list that you can check off as you go through a project. Get your developer to confirm they have done each of these steps before you sign off your website.

1. Page titles missing – The importance of these was covered in Chapter 3, yet far too many websites are set live with the page titles missing. If a developer is building your first website, there's nothing to copy across so you will need to supply these. If you already have an existing optimised website, then you may wish them to copy them across. If you do, this must be specified upfront otherwise, like providing content, the developer is unlikely to want to do this for you.

2. Header tags are used for styling – As seen in Chapter 3, any developer using a pre-built theme will be working with pre-built header tags and often, these are used out of sequence. Because it looks aesthetically better, they might use an h5 header tag where they should use an h1 header tag and your job is to make sure that doesn't happen.

3. Missing meta descriptions – Again, these are the two lines that sell what is on your webpage to anyone finding you in a search result. They need thought and consideration, and every page needs to be unique. Developers, if asked to populate them, will often simply copy and paste the same meta description onto every page to 'tick the box' and say they have completed the meta descriptions.

4. On-page copy – As already covered, every page needs content. Under no circumstances go live with Lorem Ipsum anywhere on your site. Make sure the text is clear and legible, especially on a mobile, and it's always worth using a free online plagiarism checker to make sure that everything you have written is unique. Never copy anyone else's content, no matter how good it might be, as search engines know where the original is.

5. Clear targets on each page – Back to Rule 3, 'one page, one keyword or phrase'. Make sure that every page is clear, has a purpose and fulfils that purpose before going live.

6. Image Alt Tags and original images – Every image must have an image alt tag, for the reasons covered in Chapter 3. Moreover, you must ensure that you own or have the rights to use every image on your website. Good developers will purchase them for you from reputable sources but check and get this in writing if it's part of the build agreement. Never, under any circumstances, use an image lifted from another website on the Internet. At best, you are stealing someone's copyright, and at worst, you will get a long legal letter and a demand for money from which you cannot escape. Firms who own image rights, like Getty Images, trawl the Internet daily for copies of their images and when they find them, they simply send an invoice which, in many cases, will be far more than buying 100 similar images in the first place.

7. Internal interlinking – Links between pages on your website are almost certain to be lost when you build a new website. Internal linking is essential to Google's understanding of your website. If this is the first website you are building or if it's a new site for a different project, then no internal linking will exist. In this case, it's not a problem, you can work on them once the site is live. If, however, this is a replacement website, then internal linking is likely to be lost. Most developers use tools to scrape existing websites and copy content across, but all of them will simply strip out any internal links. These links are often a key reason Google likes a page and ranks it well, so you need to ensure that they are all rebuilt before the new website goes live. Lost internal links can destroy a website's ranking overnight so pay close attention to these, as your developer definitely won't.

8. Map existing pages to their new location – When you move house, you can tell your postal delivery provider (Royal Mail, UPS, etc.) that you have moved and to redirect all your mail to your new home. This is exactly the same with urls. Every one of them on your existing website needs to find a new home on the website. If it's a page you are dropping – for example, a service you no longer provide – you need to redirect that page to the nearest possible relevant page and put the instruction in the htaccess file (your developer will know how to do this). So, if you are a builder and offer roofing services on your current website but not on the new website, then redirect the old roofing page to the new building page so users aren't left with a 404 error (no page found).

9. Check for 404 errors – Far too many new websites have 404 errors, where the Google crawler is expecting to find a page, but nothing is there. Often, this is because the redirection notice is missing, but sometimes these can be introduced by a poor website build. Google Search Console will tell you if it's encountering 404 errors on your new site or there are specialist tools such as Screaming Frog[2] that can help you spot them early.

10. Load speed – Check the load speed of your new website and make sure it meets Google's latest benchmarks as a minimum. There are plenty of free tools out there that can do this, including Google's Lighthouse[3] and GTMetrix[4] to name two. Slow load speeds kill websites and the issues that cause it are easier to solve at development stage than after the site is live.

---

2   https://www.screamingfrog.co.uk/seo-spider/
3   https://developers.google.com/web/tools/lighthouse
4   https://gtmetrix.com/

11. Include an XML sitemap – An XML sitemap is there to let Google know where all your new pages are and what your website structure is. Without it, the search engines may still crawl your website, but with it in place it's like giving them a map before they set out.

12. Your website works well on a mobile device – Mobile first indexing was addressed in Chapter 3 and this is where that advice comes into practice. Make sure that the design and build of your website is mobile first. Developers will always show you your new website on a desktop or laptop and that's fine, but when they send me the link to view it, I always open it on my phone first. Checking their work on your phone might seem like much harder work (and looks less impressive) but remember that this is how most of your customers will see your website. Some may never see the desktop version, so the mobile experience needs to be right.

13. Ensure the correct tracking codes are included – Google and Bing webmaster tools and Google Analytics all rely on a small snippet of code being inserted in the header of your website before they can track and report on your site. Developers almost always forget to copy this across. You will know if the developer has not taken this step as both Analytics and Search Console traffic will drop to zero and your graphs will look as if they are flat lining. Similarly, if you are using other tools such as Hotjar[5] or Microsoft Clarity,[6] then that code will also need to be moved.

14. Make sure your social media links work – Most websites have links to the various social media platforms. When your new website is ready to go live, click on them and make sure they take you to where you would expect them to go.

15. Make sure the website is NOT blocked! – Astonishingly, over the years I've seen too many websites where the developer has set it live without removing the search engine 'block'. This is usually a simple plug-in or button that is put in place to prevent search engines crawling and indexing an unfinished website and sending visitors to a site which is still a work in progress. This is the final check, so make sure your developer remembers it!

---

5   https://www.hotjar.com/
6   https://clarity.microsoft.com/

Conclusion

Building a well-optimised website isn't that hard, it just takes a little thought, planning and the ability to work collaboratively with your developer. If you can do this, then you have all the tools you need within this book to be able to develop a well optimised, customer friendly website that works for you and your customers.

> **Takeaways:**
> Time spent planning is never wasted.
> Think about your website from the viewpoint of your customers.
> Close working with your developer pays dividends.

What is your website worth?

Have you ever stopped to consider if your website is actually worth anything? I don't mean to you but to, perhaps, another business owner? If you are a tradesperson and you are getting a steady flow of enquiries to your website, have you thought what it might be worth to someone else? As an example, if you were looking to retire, would you plan to simply stop taking new work and turn off your website, or would you consider that someone else might want it?

The truth is that most websites have value and that value can vary enormously depending on a range of factors. Let me outline some of the ways your website could be worth money.

What is the value of a domain name?

How much is your domain name worth? Is it the £1 you paid for it in the first place, or perhaps the £10-£15 it costs you every year to renew it? Or is it more than that? Currently the highest amount that has ever been paid for a domain name is

US$49.7 million and that was for carinsurance.com, but that is scheduled to be eclipsed by the sale of lasvagas.com, which is reputed to be worth US$90 million. This is, of course, an eye watering amount of money and there are reasons why these domains have sold for so much. Your domain name probably isn't worth as much as these but knowing what makes a domain name valuable might help you if (or when) you want to sell.

Domain names that are short or memorable are always preferred to longer or more complicated names. Just looking at the list of most valuable domains on Wikipedia[7] will give you an idea of the sort of domain that attracts the big money. It's also no coincidence that all of these are .com extensions as these were the original domain names, and .com was short for commercial, meaning that people understand that it's for business.

Key to any valuation is actually owning your domain name. If you've bought it through a domain name reseller such as 123Reg or GoDaddy, then you will have your own log in to a client area where you will have to store your credit card details for future renewals. If you pay for your domain this way, you own it. If, however, the domain name is through a third party who then re-invoices it to you, the ownership usually sits with them, not you. Currently in my business, we renew domain names for several customers, but I make it clear to them that if they want to move them and take ownership at any time, we are happy to help. But not all businesses are the same. If you talk to lawyers who specialise in buying and selling businesses, they will tell horror stories of business sales held up because the business owner didn't own the domain name. In some cases, when the firm that owns it on their behalf hears about the sale, they suddenly decide that it's worth a lot more money and they ask the business owner to buy back their own domain name at a ridiculous price. Of course, this is extortion, but it happens anyway. The moral of the tale is that you should ensure that you own your domain name (or names) outright.

You may not realise, but there is also a healthy resale market for previously owned domain names. These 'dropped' domains are snapped up by companies who then remarket them, selling them on to people who want them. You sometimes see this when you follow a link to a website that has disappeared and the page that you land on has links to other websites, or just a note saying the domain

---

7   https://en.wikipedia.org/wiki/List_of_most_expensive_domain_names

is for sale. And it is big business. Some companies even go as far as recreating them as website packages and selling them as an ongoing concern. Prices for these can range from US$5,000-$40,000, and even more in exceptional cases.

How are domains valued?

The firms that buy dropped or expired domains look at a range of factors which include:
- How many backlinks the domain has.
- How many other domains link to them.
- Domain Rank.
- Year the domain was first registered.
- Number of times archive.org has taken a snapshot.

This list is not comprehensive but does give you an idea of the complexity of this market. As a rough and ready guide, however, the older the domain, the shorter the name, and the more traffic and backlinks it has had pointing to it, the more chance it will be worth money.

Now, that might not describe your website domain name, especially if you run a small local business, so in what other way might your domain be valuable?

Valuing local business websites

Does your website get traffic?

If it does, then that has some value. Buying your domain name and adding it to mine might help increase the amount of traffic that comes to my website, particularly if your website is in the same or a similar business to mine. It's even better if the traffic that you get is for an area of business that I don't currently offer but want to in the future. On this basis, a local roofing company buying a local guttering company website makes sense, if they want to offer guttering services. Once bought, they can decide whether to keep the website separate and treat it as a separate business, or to merge the pages into an existing website so the traffic comes into one place.

How many backlinks do you have?

Backlinks, as we saw earlier, are the currency of the Internet and the more high-quality links you have, the more it helps your website to rank in search. If you have managed to acquire some valuable links whilst your website has been live, those links are definitely something that an acquirer would want. Remember, quality trumps quantity, so sites with the better link profiles go for more money than those with just volume.

Do you have advertising on your website and does it make money?

Quite a number of websites are set up purely to provide affiliate traffic to other sites, such as Amazon and eBay, and in so doing they are being paid for each person that clicks through on one of the links. Other websites are set up as information hubs, but they contain a range of advertising in the forms of banners and pop-ups. A good example of this is recipe websites, most of which, whilst containing great recipe ideas, have links to places you can buy the ingredients and display advertising for kitchen and cooking related items.

Does your website deliver enquiries to your business?

This is the key measure of a smaller, local business website. If your website regularly delivers new enquiries to you, then that website is definitely worth money. Enquiries have value, and you can determine what that value is. There is no set formula for this because, as my dad used to say, "The value of something is not what it's worth, but what someone is willing to pay for it."

In the case of a plumber, for example, if you get an enquiry a day, seven days a week, and each of those, on average, leads to a job worth £100, of which there is £35 profit, then you can quickly work out how much that is worth to you. A month's enquiries are 30 x £100 = £3,000 or £1,050 profit. If you decide to sell your website for a year's worth of profit, then it's worth £1,050 x 12 = £12,600. Of course, a purchaser might reasonably argue that past performance is no guarantee of future performance and want a discount on that figure, but even so, then it's a negotiation point for you.

As your business gets bigger, the number and type of enquiries, as well as the value, will generally increase, and as part of an overall business valuation, your website becomes an asset that can be valued. The key, of course, being if you own it. Some of the websites built on platforms such as Wix, Weebly, GoDaddy, etc. will have protected key parts of their platform and whilst you might own the words you write on the page, if you've used their images, for example, they will retain ownership of them. Another reason, as your business grows, to migrate to an independent solution when you can. And remember, you need to own your domain names and your website to capitalise on a sale.

Takeaways:

Always make sure you own your domain name(s).

If you've invested money in growing your website, your domain will have a value.

As your business grows, ensure you move to an independent platform so you can sell the website in its entirety when the time comes.

CHAPTER 7

Google and The Future of Search

The biggest problem with making any predictions about the future is that the second you write them, they are out of date or just plain wrong. History is littered with people announcing that they could see what was coming, only to be proven wrong in short order. For that reason, you won't be surprised to find that this chapter is not a list of specific, detailed forecasts of things I expect to happen, more a discussion on the current direction of travel and why I believe that search engine optimisation and search engines will change significantly over the coming decades.

Chief amongst the changes I expect to happen is that I firmly expect Google to start to lose market share in the search market. Having dominated for so long, it seems almost inconceivable to imagine a world without Google. As the meme that went around a few years ago put it: "nobody says 'let's just yahoo it.'" Google's arrival heralded a sharp and almost terminal decline for Yahoo and all the other search engines. We forget all too quickly that in the late 1990s and early 2000s, almost 50% of America relied on AOL (America Online) for Internet access and other associated online services such as email.

The rise of Google almost mirrored the fall in AOL and other search engines, and heralded a new era of Internet access. Instead of access through a portal (the start page when you loaded your Internet browser), Google had a single, simple, clean page with a box where you could search for anything. All the advertising was gone. All the news and weather were gone. It was all about search – and it worked. People loved the simplicity and, more importantly at the time when dial-up Internet access was still the dominant way of getting online, the speed. The page loaded in moments and your jumping off point into the Internet was immediately accessible.

This development highlights a key element that is often overlooked in the story of Google's rise to power – as covered in Chapter 2, it was driven by people. It was driven by you and me, and our behaviour was fuelled by the things that were important to us, namely the speed at which we could get online and the accuracy of the information that we found. By developing a product that dealt with two of the biggest problems with the Internet at that time, Google became, *de facto*, the search engine of choice for large parts of the world.

Previous advertising predictions

In 1983, David Ogilvy wrote a seminal book called simply *Ogilvy on Advertising*, in which he shared the experiences he had gleaned from over thirty years working in advertising. He summarised the basic principles of great advertising in this one book. It is a classic and one that I occasionally re-read, as his insights are equally applicable in today's digital environment as they were back in the eighties, before the Internet was something we used daily. One of the most intriguing parts of it, however, is the very last chapter, which is entitled 'I predict 13 changes'. In this chapter, he reluctantly (after pressure from his publisher) predicts what will happen in the years after 1983. I won't reproduce the whole list here (you can read the book yourselves for that) but I do want to pick out a couple of very interesting predictions he made.

- The quality of research will improve, and this will generate a bigger corpus of knowledge as to what works and what doesn't. Creative people will learn to exploit this knowledge, thereby improving their strike rate at the cash register.
- There will be a renaissance in print advertising.

- Advertising will contain more information and less hot air.

- Billboards will be abolished.

- The clutter of commercials on television and radio will be brought under control.

- There will be a vast increase in the use of advertising by governments for the purposes of education, particularly health education.

- Ways will be found to produce effective television commercials at a more sensible cost.

When you consider this list, there are some which are clearly wrong – the one about billboards being an example. Of course, he could not have foreseen the rise in digital billboards, even though he correctly forecast the rise of the use of data and research in point one. And given the recent pandemic that most countries have experienced in 2020 and 2021, the point about governments and health advertising seems unerringly accurate. I include this list for two reasons: firstly, to demonstrate that even arguably the greatest advertising man of the last century couldn't get this right all the time, but also to show that these predictions were all made through the lens of his lived experiences and not a true vision of the future. His life had been in print advertising and everything he did revolved around how advertisements appeared in print. He could not have foreseen digital advertising, let alone examine what is wrong with it. That, in a nutshell, is the problem; we are quite poor at imagining something different to our lived experiences.

One of the questions I like to ask people to consider is, if you had to imagine a digital environment that would work for people, would you build what we have today? Sure, there are parts of what we have that are wonderful, but are they the best they could be? I seriously doubt it. Take email for example: how happy are you with the spam emails you get, or the phishing emails you receive? What about your search journey? How comfortable are you at seeing advertising put in front of you every time you search for something? When you visit your preferred online newspaper, are you assaulted by advertising on every page you visit? And what about 'click bait' headlines? Do you like them or are you perpetually disappointed to arrive on a page where there is a non-story, but lots of advertising?

Finally, as a business owner, how happy are you that you seem to have acquired another job to do, one that you are not trained for and didn't expect to have to do? Previously, if you wanted to advertise, the nice rep from the newspaper or directory would sort it for you, and for larger companies using radio and TV, they or your advertising agency would help you create your ads. Now you have a website instead and you are expected to do everything. You're expected to be able to know what constitutes great web design and what your customers might be looking for, you need to get your head around online advertising as it's now your responsibility to create and run your own advertising campaigns.

If that wasn't enough, you are expected to create content for your website, which you need to update regularly, and you also need to use social media to reach out to customers. You need to make sure you engage with these social channels, manage the reviews customers leave, and at the same time, you need to be looking for opportunities to link build, because as we have already established, links are the currency of the Internet and help you rank on Google. And through all of this, you need to make sure that you are following Google's Webmaster guidelines, ensuring your website is technically optimised and loads in less than a second on a mobile device and that your website has all the expertise, authority and trust signals correctly displayed.

With all this in mind, are you sure that you think what we have today is fit for purpose?

In the rest of this chapter, I want to explore some of the assumptions we currently hold about today's environment and consider what the alternative might look like.

Why do we need search engines?

This might seem like a daft question, but why do we need search engines? Or more importantly, why do we need search engines in their current format?

Historically, advertising consisted of placing your message somewhere you knew (or hoped) people would be able to see it, and relying on that message being strong enough to compel people to call, write or visit a shop and buy what you were selling.

Today, advertising assaults us at every turn. Every possible aspect of our daily lives appears to be 'monetised', as if we are simply walking cash machines and our role is reduced to unwittingly parting with our hard-earned cash.

Of all the advertising, Google's is the most dominant and arguably, the worst, and it shows it repeatedly above the search results. I have long bemoaned the death of creativity in advertising, driven by the rise in Google's pay per click model and its limitation of just thirty characters in a headline. In a study I carried out in 2015, of the top 100 all-time advertising headlines (at the time), only four of them had headlines that would fit into Google pay per click advertising. Just 4% of the greatest, most compelling, and most successful advertising headlines.

Porsche's famous advert from the 1970s had the unforgettable headline: "Porsche separates Le Mans from Le Boys". At thirty-eight characters with spaces, that's a failure. The Economist went with: "Not all mind expanding substances are illegal". Whoops. Forty-five characters so you can't write that. How about "A Mars a day helps you work, rest and play"? Also a non-starter. One of the lucky ones was Guinness with "Guinness is good for you", but that was from a time when advertising didn't necessarily have to be that truthful or accurate. The problem with Google's text adverts was, and is, that limited space means limited creativity and so much of what was initially produced was simply awful. But as Google derived over 95% of its global revenues from these, why did they need to change it?

Fast forward seven years and it has improved (slightly) as there is now more space and a little better creativity, but these text ads are still, in the main, dull. To counter this, people can now run creative display advertising, or more commonly, video advertising, particularly on social media, where the ten second format has risen to prominence. But still, to this day, search engines show advertising when there's the slightest chance that your search might result in a purchase.

We know why they do this, because that's how they make money, but is it what we want? Do all users truly understand that they are seeing advertising in these results, and do we actually need it?

Recently, I was having this conversation with my teenage son, who surprised me when he said he rarely used Google. His preferred search engine of choice was Ecosia, which uses Bing data for its search results and plants trees for every fifty searches made on it. But more importantly, his overall preference was for social media. I was astonished. I'd never considered using social media

Search Never Sleeps

for search, primarily as I couldn't imagine how it would work if I needed an emergency plumber, for example. But what he showed me next stopped me in my tracks.

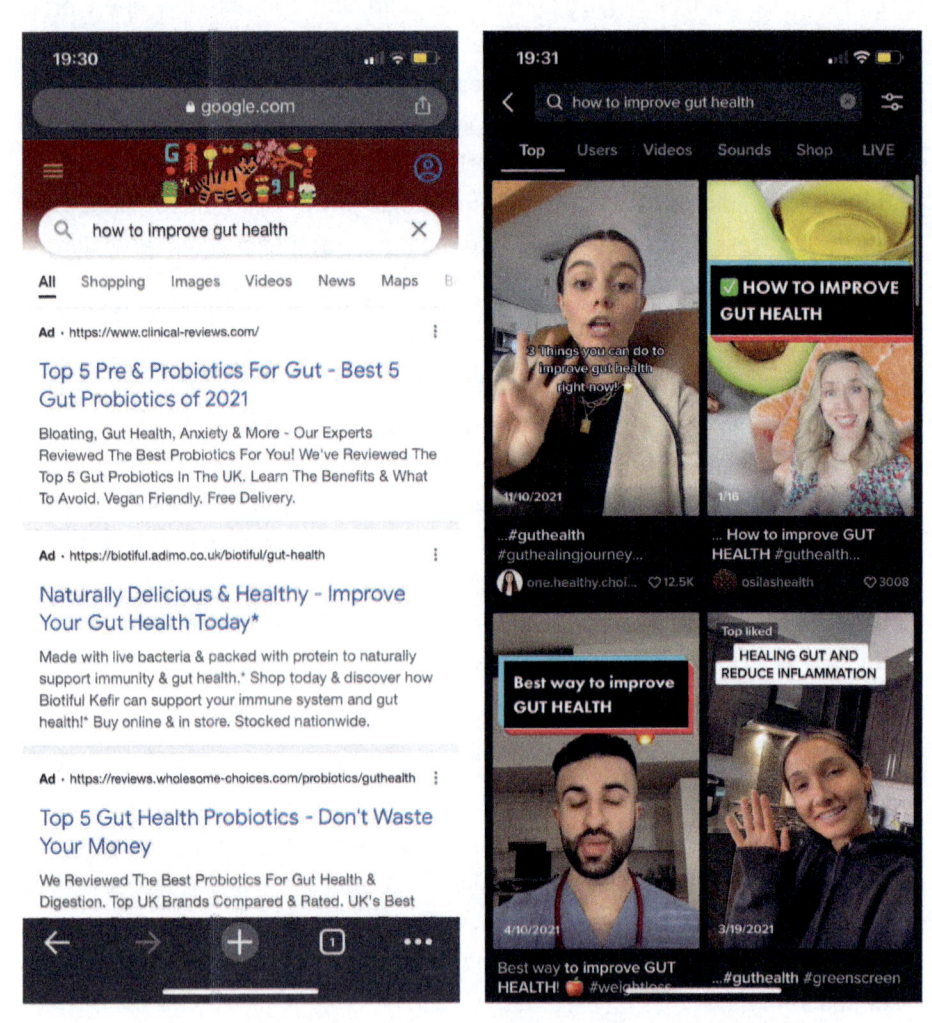

Figure 95 – Google search result for 'how to improve gut health'.

Figure 96 – TikTok search result for 'how to improve gut health'.

The problem with Google, he explained, is that no matter what he was searching for, Google's answer involved advertising. What he really wanted was to get the answer to his question without ads getting in the way. To prove his point, he pulled out his phone and searched for 'how to improve gut health' on Google. The results – as you can see in Figure 95 – were three advertisements. Sure, if he scrolled down, he would find some organic search results and perhaps some videos, but even then, the top results were websites like NHS and WebMD. He didn't want that. He wanted to understand if there were ways to improve gut health, and if so, how to do it.

His next search was on TikTok, and as you can see (Figure 96), it brought up four useful videos, all of which he watched. He reasoned that as each of these had been uploaded and available for over a year, that they hadn't been taken down by TikTok for being incorrect, and that other users had liked in sufficient numbers to push them to the top of this search result, then they must answer his query. And they did. I'm not suggesting here that TikTok will take over from Google, far from it. I'm simply saying that the current offering from Google and other search engines is not what every user wants, and amongst the younger generation, there is increasing dissatisfaction with the current set up.

If search engines make the majority of their money from showing advertising and the search results are just a vehicle for driving users, is there not a compelling case for separating these two things? Is it possible to have search results without advertising? If you look at the favourite comparator for this type of thing, do you see advertising anywhere in *Star Trek*? What you do see is people talking to a screen, which then gives them the answers they are looking for. Moreover, they inherently trust the results they are given. Do you trust the search results you currently get? Google's Senior Vice President of Search, Amit Singhal, said in 2013 that he thought the destiny of Google was to become like the *Star Trek* computer, and that this was what they were building. If they really mean that, then advertising has to disappear completely from the platform.

The bottom line appears to be that with so much available data, the rise of artificial intelligence (AI) and machine learning and people's seemingly relentless thirst for knowledge, what we really need is a system of retrieving that knowledge without the inherent assumption that it leads to consumption. What that system looks like, how it works and how it is financed is not something I can predict, but what I can say is that what we have currently isn't necessarily the best solution for mankind, so eventually, we will find another way of satisfying our needs.

> **"The destiny of [Google's search engine] is to become that Star Trek computer, and that's what we are building."**
>
> *Amit Singhal - Google SVP Search, 2013*

Do we need search engines? Probably not. What we need is an effective information retrieval system. Historically, this was provided by libraries and in our homes, things like a dictionary, a thesaurus, or the Encyclopaedia Britannica. (Whatever happened to them!?) Think back to these paper-based systems and then ask yourself, when you used them, were you assaulted by advertising every time you looked something up?

Search Engines are an extremely clever way of searching, indexing and providing a retrieval system for more information than we can even imagine. We've taken an old paper-based system and supercharged the results. But could we do it better? Is what we have ideal? I doubt, in twenty years, we will think so, and I firmly expect that this will change, because it has to. Think back to Tim Berners-Lee's original vision for the Internet. He described how he envisaged the linking of computers together into a network, which would encourage and enable sharing of data and ideas. In short, the principle he championed was that if we could link all the computers in the world together, and share what we knew, then in theory, it would be possible to solve almost any problem facing humanity. Re-reading that, you'll realise that we've strayed off the path and need to correct our course to truly benefit from the gains we've made in data creation, storage and retrieval.

As a business owner, you are currently stuck with the status quo. Google has a virtual monopoly on search in many countries, its advertising pervades everything and if you want to be able to compete online, you need to play this game, whether you like it or not. What I would encourage you to do, however, is to consider the future for your business or sector. Things are changing, and depending on what you sell and which sector you are in, change may be happening faster than you think. As I said before, lived experience can often limit our vision of what the future could look like, but one thing I do know for certain is that whichever industry you are in, you are probably better placed than anyone not in your sector to see the changes and opportunities as they arise. Remember that change is a constant and those who see the change earliest will generally thrive in the new environment.

Takeaway:

Think about how your customers use your website – could they get the information they need in other, better ways?

Why do we need websites?

On a very similar theme to the question about search engines, why do we need websites?

Websites have changed massively from the early days of the Internet. From simple, straight html pages we now have the ability to create all singing, all dancing websites in next to no time. If you want a shopping website, you can now buy a domain name and be live in a day. This used to take weeks or months to achieve, but now it's just the click of a few buttons.

Irrespective of the type of website, the framework it is built on or the complexity and size of it, Google and the other search engines have found a way to crawl, index and categorise everything they find. In most cases, they get this categorisation right and so the search results we see, by and large, include links to pages and websites that answer our query. The biggest problem now appears to be how these websites render or appear to users, as the number of devices on which we can access the Internet has increased massively.

From having to own a computer to get online, nowadays even your fridge can be connected and show you the time, weather and what you need to add to your shopping list if you are running low on an item inside it. You can search from a range of devices, including more frequently, voice search. In the case of devices like Amazon Echo (featuring Alexa) and Google Nest, these don't even need to show you a website, they just speak the answer to your query. In this kind of environment, does it make any sense to continue to build websites? With over a billion of them in the world today, consuming vast amounts of energy to keep them active, is this the best way to answer search queries?

Google has already found a way of circumventing the problems inherent in websites, and today you can search some websites directly from the search engine. Take, for example, Blue Air, who offer cheap flights to and from various European destinations. They have a website, but if you search Google for 'blue air flights' (Figure 97) you will see Google presenting a handy 'Blue Air flights on Google', which allows you to input your start point and destination, and then it gives you the flights and prices. If you click on the 'Search Blue Air Flights' at the bottom of that box, it takes you to a bigger screen (Figure 98) with a nice Google image, that allows a few more search options.

Search Never Sleeps

Figure 97 – Google search for 'Blue Air flights'.

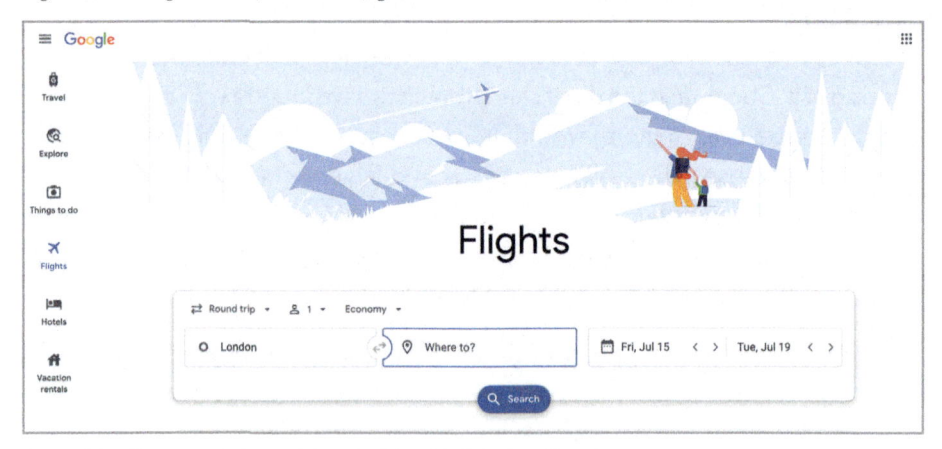

Figure 98 – The expanded search box for 'Blue Air flights' on Google.

What Google has done is to take the flight and price data directly from the Blue Air website and it is showing them to users, but on the Google Search Platform. The advantage to Google is that it can control what it shows to you and how you see it, irrespective of the device from which you are searching. In short, it's removed the need for Blue Air to have a website if the only thing users need is to be able to search for and book flights. When you remember that one of the biggest issues Google faces on a daily basis is how to crawl, understand and index websites, followed closely by how to ensure that when its users click on them in the search results, they are not disappointed, you can understand why removing websites from the equation would make it easier for Google.

So how could it do this? The answer is by using something called an Application Programming Interface (API). Essentially, this is a piece of software that sits between two systems and lets them talk to each other. What's important here is that they work particularly well as an interface between two databases – in this

Google and The Future of Search

case, the flights and price database and Google's search database. So, if Google has access to a database through an API, it can present the results it finds much better to its users.

Of course, the problem here is that you are giving Google total control over how your data is shown. This might work well for a simple flight search, but as you can see from Blue Air's home screen (Figure 99), their website is a whole lot more than just that. They use it to highlight their latest special offers, to direct you to their online check in, to manage your booking and a lot more that a customer might need. Some things, like Customer Service, simply can't be managed by API and I'm sure all of us have experienced the frustration of trying to use an automated customer service system before. Customer service needs to be handled by people, not machines. What is clear, though, is that websites don't necessarily have to be the same as they are today, and for simpler data handling tasks, there are far better and more efficient ways of dealing with this.

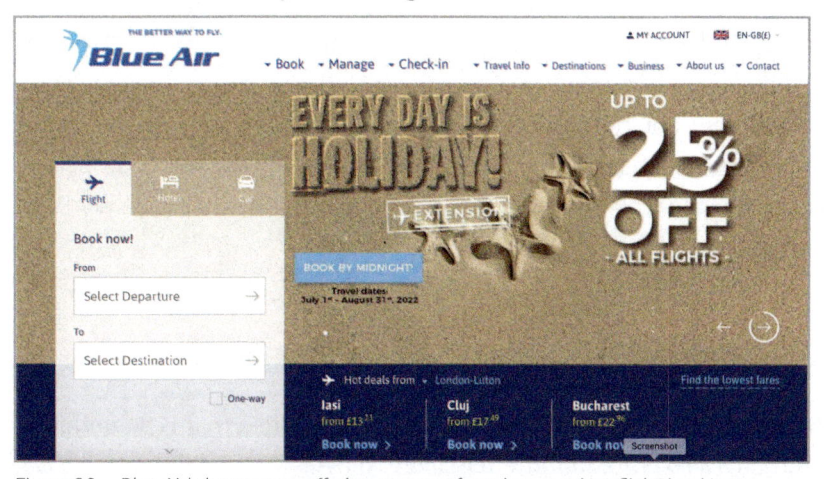

Figure 99 – Blue Air's home page offering a range of services, not just flight bookings.

As a business owner, you've ended up with a job you didn't ask for, creating and managing your website. Wouldn't it be easier if there was a way of just letting someone know what you did, why you were good at it and how much you charge, and then they sort out the problem of how to show this to people? When you stop to think about it, websites are quite a clunky way of displaying information and probably not the best way to do this. Which may lead you to ask the question, why websites? Who invented them and thought that they were a good idea?

The answer, of course, is not you and me. They were invented by someone who understood science and technology. They understood mathematics and engineering. The solution they have arrived at is only understood by half of the people who have to use them (and I'm perhaps being generous with this estimate). How many business owners do you know who can build a website? How many have ever uploaded a site to a server via ftp? How many even know what that means? When you think about it, using websites to display information is clunky, haphazard and inconsistent. They simply can't be the right answer, and if they are, we are probably asking the wrong question.

> **File Transfer Protocol**
> The way websites get up onto a server and onto the Internet

Whilst I can't predict what will happen with websites, I can say with certainty that over time, the need for them will reduce. Someone, somewhere, is bound to find a better way of displaying information, and when they do, there will be a seismic shift in the way we create, store and display information. In the meantime, as a business owner, you need to ensure that your website is as good as it gets. Until someone invents a better way of doing things, you can use the knowledge in this book and the checklist in the Appendix to make sure your website works as well as it possibly can.

The rise of machine learning

No, this isn't about Artificial Intelligence (AI), because that is something quite different. It's also not about the *Terminator* movies and the *Rise of the Machines*. It's about the rise in machine learning and that is all about how computers learn and therefore become smarter at what they do. AI is more about the way computers can become like humans. Machine learning, however, is about how they gain greater intelligence. What most people don't realise is that Google has been using machine learning extensively for a number of years. Google can harness the power machine learning delivers to help it make sense of the billions of data points it collects on users every day. There is now so much data that it wouldn't be possible in your lifetime to go through everything that is available. Imagine a beach full of sand which is being added to every day. Every twenty-four hours, the size of the beach doubles and you have to find a way of analysing it a grain at a time. It would be impossible. With machine learning, however, it becomes viable.

Google provides machine learning courses[1] which anyone can view and then sit the exams, and machine learning is now part of the algorithm for most search engines. Bing, for example, talks openly about how it is using machine learning, and over time, I expect that this will only increase. As the machines learn, they can process more data points and derive more meaningful insights from this data, like what type of behaviours an individual is likely to exhibit and what impact this might have when an advertisement is shown to them. As far back as 2015, Sundar Pichai, Google CEO said:

> **"Machine learning is a core, transformative way by which we're rethinking how we're doing everything. We are thoughtfully applying it across all our products, be it search, ads, YouTube, or Play. And we're in the early days, but you will see us — in a systematic way – apply machine learning in all these areas."**

Over the intervening years, it has become completely embedded in everything they do, to the point where it is now seamlessly integrated within Google's ecosphere, and by definition, in every touch point we have with a Google product. By 2016, Google had created AlphaGo, which, driven by machine learning, was able to play the world's top 'Go' player, Lee Sedol.[2] The machine was able to beat the human four games out of five. This kind of machine learning has been further developed and is now at the heart of our lives, whether we like it or not.

Every year, we create more and more data. By the end of 2021 it was estimated that there were more than 44 zettabytes of data in the world. A zettabyte is a measure of storage capacity, which equals 1000^7 (1,000,000,000,000,000,000,000) bytes. One zettabyte is equal to a thousand exabytes, a billion terabytes, or a trillion gigabytes. Quite apart from the question of where we can store all this data, the simpler question, and one that machine learning seeks to answer, is how can we derive anything useful from this data? Remember Figure 1 from Chapter 1?

---

1   https://developers.google.com/machine-learning/crash-course
2   https://en.wikipedia.org/wiki/AlphaGo_versus_Lee_Sedol

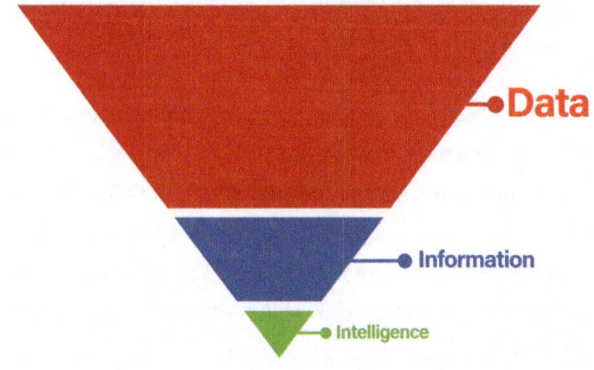

Figure 1 - The relationship between data, information, and intelligence (from page 21).

For some time, I've been using the illustration in Figure 1 to show what I think might be the answer. I've found that when dealing with SEO customers, most of them, particularly e-commerce customers, are drowning in data. There is more data than they can ever possibly hope to analyse, and they are almost paralysed by looking at the scale of the task facing them. Luckily, there are some tools which take raw data and turn it into meaningful information; Google Analytics is one of those. Leveraging all the insights Google has gained from its own machine learning, it is able to present the results in a way that you can see useful information about how many people visit your website, how long they stay and what they do. But still, this is too much. Most business owners I know simply don't have the time to get to grips with the nuances of Analytics and how the data or information in there is presented. What they want (and ultimately what they end up paying people like me for) is to turn that information into intelligence. By analysing the presented information and turning it into, for example, three simple things they should do this month, the seemingly mammoth task becomes something more manageable. It's like the old saying, the best way to eat an elephant is a chunk at a time. Deciding which chunks, however, is where the value is added.

With even more data and an increase in machine learning, there will be more and more opportunities for business owners to leverage this data to help their businesses. You, like me I'm sure, simply won't have the time to take advantage of this. Google's view is that you don't need to, just give it access to your website and let it do it for you. It already does this with its Google Ads, where it analyses the data, makes specific recommendations, and then, unless you specify otherwise, it will automatically apply them to your account. All you need to do is open your wallet and pay it for the ads it serves as it assumes that everything it does will help you make more money.

There are undoubted advantages to be gained from machine learning. Every day, our lives are touched by machine learning, even when we don't see it. The problem which is less talked about is the old problem with data, which has been around since the dawn of the computing age.

Ask any developer the biggest problem they face, and it is quality of data. Unless you start with the highest quality data, the results you get will be less than optimal, or in some cases, just wrong. Remember, 'garbage in, garbage out' (GIGO) is not just a humorous saying, it's a real issue for computers. When you apply machine learning to poor data, the results can send you in a dangerous direction. The problem is that with machines, you can get to the wrong destination even faster than before, so data integrity is critical.

Having said that, machine learning is still accelerating, and we are now able to deal with more data than ever before. As I write this, it is possible to arrange for an advertisement to appear on a digital billboard at precisely the time you know your customers will commute past it, then track that they have seen it and to insert the same advertisement into their daily life, be it on their desktop, laptop or mobile, either on the websites they visit or their social media feed. You can even arrange to send them a special offer on email and continue to track and target them at the end of the day as they watch TV or scroll through social media.

Machine learning drives all of this and the current trajectory is to do more, not less with this technology. It would be easy enough to predict that this is the way it will continue. However, I see a slightly different future. I believe there is a limit to what can be achieved by this. John Wanamaker,[3] the American businessman, famously said, "Half the money I spend on advertising is wasted; the trouble is, I don't know which half." When I was first studying for my marketing qualifications, this adage was trotted out and used to justify the nirvana state to which marketers should aspire – the ability to accurately target their advertising to only the people who want to buy it and not waste money showing it to those who won't.

Digital, when it arrived, promised to deliver just that, but in truth, it's got nowhere near. It's better than old fashioned broadcast marketing in that you can now target

---

[3] Or was it Viscount Leverhulme? Opinion is divided and there is no evidence anywhere that either of them actually said this, but it's become an accepted 'fact' as it appears self-evident.

those most likely to buy, but you can't completely eliminate waste. Nor should you because it's not wasted. It seems self-evident that showing an advertisement for a skateboard to me would be a huge waste of marketing resource. Sure, at my time of life I'm unlikely to take up skateboarding and as such, I'm unlikely to buy one. But am I equally as unlikely to buy one as a gift? Perhaps for a nephew or niece? The same with game consoles; I'm not the target audience but does that mean I shouldn't see the product? Machine learning allows for immense insights into buyer behaviour and buying patterns, but it can't predict what humans will do next. For that reason, I believe that when it comes to advertising, machine learning will reach its limits and we need to embrace the unpredictability of the human spirit.

But we should never forget Rule 1. Google may be a clever machine, but it's still a machine and it can't predict what you or I are going to do next (well, certainly not all the time). With this in mind, make sure that all the data on your website is correctly aligned for the machine so it can index it and show it to more people, more often. And who knows, perhaps the more people they show it to, the more your sales will increase?

Takeaway:
Imagine that tomorrow there were no websites at all. Review how you would promote your business to your customers.

The importance of privacy

How often do you see a pop-up on your mobile or desktop asking you to accept cookies? If you are based in the UK, then the answer is daily, without fail. These things have become so ubiquitous they are now simply an annoyance, and most people just click 'accept' to get past them and onto what they were looking for. But do you know what you are agreeing to when you click 'accept'? Similarly, when you are asked to agree to the 'terms & conditions' for any large organisation (Microsoft and Apple come to mind here, also all the social media platforms), have you ever stopped to consider what you are agreeing to? Do you know how much data you are allowing them to gather on you?

The machine learning I talked about in the previous section is driven by this type of data, and the data that is held on you is immense. Right now, for example, if you are in the UK and have a mobile phone on the EE network, are you aware of what they track? Are you also aware that they sell this data on (without your name, obviously) to companies that can then use it to target advertising to you? Have you ever wondered why, when your car insurance is due, you see more car insurance ads on TV? Have you thought it strange that you've perhaps emailed a friend about something, only to see an advertisement for that very item later that day? Do you know that Google can (and does) read all your emails that go through Gmail in an effort to better understand you as a customer and to provide more relevant and targeted advertisements to you?

Slowly but surely, as technology has advanced, our privacy has retreated. When National Identity Cards were introduced[4] in 2006 in the UK by the Labour Government, there was a huge backlash. By 2010, it became a central plank of the Conservative/Liberal coalition to abolish them, which they did. People, it seems, took unkindly to the thought that a single body could hold data on their identity.

Ironically, Apple launched the iPhone 5s in 2013, which had, as a central feature, the ability to unlock your phone by fingerprint. The fingerprint is stored securely on the iPhone and doesn't go anywhere else, but in 2015 they filed a patent to enable them to store it in the Cloud and share it across devices. Whilst they haven't done this yet, it highlights that it's being considered. So, what is the difference between the Government holding all your personal data and a large business like Apple? Do we trust one of them more than the other, and if so, why? Surely personal data is personal and should be kept private, not shared around, even in anonymised formats? We seem happy to give our data to big corporations but not to governments. Why is that?

More and more we are seeing stories of data breaches,[5] identify thefts and egregious overreach from either governments or large organisations, and increasingly people are waking up to the fact that their lives are no longer private. For all the good that technology has done for us, loss of privacy appears to have been the price. Not everybody feels the same way about this, though. I see children getting their first mobile phones, barely into their teens (or younger) and

---

4   Actually, reintroduced as we previously had them during World War Two.
5   See this website for a fabulous representation of all the biggest data breaches in the world https://www.informationisbeautiful.net/visualizations/worlds-biggest-data-breaches-hacks/

being unafraid of letting their personal data be collected by governments and business. Those of us slightly older have, perhaps, a different view, having lived through the Cold War and seen close to us in Europe, a 'papers please' society. Many older people have an inherent mistrust of governments and corporations which doesn't appear as marked in the young. Are they wrong to feel this way? Are they simply 'old fashioned'?

A fascinating study by the Pew Research Centre in the USA in 2019[6] found that the majority of Americans surveyed believed their personal data was less secure and that they were being tracked daily. The headline read:

"Americans and Privacy: Concerned, Confused and Feeling Lack of Control Over Their Personal Information"

The report went on to say: "Majorities think their personal data is less secure now, that data collection poses more risks than benefits, and believe it is not possible to go through daily life without being tracked."

The report is worth reading, if only as a snapshot of a moment in time.

The fact that these people believed (and probably still do) that it simply isn't possible to go through a day without being tracked should be of concern to all of us. A similar survey, this time by KPMG in 2021, concluded that:[7]

"A full 86% of the respondents said they feel a growing concern about data privacy, while 78% expressed fears about the amount of data being collected. Some 40% of the consumers surveyed don't trust companies to use their data ethically, and 13% don't even trust their own employers."

It seems we're not alone. Google Trends data confirms that since January 2011, our concerns over privacy have been increasing and they show no sign of abating (Figure 100).

> ## "Man is born free but everywhere is in chains."
> *Jean-Jacques Rousseau*

---

6   https://www.pewresearch.org/internet/2019/11/15/americans-and-privacy-concerned-confused-and-feeling-lack-of-control-over-their-personal-information/
7   https://info.kpmg.us/news-perspectives/technology-innovation/data-privacy-survey.html

Google and The Future of Search

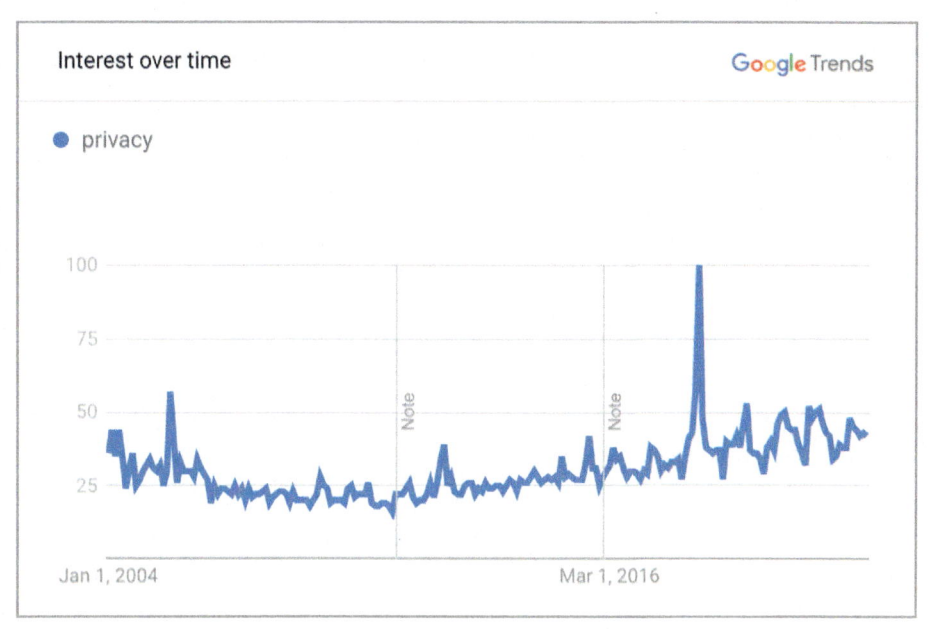

Figure 100 – Google trend of searches for 'privacy'.

What, therefore, is likely to happen? More and more data are gathered on us daily, and it seems we are becoming increasingly concerned about it. Logically, a point will come when we will draw a line and say no more. I see that coming but the only thing is I have no idea when. How much is too much? What will it take to push people into action? I suspect that a single, seismic data event, like a loss or breach, will be enough to precipitate change. When it happens, it is unlikely to be pleasant.

Takeaway:
If your business collects customer data, think about how you can use it without abusing your customers' trust.

So far in this chapter, I've covered quite a bit about the macro level factors that affect search, but what about the micro level ones? The things that affect search engine optimisation today? Here are a few of the questions that I get asked when I'm lecturing and my thoughts on these and the future of SEO.

Will there be a need for search engine optimisation in the future?

What is the purpose of a search engine? And when we use it, what are we looking for? We search daily for answers to *Life, the Universe and Everything*, knowing before we start that the answer is unlikely to be 42.[8] So, are today's search engines the modern equivalent of Deep Thought? Have we turned the planet into one big computer, connected by the Internet?

Human beings are a resourceful bunch. We managed to evolve from cave dwellings to hunter gatherers, to farmers, and with a single leap past the Industrial Revolution, we've become an inquisitive society, a people defined by information. We live in the Information Age and every day we ask billions of questions as we're infinitely curious. We've spent countless years finding ways to destroy the planet and we are now spending the same amount figuring out how to undo the damage. At the heart of all this is information, which currently is organised by search engines.

Logically, as long as we still have search engines, there will be a need for SEO. Of course, if my earlier prediction regarding search engines is anywhere close to being accurate, then this could all change! Currently, all the work we and anyone else involved in SEO is doing is to optimise websites so that search engines can crawl, understand and index the content and show the pages in the search results. If the way search engines understand websites changes or websites themselves change, then this requirement may disappear. As I've already outlined, the current system of individual websites is hugely inefficient, both from a data organisation point of view and from an energy point of view. In a world where energy might in future become a scarce resource, it won't be long before someone questions the wisdom of keeping over a billion websites globally live on servers, all of which need huge amounts of electricity to power them.

The chances of this changing any time soon, however, are slim, so at this point I will predict that SEO will definitely be around for some time to come. Busting open one of the myths from the start of the book, SEO is definitely not dead, nor is it likely to die any time soon. The thing we will need to focus on is that SEO will change. The term SEO is in itself slightly misleading, as optimising for search engines is only half of the battle. Rule 1 says that 'Google is just a machine' and as such it doesn't, by definition, have any pockets in which it can keep money.

---

8   See Douglas Adams – *Hitchhiker's Guide to the Galaxy*

Whilst we optimise for Google, the reason for optimising is so that people can find your website. People have the money that businesses need, and people are the ones who consume the content, products and services on these websites. As machines get better and slicker at what they do and technology changes, I see more value being added in People Optimisation, optimising your data, products and services for people rather than search engines. We already do this to an extent and have talked about UX/UI in an earlier chapter, so I see more value being added in this area than we have previously seen. As a business owner with a website, I would urge you to take another look at what you currently have and ask if it is set up as well as it could be for people? Remember, they are the ones you are ultimately targeting as they buy your products and services.

What's the future of data storage?

This is an interesting question and if you Google this query (Why wouldn't you?) then you will see a range of different answers, all jostling for position on page one. Some people say that we will never run out of storage space, others that there is a finite capacity. The more astute commentators know that we need to look beyond the immediate question and consider some of the other implications.

Currently, there are several competing agendas that are conspiring to create a crisis in data storage and management. Let's start at the beginning.

Forecasts vary, but conservatively there is an expectation that by 2025 we could be looking at upwards of 175 zettabytes of data stored somewhere on the planet. If you remember, by the end of 2021 it was 44 zettabytes. That's a huge growth and an awful lot of data. The obvious question is where will it all be stored? A recent story in one of the UK newspapers highlighted how in West London there is now a stand-off between developers wanting to build new homes and data centres awaiting planning permission.[9] The issue isn't as you might think, land on which to build, but the supply of electricity. Essentially, planners are saying that you can either have homes or data centres, but not both. Each data centre is forecast to need 50 MvA (Mega Volt Ampere) of electricity to run, which is enough electrical capacity for more than 5,000 homes, hence the conflict. These data centres need that much electricity not just to run the servers (which are stored in huge racks in

---

9 https://www.thetimes.co.uk/article/grid-has-no-power-for-new-homes-in-west-london-until-2035-qnrn065cb

warehouses), but for the cooling systems that are needed to ensure that they don't overheat and go up in flames. Currently, data centres account for around 1% of global electricity consumption, according to the International Energy Agency, but the demand is rising exponentially, as we can see from the forecast data volumes. This is the first strand of the problem.

Separately, politicians globally are pursuing a variety of Zero Carbon or Net Zero agendas, either looking to reduce the carbon emissions of a country to zero or to be able to at least offset those emissions. In doing so they are demanding that we move away from our traditional energy sources of oil, gas and coal and move to more sustainable sources of supply such as solar, wind and hydro. Despite the rhetoric and hype, the inconvenient truth is that currently these renewable sources deliver little more than 10% of global primary energy. Despite their best efforts, no one has come up with a foolproof plan yet to increase that figure substantially, nor to replace the electricity currently produced by gas and oil. Logically, we are therefore heading for a shortage of supply. This is strand two.

Strand three is that we are being told that we need to phase out our addiction to hydrocarbon based motoring and switch to electric cars, with the UK set to ban sales of petrol or diesel vehicles by 2030, the US following some five years later. This is going to create a massive additional demand on our electricity network which will be needed to cope with the increased charging requirements for these cars and vans.

In short, we are entering a phase of societal development where the demand for electricity will be greater than it ever has been before, at the same time as we are being encouraged to stop using the cheap, reliable sources of energy that we have traditionally relied upon. This is a problem and frankly, something has to give.

There are, of course, ways around this. The existing data storage system of using servers in buildings is, as we can see, hugely energy intensive and not at all sustainable. It relies on enormous amounts of infrastructure, energy and hardware for it to work, and at the heart of it is the issue that the devices on which we store data have finite limits. Already researchers are experimenting with different solutions to this problem, including DNA storage, light storage, and fluorescence storage, all of which sound like something straight out of a science fiction novel. Once again, I ask the question, if we had to invent a new system to store data, would we come up with what we currently have? The answer is probably not, as the limitations are clear for all to see, but finding a suitable alternative is not as easy as we might think.

The future of data storage is going to be a critical part of the narrative around the digital space over the next decade. We cannot continue to develop on our current trajectory as the resource and energy requirements are just too great. It's simply unsustainable. The solution will, I'm sure, present itself in due course. Whatever the solution, it will need to be something that allows for almost infinite storage capacity whilst using the least amount of electricity to maintain the data. Ironically, it's the sort of challenge that Tim Berners-Lee's original worldwide web was invented to solve.

Will we still need to create great content?

Someone asked me recently what Google meant by 'create great content', and in truth I found it a little hard to define. It seems that great content differs depending on who you are and what you are writing about. If it's the answer to a simple question that someone has that no one has previously answered, then that can be great content. Whilst a lot of the obvious ones have already been answered (Google knows the size of the moon, the height of the Eiffel Tower and where to find the deepest part of the ocean), there are still more questions that need simple answers and more and more of these questions arise every day. Typically, Google sees up to 25% of all queries it is asked in a year being brand

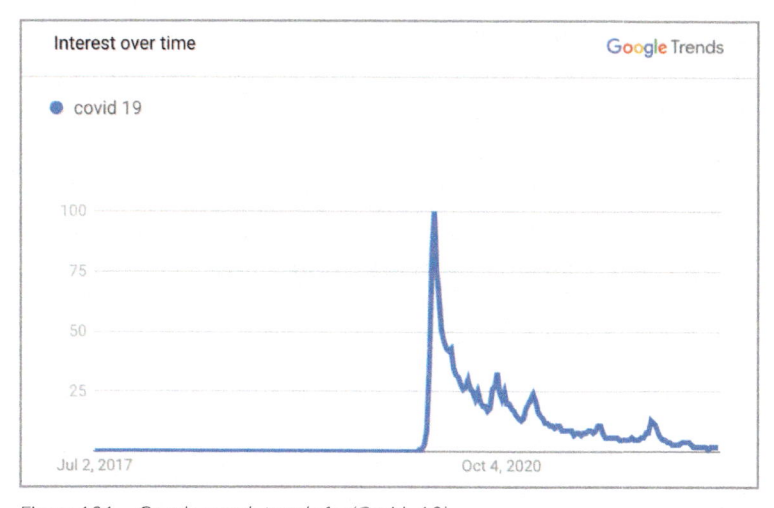

Figure 101 – Google search trends for 'Covid-19'.

new, questions no one has ever asked before. As an example, until 2020, no one had ever asked Google about Covid-19 (Figure 101).

Great content can also be a more comprehensive answer about something not previously recorded. Alongside writing this book, I'm also co-authoring several research papers on a completely different subject. We've looking at an aspect which, to date, has been largely ignored. When our next article is published, it is likely to be the 'definitive' paper on this subject and one, we expect, that will be referenced and cited for years to come. The reason we are writing this is because we spotted a gap in the existing literature and have gone out of our way to find the answers. The article will be published online and, in time, will rank number one on Google for a search for that item. It will be 'great content'. But great content can also be opinions. Every day, newspapers produce what they consider to be great content, and whilst large parts are news, there is almost as much opinion. Many of these articles rank highly in search and are valuable insights into human knowledge or behaviour.

> **"If I have seen further, it is by standing on the shoulders of giants."**
> *Sir Isaac Newton*

Our natural curiosity as a species means that we will continue to ask questions, research the answers to problems, and because we live in a connected society, we will continue to share those solutions and answers online so others may benefit. This would take us nearer the original vision Tim Berners-Lee had about the Internet. We will continue to add to the sum of human knowledge, and if you are doing that, you will still be adding great content. There won't be a shortage of people looking for answers, so the simple answer is yes, we will still need to create great content. It might not always be for Google but think of it as adding to the canon of work on your subject, and if you only add things that add value, you can be sure that your work is not wasted.

CASE STUDY

I'm including this here as a case study in how not to approach content. We took on a business who operated in the hobby market and created a great content strategy for them. We started writing blogs and pages for them in line with this strategy and sent them, as they were written, to the customer for approval and sign off. Unfortunately, they didn't sign off anything and therefore this valuable content was not being uploaded onto their website. Because no one was following this up, six months into the project the customer complained that their SEO wasn't working. They complained that we had not spent enough time inside the back end of their website (which they measured by how often we logged into their website) and therefore they believed that we had not done any real SEO. Meanwhile 20,000 words that would have driven traffic sat wasted on their desk. This was a perfect example of how not to do SEO. You can't measure the success of your SEO by how many times your SEO firm logs in, nor can you ignore the content when it has been created. It also taught us that we needed a more robust chase process to ensure this never happened again!

Takeaway:
Engage with your SEO team and talk regularly to ensure you are all working towards the same end goal.

What about link building, will we still need to do that?

Why exactly are we link building? For me, this is a real elephant in the room. Almost every other book and all of the online resources I have read on the subject of SEO cover link building as an accepted part of search engine optimisation. No one challenges the question of whether we should be link building at all; it's taken for granted that we should just get on with it. But I'd like to stop for a second and ask why?

We are told we should create a 'natural link profile' but we're not told or shown what 'natural' looks like. Moreover, if this natural profile is dependent on who links to you and what anchor text they use, how can you control this if you don't own the website from which you get the link? Surely, it's up to the owner of that website what the link looks like and what anchor text they choose? Just because Google has determined that links are important for its product to work, why does this become your problem? How can a normal business owner be expected to firstly understand the nuances of link building practices and secondly, to invest time into doing it? For most people, it's impossible. They are being forced to become experts in something in which they have no expertise, nor in most cases, any desire to become experts. They are specialists in their own field, which is presumably why they started their own companies. They didn't start up to become beholden to Google and help Google become more profitable.

Somewhere in the dim and distant past, we all became subservient to Google. We surrendered any form of free will and simply fell in line with what we were told to do. When Google said that we all simply needed to 'create great content', we went along with it, even though this has helped Google more than it helped us. Over the years, I have written and published hundreds of thousands of words on a variety of websites in an effort to get them to rank highly in the search results, but the very act of doing this has helped Google to improve its search results by providing it with more and better material with which it can answer your questions. Looking back, I can see that the time I have invested will never yield me a return.

Google's current business model is to take everything that is created and published on websites and then use it to answer the questions it gets asked. And if there is an opportunity to show an advertisement in that search result, it will do. We all forget that the material it is using to answer people's queries is the stuff we created. Google take it and use it and we don't get a penny in return. As we became content creators for a higher power, we also accepted that we all need to be experts in everything that they want. Business owners are now expected to build great websites, create great content and make sure their website is fast, usable and accessible. Moreover, they are also expected to share that great content they have created on social media platforms in the hope that it will gain traction, and on seeing it, people will link back to their content as being valuable. I think you can see by now that the entire model is geared towards Google, not users.

If you are sat reading this and you run, for example, a scaffolding company, I'm betting that writing content, sharing it on social media and outreaching to try and create backlinks for your website are not top of your 'to-do' list. I'd wager that erecting scaffolding, running your business, generating employment opportunities, and making a profit are much higher up your agenda. Since when did business owners have to be digital experts? In the days of printed media, there were few small business owners with anything more than a passing interest in advertising and marketing and even fewer who would take it upon themselves to create their own advertising. They expected either the media in which they bought the space or an advertising agency to create the adverts. As I've said earlier, every business owner is now expected to be an expert and the only reason for this is because it suits Google. For me, this is a fundamental flaw in the system and one which will eventually drive the change that moves us away from the current search engine model. In the meantime, we still need to create backlinks, or more specifically, the search engines will still look at, count and evaluate the relevance and importance of links from other websites to your website. Over time, however, I see that changing.

The original driver for link building was hard wired into Google's first patent, as we discussed earlier in the book, but since then, times and information have moved on. We shouldn't have to even consider this now, as the ability of search engines to make their own determination on the value of content has increased significantly. Using backlinks as a raw signal of the value of a page or website is quite crude, and given the current state of the market, probably a poorer indicator than it once was. For now, it seems that we will still have to pursue backlinks, but over time, I forecast that the importance of this signal will decrease, and eventually be removed altogether.

Currently, it's too easily manipulated. Daily, I see examples of websites that have 'gamed' the system. One of my local competitors has done just that and managed to fool Google into putting them top for a range of search results. They did it by buying cheap, high value backlinks. Four years on from doing this, they are still top, despite it being an obvious breach of Google's guidelines. So for these reasons, I'm calling time on backlinks and predict that they will, over time, lose their value and potency in the quest for search rankings.

Should you use an SEO company?

In some respects, this is the $64,000 question, and if there was a simple answer it would make this a very short section of the book. Unsurprisingly, it's not a straightforward question to answer, because context is everything. As we have seen throughout this book, websites need, at their heart, optimising for search engines. Until and unless we have a different way of accessing information online, the **3 Rules of Google** still apply, and you have to do everything within your power to help the machine understand what your website is about and give it reasons to show you in the search results.

Your starting point, if you accept that SEO is needed, is around the time and expertise required to do this work. Do you have the time? Do you have the knowledge? (This book should have given you a lot of that.) And do you have the inclination to do this yourself? If so, crack right on and have a go. Many small businesses do exactly this and I have met many business owners who are happy with their well-optimised websites and the work it brings. In many cases, the work they do is all that's needed. If you are running a small business where the website is not your primary source of leads and income, then the work you do on your website may be sufficient. Of course, if you ask a professional to review it, they will probably find a lot more that needs attention, but that's to be expected. If you work day in, day out in SEO then you know what to do and how to do it and you will also understand where most issues lie. What professionals have that you don't is knowledge and, in most cases, time-served expertise.

Things get slightly more interesting if you are in an industry where your competitors are using SEO firms. In these cases, it becomes inevitable that at some point you will need professional SEO help, if only to help you understand what your competitors are doing and if some or all of it is working for them.

The next question will be around budget and timescales, and whilst this is variable across SEO firms and different industries, the following gives you a flavour of what might be required. Please don't take this as being set in tablets of stone; it's more about letting you know what to expect at different levels.

As you can see, prices vary considerably and if you are in certain industries, such as gambling, prices will be significantly higher. For the purposes of this book, however, let's assume that you run a small to medium large business and if you do, then hopefully you can recognise where your business might sit in this table.

Business Type	Typical staff numbers	Type of website	Typical work needed and cost
Start up or small business	1-5	Simple design, few pages, minimal content.	Addition of extra content, few backlinks, some technical SEO. Cost - from a few hundred pounds up to £1,000 a month
Small to medium large business	6-50	Bigger website, a growing number of pages and content, a sales and/or lead generator for the business.	Ongoing technical SEO, content creation and link building, competitor analysis. Cost - from £1,000 a month up to £5,000 a month
Medium large to enterprise level business	51+	Large websites with a significant digital footprint.	Deep technical audits and analysis, ongoing content creation strategies, outreach strategies, competitor analysis and press & PR strategies. Cost - over £5,000 a month

The bottom line is that every website needs optimising as long as we have search engines. Organic is the predominant source of traffic on the Internet, and despite the revenues it generates, paid traffic typically is measured to be a relatively small percentage, with surveys regularly pegging it at no more than 15% of all traffic. This means that anywhere between 80-100% of the traffic arriving on your website is organic and therefore free. It's also long lasting; if you can gain visitors to your website without paying for them, simply by virtue of where you appear in the search results, then unless something drastic changes, you are likely to continue receiving this traffic. Of course, competitors often spot this and will target your best performing pages, so it's up to you to optimise what you have to ensure lasting success with organic traffic.

All of which brings us neatly round to the fact that you should invest in securing your organic traffic and the best way of doing this is to invest in SEO. If you have the time (and frankly, if you are unused to doing this it could be an infinite time sink), resources, ability, skill and desire to do it yourself, then your investment need go no further. You could even try doing a little bit yourself to see if it makes a difference, such as writing some additional content or optimising the on-page elements. If, however, you are in a growing business and don't have the time, or are surrounded by competitors who rank above you, then you really should consider using an SEO professional to help you rank well on Google.

When you start talking to SEO companies, you will find that there are a range of options available to you. Having read this book, if you feel that there are some elements that you want to do yourself then tell them upfront. Most firms will be happy to work with you on a 'hybrid' basis where you can split the tasks between you. However, in this type of arrangement, don't be scared of asking their opinion of your work, or asking for help if you get stuck. Remember, these companies are professionals in this area and if they are any good, will be up to date on the latest changes in the Google algorithm and what will help you rank above your competitors.

Having made the decision to hire an individual or company, you will need a way of assessing whether they are a good partner for you. There are numerous checklists of questions online that you can ask potential partners and some of these are useful. Rather than reproduce them here, let me give you a much shorter list. In essence, you are simply buying time and knowledge; time to do the tasks required and the knowledge to know which ones to do. On that basis, the questions you need to ask are:

1. How long have you been working in SEO?
2. Can you show me examples of your work?
3. If I engage you, what will you do for my website?
4. How will you report what you have done each month?

Many of the other checklists will tell you that you need to ask about link building strategies, content creation, insurance, awards and contract length, and whilst all of these are valuable questions, ultimately it boils down to: 'Do I trust you to help my business?' I'm a huge believer in trust and that people buy people, so whoever you choose, it must be about trust. Trust typically comes from a belief that the person you are talking to understands you, your business, and the process of SEO and if you can satisfy yourself that these needs are met, then you should have enough confidence to use them.

Often, you can choose suppliers from personal recommendation as this carries with it an inherent trust signal. When choosing an SEO firm, this can be the difference between success and an expensive mistake. Asking other business owners that you trust who they use for their SEO will help develop a shortlist. But remember, success with one firm does not guarantee success with the next. Every website is unique, and whilst the techniques and processes described in this book remain constant, there is no guarantee that applying them equally to two different websites will yield identical results. What you will get, however, is the confidence that the company your fellow business owner recommends will be trustworthy and do everything they can to help you and your business.

So if you want to engage an SEO firm, you can do so in the knowledge that what you have learned from this book will give you the confidence to ask the right questions, at the right time, of whoever you choose to help you.

Conclusion

As I said at the start, I'm not in the business of making predictions, and even of those that I have ventured throughout this chapter, I firmly expect to be wrong at least half of the time. It's not that I'm doubting what I have written, far from it. More that I'm seeing this through my lived experience and as such, I'm likely to miss the 'unknown unknowns' that have a habit of changing history. What I stand by, though, is the general direction of travel. We've created an unnecessarily complicated system of data storage, retrieval and management which desperately needs to change. When it does, I have no doubts that what comes next will radically change what we see today. Google, I am sure, would love to be at the forefront of that change, for as Steve Jobs from Apple so eloquently put it many years ago, "If you don't cannibalize yourself, someone else will."

Google will either have to invent a completely new system, away from websites, or risk that someone else will. Perhaps this is already underway, as right now we see websites becoming a relic of the early Internet, and in many cases, an irrelevance. Billion dollar businesses now exist as an app on a mobile phone with their base in the cloud. They have no physical presence, make nothing tangible and have no desire to create content for a website to which no one will go. As this trend continues, websites will become little more than shop windows and with this will go the relevance of content and links. Where then for Google, for information and for the way we slake our thirst for knowledge? Oh for a crystal ball…

Having said all that, if you are looking for ways you can futureproof your website for the next few years through search engine optimisation, here are my takeaways:

Takeaways:

Create great content – irrespective of Google, human beings (who will buy what you are selling) will always appreciate great content.

Keep it simple – you might be shown the latest flashy 'technological breakthrough' for websites but remember, simplicity always works.

Do the basic optimisation tasks well – If you can't do them through lack of knowledge or time, pay someone to help.

Never forget Rule 1 – Google is just a machine.

CHAPTER 8

Resources and Tools

Throughout this book, I've referred many times to the 'resources' section at the back of the book, so this is it. Everything you might usefully need to know to help you with your search engine optimisation. I don't mean that this chapter contains everything you need to know, far from it. What it does is give you a starting point to jump into any topic I've covered in the book and help guide you to what's good on the Internet.

I've broken this down into sections which roughly correspond with the chapters in the book. Some of these resources will, of course, spread across more than one chapter and if so, I'll cross reference them for you rather than listing them twice.

As I mentioned earlier in the book, the aim of this was not to create another 'how to' guide; there are plenty of those already. The aim of this book is to help you understand what SEO is about and why is important. If, from there, you want to have a go at doing it yourself, the following resources should point you in the right direction.

Here are the resources. Everything mentioned earlier in the book: links, footnotes and mentions, summarised in one place.

Preface

If you have no idea about SEO but fancy learning more, these two websites will give you an excellent basic grounding.

Google's Starter Guide to SEO –
https://developers.google.com/search/docs/beginner/seo-starter-guide

Moz Beginners Guide to SEO –
https://moz.com/beginners-guide-to-seo

Chapter 1

This chapter is all about how Search started, and these are the resources mentioned in that chapter.

- https://en.wikipedia.org/wiki/Search_engine
- https://analytics.google.com/analytics/web/
- https://developers.google.com/search/docs/advanced/guidelines/webmaster-guidelines
- https://www.gov.uk/government/statistics/business-population-estimates-2019/business-population-estimates-for-the-uk-and-regions-2019-statistical-release-html/
- https://www.statista.com/statistics/282241/proportion-of-businesses-with-a-website-in-the-uk/
- https://www.ons.gov.uk/peoplepopulationandcommunity/householdcharacteristics/homeinternetandsocialmediausage/bulletins/internetaccesshouseholdsandindividuals/2020

Chapter 2

This is where I introduce **The 3 Rules of Google** and as you might expect, there is no resource for this anywhere online. Yet.

Chapter 3

As this is a major section in the book, there are lots of resources and references.

Here are the links to these in the order they appear in the chapter.

- https://developers.google.com/search/docs/beginner/how-search-works
- https://www.bbc.co.uk/news/world-australia-55760673
- https://www.cityam.com/google-to-pay-uk-publishers-for-news-as-global-pressure-mounts/

An overview to Meta data –
- https://www.metatags.org/all-meta-tags-overview/

A report into our attention span –
- https://www.eurekalert.org/pub_releases/2019-04/tuod-aoi041119.php

Three good sources on how to write meta descriptions –
- https://developers.google.com/search/docs/advanced/appearance/snippet
- https://yoast.com/meta-descriptions/
- https://moz.com/learn/seo/meta-description

Keyword stuffing examples –
- https://www.searchenginejournal.com/the-complete-list-of-google-penalties-and-how-to-recover/201510/

Mobile searches are often for local businesses –
- https://www.thinkwithgoogle.com/marketing-strategies/app-and-mobile/mobile-search-trends-consumers-to-stores/

One of the great free resources (and even better if you pay for it) is Answer The Public – https://answerthepublic.com/

Free image resources –
- https://www.pexels.com/
- https://pixabay.com/

There are hundreds of tools for measuring keyword positions so any list I produce will be missing some of them. I've used quite a few in my time and the following are just some of those tools. As with everything, try different ones (most offer a free trial) and then decide which is best for you and your business. Some are free, some are paid; just choose whichever suits you best.

Google Search Console –
- https://search.google.com/search-console/about

It's free and it's from Google so it will show you a lot of what you need. Can be used stand alone or in conjunction with the others in this list.

- SEMRush – https://www.semrush.com/
- Ahrefs – http://ahrefs.com/
- Moz – https://moz.com/
- AccuRanker – https://www.accuranker.com/
- Raven – https://raventools.com/
- SERanking – https://seranking.com/
- SEO Power Suite – https://www.link-assistant.com/
- Advanced Web Ranking – https://www.advancedwebranking.com/

Anchor text types –
- https://www.semrush.com/blog/what-is-anchor-text-and-how-can-i-optimize-it/

Resources for link building –
- This is a great article from Brian Dean – start here and you won't go wrong – https://backlinko.com/link-building-tools
- Majestic – https://majestic.com/
- SEO Power Suite – https://www.link-assistant.com/

Try this blog at Wordstream for different tools you can try –
- https://www.wordstream.com/blog/ws/2013/09/18/best-keyword-research-tools

Stats of mobile v desktop v tablet usage –
- https://gs.statcounter.com/platform-market-share/desktop-mobile-tablet/worldwide/#monthly-200901-202210

Website security resource –

As this is an ever-changing field, I'd recommend searching online and reading up on specific solutions for your website, depending on which framework you use.

A good general list can be found here –
- https://blog.hubspot.com/website/website-security-threat-services
- and here – https://www.getapp.com/all-software/website-security/

For WordPress, we typically recommend this installation of Word Fence, All in One WP Security or Suciri. For a bigger list, try this blog post –
- https://optinmonster.com/wordpress-security-plugins/

As always, if in doubt, ask other website owners what they use or consult a professional web building or SEO firm for advice.

Chapter 4

There are several good resources for Local SEO. However, the team at Bright Local have put together a decent collection which will help any business rank locally.

- https://www.brightlocal.com/resources/
- https://blog.hubspot.com/marketing/local-seo
- https://moz.com/learn/seo/local

Website Security –
There is a pretty good list of WordPress security plug-ins that has been complied by the team at HubSpot and they tend to keep it up to date. All of these are tried and tested and will keep out all but the most determined hackers.

- https://blog.hubspot.com/website/best-security-wordpress-plugins-secure-blog

For Drupal, you can see a list at this blog –
- https://fivejars.com/blog/top-security-modules-your-drupal-website

Magento has its own security modules, and a list can be found here –
- https://serverguy.com/magento/best-5-magento-extension-security/

For all other platforms, simply type into Google 'top security for [platform name]' and it will present you with an up-to-date list of the best tools around. Do your research and you will be able to find something that suits your website and budget.

Chapter 5

E-commerce is awash with resources for anyone looking to develop a website. Start by signing up for the daily email from Shopify –

- https://www.shopify.com/blog
  – as it usually contains some excellent tips for website owners.
- https://ecommerce-platforms.com/resources
- https://builtwith.com/

Chapter 6

If you want to build a better website, then use the checklist at the back of this book and then these tools to get the result you are looking for.

- https://www.screamingfrog.co.uk/seo-spider/
- https://developers.google.com/web/tools/lighthouse/
- https://gtmetrix.com/
- https://www.hotjar.com/
- https://clarity.microsoft.com/

Books to Read

These are the books I mention throughout the text that I consider worth reading. Some of them might seem quite dated now, but they are still a worthwhile investment of your time.

- Berners-Lee, T (1999) *Weaving the Web*, London: Orion Publishing
- Ogilvy, D (1983) *Ogilvy on Advertising*, London: Pan Books
- Sheridan, M (2017) *They Ask, You Answer*, New Jersey: John Wiley & Sons

Appendix
Checklist for website development

The following list is not a definitive list of everything that everyone will need for a successful website. I feel the need to stress this upfront as it's impossible to second guess every requirement that could possibly exist. What this list does, however, is to help you to focus your thinking on the sort of questions that a competent developer might ask you when being engaged to build a website.

What they are looking for is a clear idea of what you are trying to achieve, and from their point of view, what things could go wrong with the build. Experienced developers know certain pitfalls await them and often it's the smallest things that can make a difference.[1] Elements such as the sourcing of images, supply of content, access to a payment provider or links to other systems, either internal or external, all take time to do properly, and unless they are planned for and built into the cost, will inevitably end up causing delays or disagreements. The clearer your instructions at the start, the better the outcome at the end; or as someone once neatly put it, "time spent planning is never wasted".

At the end of this checklist, you should have a clear picture of what functions are required in your website and more importantly, a plan for the website you need to build.

---

[1] I once delivered a website for a customer that worked perfectly on mobile, tablet and desktops but the client was still using a ten-year-old version of Windows on all his computers and of course, we'd designed it for the latest version. Putting that right cost more than the entire cost of the job and became an expensive lesson in how not to plan a website build.

Who and Why?

- Who are you targeting?

- What will they come to your website for? (articles/reviews/contact details/pricing?)

- Why will they visit you and not your competitors?

- What do your competitors do well and what, as a minimum, does your website need to do?

- Will anyone be allowed on all of your website or are you going to have a log in, members only area?

Look and Feel

- What designs and layouts do you like and admire and why?

- Do you have a design in mind? Draw it out, even if it's just boxes on a page.

- How many pages do you expect the site to require? (it's OK to estimate this if you don't know)

- Will you require different template layouts between pages, or will the layout remain largely the same throughout the site?

- What specific features (other than core content display) will the site require? For example: discussion forum, newsletter subscription, online shop (e-commerce), user registration and accounts, blog, gallery, search function, etc.

- Branding & Design – Do you already have a clearly defined brand, or will you require your designer/developer to create something?

- Website Colour Scheme (a website's colour scheme is typically drawn from the company logo in order to promote the brand)

- Describe the style of the site. Use as many keywords as you feel is necessary. For example: modern, bright, colourful, dark, retro, minimalist, neutral, corporate, newspaper, etc.

- Who is supplying images and how can you guarantee that you are permitted to use them?
- What do you want people to do when they get to the site? For example, buy from the shop, complete an enquiry form, call you, read lots of articles, sign up to the newsletter, etc.
- Will most of your customers be on a mobile, tablet or a desktop and how easy is it for them to do the action you want on that device?
- What are the two most important calls to action that will be on the home page?
- Is your website going to be e-commerce and if so, how many products will you be selling?
- Who is your payment gateway provider? How can a developer gain access to test this on your new website?

Marketing & SEO

- What keywords or phrases are you trying to target? From these, do you have a set of priority keywords and phrases?
- Who's writing the content? When will it be available?
- Are you copying content over from a previous website and if so, who is copying it across?
- List the subject areas – from most important to least, focus on topics and clusters. (which can then become the site map)
- Is there a variety of content available to tell the story? (photos, videos, text, diagrams, etc.)
- Do you need a contact form on the website? Do you need different forms for different pages? Where will the enquiries go (email address)?
- Do your contact forms need to harvest emails into a database?

Social Media and Sharing

- What avenues do you need for sharing your content? (links on the page using Social Sharing to LinkedIn, Facebook, Instagram, Twitter, TikTok, etc.)

- What Social Media presence do you have (or need) and how is that going to be presented on the site? (Facebook Like box, Follow us on twitter, your Twitter stream, etc.)

Housekeeping

- Do you have a Privacy Policy & Terms of Use? You will need them and a Google-friendly privacy statement if you plan on using Google Ads, AdSense, etc.

- Do you need other statements covering things like Modern Slavery policy, GDPR compliance, Bullying & Harassment policy, Corporate & Social responsibility policy or a Customer Charter?

- Do you have a Google tracking code?

- Do you have Bing tracking code?

- Do you have other bits of tracking code that might need to be transferred to a new website from an existing website?

- Do you have any linked dependencies? i.e. your website needs to link to an accounting system, a CRM system, advertisers, or affiliates or a third-party data provider?

- Where is your domain name? Who owns it and how can you access it?

- Where are you planning on hosting your website?

- Who is arranging for the SSL certificate (secure sockets layer) on your hosting?

- What security measure are you planning on putting in place to prevent it from being hacked?

As I say, this is not a complete list but if you can answer all of these questions satisfactorily, then you are on your way to creating a great website.

Glossary of Terms

Term	Description
404 error	This is a page or file not found error message in HTTP standard response code.
Above the fold	The upper half of the front page of a newspaper where an important story or photograph can be found. In web design, it refers to sections of a webpage that are visible without scrolling or clicking.
AdWords	Google AdWords – now known as Google Ads – is a pay per click (PPC) online advertising platform, where advertisers bid to display digital adverts, product listings, or videos to web users.
Algorithm	A set of instructions designed to perform a specific task. Google search uses algorithms to rank websites.
Alt tags	Also known as 'alternative attribute' – a HTML attribute applied to image tags as a text alternative for search engines.
Alt text	A shortened version of 'Alt Attribute Text'. It is used in HTML code to describe the appearance or function of an image on a page when it cannot be rendered.

Analytics	The systematic computational analysis of data. Google Analytics, for example, is a web analytics tool that tracks and reports website traffic.
Artificial Intelligence (AI)	The simulation of human intelligence by computers that are programmed to think like humans and mimic actions such as learning and problem solving.
Authority website	An 'authority' website is one which Google (and users) find to be reliable, reputable and a source of good information.
B2B	Business to business.
B2C	Business to consumer.
Backlinks	Any electronic link from one place on the Internet to another.
Bing	A search engine owned and operated by Microsoft.
Black hat	Unethical search engines optimisation practices that go against search engines guidelines and artificially boost website rankings.
Blog	Short for web log, this a website or webpage that is updated regularly and typically written as discrete text entries in an informal or conversational diary style. Blogs are generally displayed in reverse chronological order, with the most recent first.
Bounce rate	When someone visits your website, lands on a page, and then leaves your website without visiting any other pages.
Citation flow	A score which reflects the quantity of links that point to any given website.
Click Through Rate (CTR)	The ratio of users who click on a specific link, compared to the number of total users who view the page as a whole.
Comment spam	A general term used to describe unsolicited spam advertising left by a spambot or spammer in the comments section of a blog, online forum or social media post.

Glossary of Terms

Conversion rate	The percentage of customers or users that perform a desired action as a result of visiting a website or engaging with an advert or other marketing initiative.
Crawl budget	The average number of pages a bot or spider will analyse on your website.
Directory	A file system cataloguing structure which contains references to other files and directories. A web directory or link directory is an online list or catalogue of websites. Formerly paper based, like Yellow Pages
Disavow	The process of discarding harmful or low-quality links pointing to your website or asking a search engine to not take specific backlinks into account when ranking your website.
Domain authority	A search engine ranking score that predicts a website's ability to rank on a search engine's results page. Domain authority indicates a website's relevance for a specific subject or industry sector.
Domain name	A unique name, comprising numbers, letters and some special characters, that identifies your website.
Duplicate content	Identical content that appears on the Internet in more than one place.
EAT	Expertise, Authoritativeness and Trustworthiness – attributes checked by Google Quality Raters.
Exact match search	A search where you use double quotation marks at the start and end of the phrase you are searching for.
External link	Hyperlinks that point to webpages on a different website domain.
Favicon	A small image that is associated with that website – often the company logo or, for personal websites, a face.
Featured snippet	Elements of text that appear in highlights at the top of a Google search result.
File Transfer Protocol (FTP)	The way websites get up onto a server and onto the Internet.

Google Analytics Tracking Code	A few lines of code that acts as a unique identifier to your website. This allows Google Analytics to collect data on your website and report that data back to you as the website owner.
Google crawl	A process whereby search engines send 'bots' to examine websites and report back what they find.
Google My Business	A free Google listing service used to find local businesses. Often abbreviated to GMB.
Google Quality Rater Guidelines	Quality control guidelines that are given to Google-employed search quality raters to evaluate search results. They are based on what Google believes the search users want.
Google Search Console	Formerly known as Google Webmasters Tools, this is a web service that audits the indexing and optimisation status of a website.
Header tags	HTML tags used to separate headings and subheadings on a webpage. Also known as heading tags.
Hyper Text Markup Language (HTML)	The standard markup language for documents designed to be displayed in a web browser.
Hypertext Transfer Protocol (HTTP)	The fundamental building blocks of the World Wide Web. It is used for load webpages using hypertext links.
Hypertext Transfer Protocol Secure (HTTPS)	A secure version of HTTP used to exchange data between a website and an Internet browser.
Inbound link	A link directed at your website from another website.
Indexing	A process of analysing the content of the page, cataloguing images and video files embedded on the page, and generally trying to understand the page.
Internal link	A link on your website that points to another location on your website.

Glossary of Terms

IP address	A unique address, made up of characters (letters and numbers) that identifies a device on the Internet or a local network.
Keyword	A word, phrase or question a user enters into a search engine as a search query.
Keyword research	An SEO practice aimed at researching appropriate keywords for finding specific products, services or online information.
Keyword stuffing	A black hat SEO technique where excessive keywords are loaded into a webpage to boost search engine rankings. It is often referred to as Webspam or spamdexing.
Knowledge Panel (aka Knowledge Box)	Information boxes that appear on Google when you search for entities (people, places, organisations, things) that are in the Google Knowledge Graph.
Landing page	A webpage that users are directed to when they click on an advert, marketing promotion, marketing email link, or campaign call-to-action.
Link building	The process of getting other websites to link back to your website.
Link equity (link juice)	The concept that individual links pass a value and/or authority from one page to another.
Local pack	A search engine results page feature that displays useful information in response to a local search. e.g. map of a business' location.
Long tail keyword	Longer search terms or key phrases that are used by searchers that have more specific and complex search requirements. They typically have lower search volumes but higher conversion rates.
Lorum Ipsum	Dummy text, historically used in the printing and typesetting industries.

Machine learning	The application of artificial intelligence (AI) to enable computer systems to learn from experience without being programmed. Search engines use machine learning to better answer search queries and far faster than could be done manually by a human.
Manual action	Search engines can issue 'manual action' against a website if it deems the website to be non-compliant. This is typically in response to a review by a human working for the search engine rather than automated.
Metadata	Metadata is a summary of a set of data.
Meta description	A HTML element that details the contents of a webpage, for the benefit of users and search engines (also called a meta-attribute or tag).
Meta keywords	A type of meta tag found in the HTML source code of a webpage that describes its content.
Meta tag	Descriptors in a webpage's HTML source code that tell search engines what the webpage's content is about.
NAP	Name, Address and Phone number.
No follow	A HTML instruction to search engines to ignore crawling and indexing specific links.
No index	A meta tag that instructs a search engine to avoid indexing a page.
Organic search	Placement in search results that is achieved without the help of paid adverts.
Organic traffic	Internet traffic that occurs without being driven by paid advertising.
Page rank	A metric that predicts how well a webpage will rank on a search engine result page.
Page speed	A measurement of how fast a webpage and its content loads.
Page tab	A clickable area at the top of a window that shows another page.

Glossary of Terms

Page title	The title of a webpage that features at the top of a browser and on a search engine results page.
Panda	The name given to a Google algorithm update that was specifically developed to reduce the appearance of low quality, thin content in the search results.
Paid search	This typically refers to pay per click (PPC) advertising on search engine results pages using advertising platforms such as Google Ads or Bing.
Pay Per Click (PPC)	An online advertising model, where advertisements are served to potential customers and the advertiser is only charged when someone clicks on the advertisement.
Penguin	A Google algorithm update, specifically aimed at penalising websites with unnatural backlinks pointing to them.
Penalty	A Google penalty is enforcement issued by Google for breaking its guidelines. A Google penalty typically results in a website no longer being listed in search results, or a significant drop in rankings.
Pixel	A 'picture element', a tiny area of illumination on a display screen, a group of which make up an image.
Plug-in	Something you can add on to a website to give it additional functionality.
Position zero	Whatever appears at the very top of the organic search results, often a Featured Snippet.
Private Blogging Network (PBN)	The linking together of websites to build link authority and manipulate search engine results. This is a black hat SEO technique and should be avoided.
Query	Search words, terms and phrases entered into a search engine.
Rank	The order of relevant search results in response to a search engine query.
Rank Brain	A machine learning element of Google's core search algorithm.

Ranking factor	Any aspect that has a direct impact on a website's position on a search engine results page.
Redirect	An automated instruction that directs a browser from one URL to another URL.
Schema	A semantic vocabulary of data tags that can be added to a webpage's HTML code to improve the way search engines read and present the page in a search.
Scraper software	An automated programme that scours the Internet looking for email addresses to add to their contact list.
SERPS	Search Engine Results PageS
Search engine	A software system designed to carry out searches and find items and content, particularly on the World Wide Web. e.g. Google, Bing, Yahoo, Duck Duck Go.
Search Engine Optimisation (SEO)	The process of improving the amount and quality of organic traffic driven to a website or webpage by a search engine (see my definition on page 27).
Search Quality Rater Guidelines	Guidelines given to Google employees for the purpose of rating websites. Google's raters are spread across the world and are trained to give feedback and suggestions on how search could be improved.
Search term	The word or phrase someone types into the search engine search bar or asks a search engine to find results for.
Sitemap	A file where a website owner can provide information about the pages, videos and other files on their website, and the relationships between them.
Software-as-a-Service (SaaS)	Occasionally referred to as software-on-demand, this is a software licencing model where the right to use the software is sold on a subscription basis. Examples include Microsoft Office 365 and Adobe Creative Suite.
Spam comments	A comment left on a website expressly for the purpose of building a link and not relevant to the page, article or website on which it is placed.

Glossary of Terms

Spammy links	A spammy link is a link to your website from a poor quality or low value domain.
Structured data	Standard formatted information that allows search engines to understand the content of a webpage.
Title tag	HTML that states the title of a webpage. In SEO, the title tag should contain all the keywords you want that page to rank for.
TL;DR	Abbreviation for 'Too Long; Don't Read' (or sometimes 'Too Long; Didn't Read).
Trust flow	The quality of links that point to URLs and websites.
Uniform Resource Locator (URL)	Otherwise known as a website address.
User Experience (UX)	An individual's feelings, perceptions and emotions when using a system, product or a website. UX web design is a process that focuses on developing the best possible, relevant experience for a website user.
User Interface (UI)	The point at which human interaction with a machine or software system occurs. A graphical operating system or Graphical User Interface (GUI) such as Microsoft Windows or Apple iOS are good examples of a User Interface.
Webmaster Guidelines	Guidelines issued by search engines that give details of how best to optimise a website so that it can be easily found using a search.
XML Sitemap	A file containing a list of all the pages of a website. They provide information to search engines about the structure of a website.
Your Money Your Life (YMYL)	Pages or topics that could potentially impact a person's future happiness, health, financial stability or safety.

About the Author

Specialist speaker and writer on SEO, digital marketing and online reputation management, Jonathan has over forty years' experience in sales and marketing and has been a chartered marketer for over twenty years. He helps people cut through the jargon surrounding digital marketing and writes in plain English, so everyone can understand. He is allergic to technical BS.

In his spare time, he is a philatelist, a bird watcher and loves reading. His wife thinks he's a bit of an anorak.

Acknowledgements

Writing a book turned out to be a much longer and harder process than I had imagined. Apparently, you can't just dump your thoughts on paper and send it to a printer. As such, without the support and encouragement of the following people, none of this would have been possible.

Firstly, I need to thank my lovely wife, Emma, for her unwavering support and her understanding when I disappeared into the office for hours on end to do another 'bit of the book'. Without your support and leading the way by publishing your own book during lockdown, this definitely would never have happened.

Thanks also are due to Siân-Elin, my editor, for helping wrangle my disjointed prose into something resembling the English language and for questioning everything. You even went as far as to actually understand SEO and simplify what I was saying when it didn't make sense. That's definitely above and beyond the call of duty.

I need to thank my friend Kristian, our marketing director at Aqueous Digital, for asking me initially if I'd write a short article for the website on the 3 Rules of Google and then telling me that at 5,000 words it was a bit too long, but it might make a good book... Eighteen months later he was kind enough to sit and read the draft manuscript that I'd churned out and offer sensible suggestions and changes to the text.

To my children Gabriella, Marcus, and William, for patiently suffering 'Daducation' and for letting me get way with the awful dad jokes. Also, to Gabriella especially for her help in designing the cover of this book – you made a vague idea come to life.

To Ian, my friend and fellow director at Aqueous Digital, for asking me, continually, when the book was going to be ready. Nothing like a target to keep you focused!

To Paula, our operations director, and the team at Aqueous Digital for continually keeping me on my toes by asking me questions about SEO. Having to explain my thoughts to you was an essential part of distilling the knowledge that needed to be shared in this book.

To Andrew Collier for the photography in the book. Thanks for traipsing around looking for portable buildings to photograph for me! Thanks also to Just Headshots for making my author photos look the best they can be.

To Geraint Roberts and Rod Duncan, both successful authors who have no idea that watching them inspired me to give it a go.

To Julian and his team at Farrer & Co for ensuring my use and attribution of copyright and intellectual property was all above board.

To every customer who has ever been a part of the Aqueous story. All the successes, and failures, have been an integral part of getting me to this book. I hope you find it useful.

To get a book looking this good, takes time and patience. It is, therefore, in no small measure due to the hard work of Tanya Back for all your help with typesetting, design, and layout. Thanks also to Noel at Fountain Creative for providing ideas, alternatives, and inspiration for some of the layout and Dan at Para Studios for casting a critical eye.

And finally, any errors in this book are mine and mine alone, as are all the opinions.

Printed in Great Britain
by Amazon